Driving Innovation from Within

KAIHAN KRIPPENDORFF

DRIVING
INNOVATION
from
WITHIN

A GUIDE for
INTERNAL ENTREPRENEURS

Columbia University Press
Publishers Since 1893
New York   Chichester, West Sussex
cup.columbia.edu
Copyright © 2019 Kaihan Krippendorff
All rights reserved

Library of Congress Cataloging-in-Publication Data
Names: Krippendorf, Kaihan, author.
Title: Driving innovation from within : a guide for internal entrepreneurs /
Kaihan Krippendorf.
Description: New York : Columbia University Press, [2019] |
Includes bibliographical references and index.
Identifiers: LCCN 2019021922 (print) | LCCN 2019980593 (e-book) |
ISBN 9780231189521 (hardback) | ISBN 9780231548366 (e-book)
Subjects: LCSH: Intellectual capital—Management. | Creative ability in
business. | New products. | Technological innovations—Management. |
Organizational change.
Classification: LCC HD53 .K74 2019 (print) | LCC HD53 (e-book) |
DDC 658.4/063—dc23
LC record available at https://lccn.loc.gov/2019021922
LC ebook record available at https://lccn.loc.gov/2019980593

Columbia University Press books are printed on permanent
and durable acid-free paper.
Printed in the United States of America

Cover design: Noah Arlow

For Lucas, Kaira, and Makar.
May you do what you love.

Contents

Foreword

RITA GUNTHER McGRATH

OVERHEARD AT A recent conference: "Today is the slowest day of your life." As the pace of change accelerates exponentially, established corporations are increasingly waking up to the reality that the rules have forever changed. Sustainable competitive advantages are growing shorter, less attainable, and more difficult to sustain. Meanwhile, growth by acquisition holds little value for investors, the old ways of organizing are dying off, and formal, structured innovation programs such as hackathons and incubators are often nothing more than "innovation theater," doing very little to actually drive real business impact.

What, then, is the answer?

Kaihan Krippendorff's key insight is that the successful companies of tomorrow are finding a new way to compete by empowering the true drivers of innovative growth: their employees. These companies are implementing an entrepreneurial mind-set and creating organizational platforms that free employees to identify and seize innovative opportunities themselves—thereby merging the advantages of scale with the agility of a startup. While this was once deemed a nearly impossible task, tech giants born from lean approaches—the likes of Google, Alibaba, and Netflix—are undeniable proof that this is not only attainable but absolutely vital.

In *Driving Innovation from Within*, Krippendorff offers a simple guide for how large corporations can move at the speed of startups by activating internal innovators. Drawing on five years of in-depth research and more than 150 interviews with employee innovators and the world's top experts, he unites several of today's most important strategic concepts—corporate entrepreneurship, lean startup methodology,

human-centered design, entrepreneurial intention, agile team-based structures, and self-coordinating organizations—into a single applicable framework for leading an organization of employee entrepreneurs.

The IN-OVATE framework that Krippendorff introduces in this book compiles a set of proven tools and practices into an accessible structure that readers will be able to apply immediately within their own organizations to build a pipeline of competitive advantages. This framework identifies seven of the most common barriers to innovation and outlines the contours of a new type of organization that successfully unlocks the value of employees' ideas.

- Intent: Turn your employees into intrapreneurs.
- Need: Communicate simple statements of purpose that describe what the market needs.
- Options: Generate disruptive business ideas in hallways, not boardrooms.
- Value blockers: Predict and neutralize business-model conflict.
- Act: Adopt an act–learn–build approach (rather than prove–plan–execute).
- Team: Assemble agile teams instead of siloed, hierarchical structures.
- Environment: Shift to open platforms that allow employees to rally resources.

While there are plenty of books available offering senior leaders a top-down view on the challenge of innovative growth, Krippendorff writes instead for the employee, arming readers with a set of practical tools to more effectively drive innovation within an established organization. After reading this book, employees will be able to better understand their organization's strategy so that they can focus their efforts on fertile ground and learn what hinders their passionate pursuit of innovation so that they can build the game-changing ideas their organizations need to survive. Leaders, in turn, will walk away with a broader understanding of key organizational factors—including culture, structure, and talent—that block internal entrepreneurial activity so that they can move beyond innovation theater and focus on what really works.

As a seasoned strategy consultant and one of the world's premiere transformation experts, Krippendorff is an authoritative guide

to navigating organizations through this era of transient advantage. While we still do not have an absolute, proven system for innovative growth, this book provides one of the most comprehensive paths I've seen, uniquely combining the breakthrough ideas of Steve Blank, George Day, Steve Denning, John Hagel, Alex Osterwalder, myself, and other leading thinkers into a single framework that can be easily activated within any organization. Through the IN-OVATE framework, readers will learn how to shift their organizational mind-set, break free from traditional thinking, and challenge the outdated status quo in order to embrace transformative possibilities, deploy disruptive ideas, and deliver bottom-line results.

The organization of tomorrow will gain a sustained competitive advantage by asking its employees to paint outside the lines. Let Kaihan show you how to create a masterpiece.

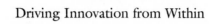
Driving Innovation from Within

Introduction

What My Clients Taught Me

I THOUGHT I knew everything.

For more than fifteen years, the entire focus of my professional life had been on the dynamics of strategy and innovation. I had conducted some one thousand workshops and seminars across a wide spectrum of organizations and industries, helping managers generate creative business ideas to drive growth. Almost always, those workshops produced terrific ideas that left participants feeling enthusiastic and eager to proceed.

But their organizations rarely acted on these ideas.

I concluded, reluctantly, that getting an innovative idea through the bureaucracy of an established company was hard work and carried a low success rate. It seemed that large organizations, even when well intentioned, simply set up resource-allocation structures that tend to kill off radical ideas. An intractable dead end.

Then, in 2015, I learned how wrong I was.

I happened to hear a program on National Public Radio about a leading New York publishing company that was using a new approach to engage aspiring writers. *Wait*, I thought, *this sounds familiar*. As I

listened to the details, I realized that this idea had emerged out of a workshop we had facilitated a couple of years earlier.

So I excitedly called our client. Could I come talk with them about how they had pulled it off? Of course, they said. And so I made my way to the offices of Macmillan Publishers' Children and Young Adult division, in the historic Flatiron Building in Lower Manhattan.

I didn't realize it at the time (we seldom do), but that meeting started me on a path that led to an entirely new way of thinking about innovation.

My education came in two parts: First, the Macmillan story, remarkable and illuminating in itself. Then, as I began analyzing that success in detail, I uncovered new research that revealed even deeper insights.

The hero of the Macmillan story is Jean Feiwel, the editor behind phenomenally successful series like Goosebumps and The Baby-Sitters Club. You will get to know her well in the pages that follow, for her story illustrates all the key elements presented in this book.

When Jean attended our original workshop, she had proposed an idea she was calling "Romance 2.0." Through her hard work and relentless dedication, it eventually evolved into the new initiative known as Swoon Reads—today the leading crowd-sourced platform to help undiscovered romance and young-adult writers refine their manuscripts and find their audience. It has been lauded in the industry press as an uncommon example of an established publishing company introducing the kind of innovation we usually expect from Silicon Valley.

In the Flatiron offices that day in 2015, Jean and her team laid out the steps that took them from the kernel of an idea to what it is today. In the chapters ahead, you will be able to watch those steps unfold.

But what struck me most that day was what I *didn't* hear.

- I expected to hear that an internal innovation group or center of excellence had adopted and incubated Jean's idea. Nearly every large company today has established some kind of formal program to build out new innovations. But no such formal program was involved.
- I expected to hear that Jean's boss, Jon Yaged, president of Macmillan's Children's Publishing Group, had greenlit the project with funding. He hadn't.

- I expected Macmillan would have given Jean and other employees time to work on it, following the "20 percent rule" popularized by 3M and Google, in which employees are allowed a portion of their time to advance their innovative project. No such extra time was given.
- I expected Jean would have won some kind of business-plan competition. She didn't.
- I thought Jean would have left the company to pursue the entrepreneurial effort on her own. After all, isn't that what usually happens when good ideas confront bureaucracy? She didn't leave.

Swoon Reads's path from idea to realization involved none of the formal structures or practices espoused by innovation experts. Instead, the journey was entirely spontaneous, organic, self-directed, and, for much of its path, done without the approval of funding or extra time. It was a labor of love, a movement generated by a group of passionate employees who saw a possibility and worked collectively to realize it.

How did that happen? More to the point, could it be replicated? I started to look more closely at this particular story, and that's when the second phase of my education kicked in. I eventually interviewed more than 150 experts and internal innovators, looking for a way to ensure that more of the creative ideas from our workshops would find their way into the real world. What I discovered instead was far more meaningful.

In a nutshell, I found that:

- This path of self-directed, employee-generated innovation has historically been far more prevalent than we understood. Indeed, the innovative ideas of employees have done more to shape society than those of entrepreneurs.
- With remarkable consistency, the 150 innovators, when asked what they saw as barriers to driving internal innovation, named the same seven key problems.
- A set of emerging concepts precisely address these seven barriers, opening up a pathway for internal innovators.
- Far more is known than I realized about what it takes to unleash the potential of would-be internal innovators.

In the chapters ahead, I have synthesized these findings into a framework and set of tools that anyone with a creative idea can use,

no matter their industry, special skill, or place in the company hierarchy. I am writing primarily for the internal innovator, not the boss, with the exception of chapter 10: For Leaders.

The book draws on stories from many interviewees held during the preparation of this book. For reasons of confidentiality, where my interlocutors are not identified in the text, I have also not cited or otherwise identified these sources in the notes.

I don't claim to have all the answers—indeed, new approaches to removing the barriers to internal innovation are being developed all the time—but I do know that the tools outlined here have worked. Some of the concepts may be familiar. My hope is that pulling them together into a holistic framework, with good fortune and hard work, can not only help generate new revenue and growth for the organizations that adopt them, but also contribute to greater happiness, fulfillment, and health for us all. These passionate innovators will indeed change the world.

CHAPTER ONE

The Real Innovators Among Us

YOU KNOW THIS story:

A super-smart kid comes up with a big idea, quits college, and moves to the West Coast, where he sets up in a garage with a small team—"a hacker, a hustler, and a hipster" as Silicon Valley folklore holds it—to build a breakthrough innovation, then launches a company that disrupts an existing market and makes him and his team rich.

Here's another version:

A super-smart employee, maybe no longer a kid, comes up with a great idea related to the company's core business, but nobody in senior management wants to listen. So she quits the job and starts a new company on a shoestring, builds it into a huge success, and sells it to her former employer's competitor.

The entrepreneurial narrative is innately, inevitably moving. It speaks to the power of human will, unifies public sentiment behind the ideas of a better world, fresh thinking, freedom, and self-realization—all while also promising wealth.

There's just one problem with this particular narrative. It isn't true.

The well-loved entrepreneurial story is more myth than reality, as entrepreneurial guru Michael Gerber points out in his enormously influential book and concept, *E-Myth*. The true story of innovation is less sexy, less sticky, and more complicated, which is why we don't discuss it as often.

Here is what the true path of innovation looks like.

In late 1969, the same year the first human landed on the moon, Elliott Berman started thinking about the future—not just his future but everyone's future, and not just the next year but thirty years ahead.

Much of the world was also worried about the future that year. Amid rising global inflation, political unrest, and ever-present racial, social, and economic tensions, energy dominated Berman's thoughts. He believed that by the year 2000 the cost of electric power would reach the point at which we would need to look beyond fossil fuel. He became determined to help make alternative energy sources a reality.

Solar power was an obvious alternative, but at more than $100 per watt, it was far too costly. Berman decided he needed to find a way to bring down the cost. He was a scientist himself, but he knew he could not do it alone, so he assembled a team to research, experiment, and find a solution. They calculated that if they could somehow bring the price down to $20 per watt, they would open up a considerable market, which would lead to profits. They would also change the world.

Until that point, most solar cells had been used in space and so required expensive materials and wiring. On Earth, with different requirements, the team experimented with printed circuit boards. They found that they could glue circuit boards directly to the acrylic front layer of the solar cells with silicon. And instead of using silicon from a single crystal, the accepted rule at the time, they experimented using silicon from multiple crystals. Instead of using expensive, customized components, they looked for ways to use standard parts available from the electronics market.

Each innovation challenged the prevailing norms. None seemed particularly radical. But together, these changes enabled Berman's team to bring the price of solar energy down fivefold, to $20 per watt.[1]

Innovation in hand, in April 1973 Berman founded a company, Solar Power Corporation (SPC), to commercialize the product he and his team had developed. They initially tried to sell their technology to the Japanese electronics conglomerate Sharp, but the two sides couldn't

agree on a price. So SPC decided to bring its innovation to market on its own. In its first year, SPC's business development team convinced Tideland Signal to use SPC panels to power navigation buoys for the U.S. Coast Guard.[2]

Then they tried to convince Exxon to use their panels on oil-production platforms in the Gulf of Mexico. No thanks, Exxon executives said, we already have power. So Berman's team flew to visit the people working on the platforms and found that the story on the ground was very different. Eventually they convinced Exxon to use SPC solar cells, and that led to solar cells' becoming the standard power source for oil-production platforms around the world.

By bringing down the cost of solar cells so dramatically, founding SPC to commercialize his innovation, and passionately selling the innovation, Berman engineered a major leap in the evolution of the solar cell. Were it not for his entrepreneurial effort, solar-power technology might be ten years behind where it is today. Berman is admired as one of the most important pioneers of solar technology, with more than thirteen patents and innumerable research papers.

You could say that Elliott Berman was the Elon Musk of the 1970s. And yet you have probably never heard of him.

Why is this?

Because although his story is familiar in so many ways, one wrinkle makes it unusual. Berman was an employee of Exxon when he started his research, and the company he founded, SPC, was a wholly owned subsidiary of Exxon. Although few at the time knew the word, Berman was an *in*trapreneur,[3] not an *en*trepreneur. With a fierce belief in his idea, he significantly changed his slice of the world, and he did it without quitting his job.

The Truth About Innovation

Innovation and growth, as I've mentioned before, are the primary focus of my professional life. I realized early in my career that my mission is "people loving what they do." I believe that having the freedom to innovate is a major contributor to loving your work. So, twenty years ago, when I felt I was not fulfilling this mission through my work at a global strategy consulting firm, I quit. If I was to be of service to organizations in their search for dynamic growth, and to individuals

creating work they loved, I needed to understand as much as I could about how innovation really works.

But we should pause briefly here for a definition. The concept of innovation has been written about so often that there are many opinions about precisely what it entails. In this book, when I use the term "innovation," I specifically mean something that meets these three criteria, on which a majority of definitions align:

1. *Newness:* A solution, idea, model, approach, technology, process, etc. that is considered significantly different from those of the past. We might say that for something to be an innovation, it must be surprising.
2. *Adoption:* Being surprising is not sufficient in itself. To become an innovation, a new idea must be adopted (or diffused).
3. *Valuable:* For something to be an innovation, it must be deemed valuable to relevant stakeholders (e.g., customers, investors, partners, and other stakeholders). Peter Drucker oriented his definition of innovation toward value when he wrote:

> Innovation is the specific function of entrepreneurship, whether in an existing business, a public service institution, or a new venture started by a lone individual in the family kitchen. It is the means by which the entrepreneur either creates new wealth-producing resources or endows existing resources with enhanced potential for creating wealth.[4]

With that definition as a filter, I was ready to delve more deeply into the essence of innovation. I wanted to understand if Jean Feiwel's story was an exception or the norm; I wanted to understand if, in order to innovate, employees needed to quit their jobs and become entrepreneurs, as is commonly believed and as I had done myself.

That search led me to a list of innovations that had most transformed our world in the recent past. A few years prior, the PBS business news program *Nightly Business Report* had partnered with the Wharton Business School to answer the question "Which thirty innovations have changed life most dramatically during the past thirty years?"[5] They asked the show's viewers from more than 250 markets across the country, as well as readers of Wharton's Knowledge@Wharton digital magazine from around the world, to suggest innovations they thought had shaped the world in the previous three decades. After receiving

about 1,200 suggestions, a panel of eight experts from Wharton reviewed and selected the top thirty of these innovations. The list appears in the first column of table 1.1; as you can see, it includes major innovations like the PC, the mobile phone, the internet, and magnetic resonance imaging (MRI).

My research assistant and I then dug into the histories of these innovations. In particular, we tracked the three stages that are common to every journey:

1. Conception: Who conceived of the idea?
2. Development: Who developed the idea into something that works?
3. Commercialization: Who brought the idea to market?

Table 1.1 summarizes our findings.

According to the hero narrative we like to retell, the answer to all three questions is the same: the entrepreneur conceives of the idea, develops the idea either on his/her own (Michael Dell in his dorm room building computers) or with a small team (Steve Jobs and Steve Wozniak in their garage), and then launches a company (Dell, Apple) to commercialize the idea. But let's look at the facts.

Question: Who conceives of transformational ideas?
Answer: Employees.

Only eight of the thirty most transformative innovations were first conceived by entrepreneurs; twenty-two were conceived by employees. Without their inventiveness, we might not have a mobile phone to reach for in the morning, an internet to connect it to, or an email to send. If we got sick, we would not be able to get an MRI or have a stent implanted.

Question: Who develops the idea?
Answer: Corporate and institutional collaboration.

The second chapter of the entrepreneurial hero story has the entrepreneur working alone or with a small team to develop the idea. Actually, only seven of the thirty were developed this way. Most transformative innovations come to life when a larger community forms around the idea to develop it. In this stage, academia and institutions start to play a major role, particularly when the innovation has significant social value.

For example, in the midst of the 1973 oil crisis, a Danish carpenter named Christian Riisager grew interested in developing a large

TABLE 1.1
The Thirty Most Transformative Innovations of the Past Thirty Years

Legend:
- Entrepreneurs
- Competitors
- Academia and institutions
- Internal innovators

Conceived	Developed	Scaled
>	>	>
Open-source software	DNA testing and sequencing/Human genome mapping	Microfinance
Large-scale wind turbines	Liquid crystal display (LCD)	RFID and applications (e.g., E-ZPass)
Biofuels	Noninvasive laser/robotic surgery (laparoscopy)	Magnetic resonance imaging (MRI)
Ecommerce	Mobile phones (personal handheld phone)	Large-scale wind turbines
Noninvasive laser/robotic surgery (laparoscopy)	Microprocessors	Biofuels
Social networking via the internet	Microfinance	Photovoltaic solar energy
Genetically modified plants	RFID and applications (e.g., E-ZPass)	Graphic user interface (GUI)
Radio frequency ID (RFID) technology and applications	Photovoltaic solar energy	Bar codes and scanners
Internet, broadband, WWW (browser and html)	Graphic user interface (GUI)	ATMs
Email	Bar codes and scanners	SRAM flash memory
Media file compression (jpeg, mpeg, mp3)	ATMs	Ecommerce

Stents	SRAM flash memory	Liquid crystal display (LCD)
Antiretroviral treatment for AIDS	Ecommerce	Noninvasive laser/robotic surgery (laparoscopy)
DNA testing and sequencing/Human genome mapping	Internet, broadband, WWW (browser and html)	PC/laptop computers
Magnetic resonance imaging (MRI)	Email	Fiber optics
Photovoltaic solar energy	Media file compression (jpeg, mpeg, mp3)	Digital photography/videography
Graphic user interface (GUI)	Stents	Social networking via the internet
Bar codes and scanners	Antiretroviral treatment for AIDS	Genetically modified plants
ATMs	Open-source software	Internet, broadband, WWW (browser and html)
SRAM flash memory	Magnetic resonance imaging (MRI)	Email
Liquid crystal display (LCD)	Large-scale wind turbines	Media file compression (jpeg, mpeg, mp3)
PC/laptop computers	Biofuels	Stents
Fiber optics	PC/laptop computers	Antiretroviral treatment for AIDS
Digital photography/videography	Fiber optics	Open-source software
Mobile phones (personal handheld phone)	Digital photography/videography	DNA testing and sequencing/Human genome mapping
Microprocessors	Social networking via the internet	Mobile phones (personal handheld phone)
Office software (spreadsheets, word processors)	Genetically modified plants	Microprocessors
Light-emitting diodes	Office software (spreadsheets, word processors)	Office software (spreadsheets, word processors)
GPS systems	Light-emitting diodes	Light-emitting diodes
Microfinance	GPS systems	GPS systems

windmill that could generate enough power to be commercially viable. He designed one that could produce 22–55 kilowatts of power. After building and selling a few of these, he didn't launch a company to further refine his design so it could be mass-produced. Instead, a community formed around his idea. This group, called the Tvind School, was formed by innovators and backed by other technology firms, including Vestas, Nordtank, Bonus, and later Siemens.

This pattern of community developing is common in medical innovation (e.g., magnetic resonance imaging, antiretroviral treatment for AIDS, and stents) but also in many other transformative innovations such as email, media file compression, and open-source software. Innovation more often comes from the collaboration of corporate and institutional employees than from small teams of mavericks.

Question: Who commercialized the idea?
Answer: Competitors.

As it turns out, only two of the thirty innovations were scaled by the original creators. And one of those innovations, microfinance, developed by Muhammad Yunus from my mother's home country of Bangladesh, was scaled by the innovator himself only because he could not convince other organizations to copy him. He won the Nobel Peace Prize for his effort.

Rather, more than 50 percent of the time (16 out of 30) the innovator loses control of the innovation. Competitors take over. Then, through a battle of players seeking to commercialize the innovation, the innovation scales.

Consider the Italian manufacturer Olivetti, which in the early 1960s was struggling to compete with large U.S. firms building massive mainframe computers. The company's CEO, Roberto Olivetti, came up with a radical, seemingly impossible idea: to make a computer that was small enough to sit on a desktop.

He then handed the idea to a five-person design team, led by Pier Giorgio Perotto. The Olivetti team eventually achieved the impossible: a computer small enough to sit on a desk and economical enough to be acquired by an individual. The personal computer was born.

But management didn't fully understand what their personal computer (called the Programma 101) was, and they didn't appreciate its market potential. So for their display at the 1964 World's Fair, Olivetti put a mechanical calculator front and center in its booth, and put the

Programma 101 in a back room as an interesting oddity they were experimenting with.

But when an Olivetti representative showed the audience what the Programma 101 could do, they were stunned. This little device could perform intricate calculations—like the orbit of a planet—that until then had required mainframes that filled entire rooms. Market response was electric. Olivetti quickly started production. NASA bought at least ten to perform calculations for the 1969 Apollo 11 moon landing. The company sold 40,000 units at about $20,000 each in today's dollars.

Olivetti had a hit that would transform the world.

Then the competition took notice. In 1968, HP launched its HP9100 series, which was later ruled to have copied several aspects of the Programma 101. That was soon followed by copycat products from innumerable competitors, including the Soviet Union MIR program, Commodore, Micral, IBM, and Wang.

New ventures don't scale innovations; competitors do.

What I hope this quick analysis will show is that the entrepreneurial hero narrative is more myth than reality. We owe much of the modern world to the efforts and passions of internal innovators. To tell the true story of innovation, we would have to say that employees conceive of innovations, communities composed of corporations and institutions build them, and then the competition takes over to scale them.

The Double-Sided Advantage of Scale

Among the many advantages of innovation from within a company is the reciprocal relationship to scale. Being an innovator working from within an established organization can enable you to scale more quickly. And growing in scale makes more innovation possible. Let me tell you two stories to illustrate.

Heather Davis is a senior managing director at TIAA, a leading manager of retirement funds. The $45 billion private equity fund she helped build is one of the largest owners of wineries, farms, and other forms of agricultural real estate in the world. By investing in agricultural real estate and in technologies to increase farmer productivity, she is pursuing a mission to help prevent a world food crisis.

She has even used this platform to launch social efforts. When many of their farms were having trouble recruiting workers, Heather flew over to assess the situation. In a large apple orchard, she observed workers carrying heavy loads, performing repetitive tasks. Heather is also the mother of an autistic child, so it became immediately evident to her that such work was ideal for people with autism. She launched the Fruits of Employment program, which strategically employs workers with autism and other disabilities at agricultural sites such as apple orchards and vineyards. By doing this within TIAA, to the benefit of society *and* TIAA, she was able to achieve instant scale, quickly reaching a level of impact that might have taken years to achieve on her own.

I'm sharing Heather's story to illustrate the importance of scale. Startup companies are young, disruptive, and risk-taking. But once they find a business model that works, they start repeating that model in order to scale up. To do this, they turn to the bureaucracy they once scorned. They start narrowing tasks and tightly monitoring the performance of those tasks. They become risk-averse. Their level of innovation drops.

However, as they continue to grow, four factors come into play that invigorate internal innovators and give them great advantage:

1. They have scale that entrepreneurs cannot easily match.
2. They have access to multiple capabilities under one roof, tapping technology and experts from across the organization.
3. They can take advantage of resources their company has to invest (academics call these "slack resources"). Entrepreneurs must fundraise continually.
4. They can diversify risk. By making multiple bets, knowing some will fail but others will work, they can make the returns from innovation predictable.

One internal innovator explained it this way:

I could quit and start my own company, but if I do it here, I get immediate access to support, like legal and accounting. I get a brand that people recognize. When I make a phone call to a potential partner, I can get the meeting immediately. If I were a start-up, I'd have to make ten phone calls to get that meeting.

A few years ago I was visiting my mother at her home in Bangladesh and had the opportunity to meet Kamal Quadir. An MIT graduate and technology entrepreneur, he founded a mobile ecommerce business in Bangladesh called CellBazaar, quickly expanded it, and sold it to the Norwegian-based telecommunications company Telenor.

Kamal's next big idea was to create a mobile P2P (person-to-person) payments solution. At the time (2010), mobile P2P was nearly unheard of by most U.S. consumers, though it was universal in Kenya and Nigeria, where more than 95 percent of adults used mobile phones to transact with each other. Kamal was ahead of his time.

If he set out on a typical entrepreneurial path, Kamal would get funding, code, then launch a company. Instead, he saw that he could scale much more quickly if he built the business from inside a larger organization. He brought the idea to BRAC, the largest nongovernmental organization in Bangladesh, which, among other things, operated one of the country's largest banks. Within five years, he was able to reach fifteen million fishermen, small business owners, and others using his platform. As of this writing, his company, bKash, in which he retains partial ownership, has more than thirty-five million users.

Employees' Ideas Often Matter More Than the Founders' Ideas

Another assumption within the entrepreneurial myth is the notion that today's successful enterprises spring entirely from the entrepreneur's original business concept: Steve Jobs's vision of a beautiful computer, Ingvar Kamprad's vision of furniture sold in flat boxes, Jeff Bezos's vision of an "everything store."

In 1962, the physicist and historian Thomas Kuhn introduced a theory of "scientific revolution." It posits that advances in science follow a pattern in which one revolutionary introduces a new paradigm and then other scientists follow to build out the details.[6] It's often assumed that great companies follow a similar pattern.

But when we study what actually makes great companies great, we see that success depends more on the founder's ability to create a system in which employees can bring ideas to reality. The ideas that turn organizations into market-shaping disruptors often come years after the original founder's vision.

Consider IKEA.

Gillis Lundgren, a young employee of a little-known mail-order furniture company called IKEA, was trying to deliver a table in 1953 when he discovered that it wouldn't fit into the back of his small car. His solution: remove the legs. His boss, Ingvar Kamprad, immediately saw the value of this simple idea.[7]

IKEA at the time was a catalog business delivering furniture and other products mostly to homes in Agunnaryd, a small city in Sweden where Kamprad was born. Flat-pack packaging and self-assembly quickly became IKEA's centerpiece business strategy. And you know the rest. As of 2015, IKEA had more than 150,000 employees running twenty-nine stores and distribution centers, with 800 million people shopping at the stores and 2.5 billion visiting the website. All this produced an annual revenue of more than $36 billion.[8]

Lundgren, who was IKEA's fourth employee, worked for the company for more than sixty years. The former delivery driver was a talented designer, and Kamprad was wise enough to recognize it. Lundgren was eventually named head of design, where he played a major role in the company's worldwide success. Altogether he designed more than two hundred IKEA products, and in 2012 he was awarded the Tenzing Prize, Sweden's highest innovation award.

The IKEA story is compelling, but it is by no means unique. The pattern we see in most successful large organizations is the same. Growth comes not from the founder's original idea but from his or her ability to activate the innovative prowess of employees.

Amazon does not generate significant value from selling stuff online, but rather from its services, from video to logistics to technology. Apple does not generate value from selling computers, but instead from iPhones, iPads, and other consumer services—ideas that were primarily advocated for by employees. The founder and CEO of Urban Outfitters, Dick Hayne, one of the fastest-growing and most profitable apparel retailers in the United States, told me that the innovations that propel its growth come from employees who bring in new ideas every day.

What About the Future?

I hope I've convinced you that our love affair with the "hero" lone entrepreneur and his/her role in our economic landscape is overstated.

In point of fact, we now know that internal innovators have had a more significant effect on our lives than entrepreneurs.

Yet, when I lay out the facts at my workshops and speeches, I am often challenged by those who protest that my data are too old, that entrepreneurs are now taking the lead in innovation. The future, these skeptics claim, will once again belong to daring entrepreneurs.

Are they right?

I needed to dig deeper. So, with the valuable help of my research team, I analyzed recent data on innovation trends from respected sources such as *Forbes*, *R&D* magazine, and the Kauffman Foundation, the leading research institution dedicated to the study of entrepreneurship. Details of the research, including graphic presentations of the findings, are included in appendix A. For the moment, I'll summarize.

In a sense, the skepticism of those who insist the future belongs to entrepreneurs is understandable. For one thing, startup costs are coming down, thanks to access to cloud computing, 3-D printing, on-demand workers, and so forth. This should even the playing ground, making it easier for startups to compete with large incumbents.

Also, large companies are failing faster and earlier than before. A recent study of more than thirty thousand public companies over a fifty-year time span[9] shows that public companies today have a one-in-three chance of being delisted in five years (because of bankruptcy, M&A, liquidation, etc.). That is six times more likely than forty years ago. They are also dying younger. The average age of a company delisted in 1970 was fifty-five years. Today it is thirty-one.

More evidence: A famous study from Clayton Christensen's consulting firm, Innosight, measured how long companies that made it onto the Standard & Poor's 500 list stayed on the list. In 1960, they lasted about sixty years. Today, they last only about fifteen. And the Kauffman Foundation has shown that the length of time that Fortune 500 companies remain large enough to qualify for the list has been consistently dropping for the past five decades.

All of these facts fuel the idea that big companies are failing, leaving room for the small ones to take over. It's a heartwarming David-and-Goliath story, but—and this is a big "but"—is it real? For this theory to hold up, we should see a parallel growth in entrepreneurship, with new startups popping up everywhere and pulling profits away from large companies.

It's not happening.

The Kauffman Foundation found that the number of startups per 100,000 adults has been steadily declining. It started at more than 250 in 1997 and has been dropping steadily over the past two decades, though we saw an uptick in startups in 2016.[10]

If it were true that entrepreneurs are increasingly becoming the innovators, we would expect to see that the lists of highly innovative companies are headed by younger companies. That isn't happening. Using the *Forbes* list of the most innovative companies from 2011 through 2017, we calculated how old each company was when it made the list. If younger companies are starting to replace older ones, the average age should come down. It doesn't. We may *think* old companies like GE and J&J are being replaced by younger innovators like Tesla or Spotify, but the data don't support that. If anything, the most innovative companies are getting older.

Then I wondered if "company" was the wrong unit of measure. After all, smaller entrepreneurial companies don't yet have the scale to launch multiple innovations in any given year, so the "most innovative companies" list might skew toward larger organizations. I looked at the frequency of innovations, using *R&D* magazine's annual list of one hundred top innovations from 2013 to 2017. If younger companies are starting to out-innovate incumbents, we should see the prevalence of innovations launched by younger companies increasing on the list. What we found, however, showed no such trend.

All this was running through my mind as I tried to formulate a response to the skeptics. And I came to the realization that when we set out to understand the full dynamic of innovation and think carefully about what lies ahead, the first thing we have to recognize is that the story is not one of big versus small companies, or startups versus veterans. *Both* struggle to endure. Something else is happening. What is driving the changes we are witnessing? A compelling answer is an acceleration in the pace of change.

Digitization and Acceleration

In 2017, electric-car manufacturer Tesla discovered a problem in their passenger-side airbag. They would need to issue a recall. In the same situation, most car companies would send letters out to drivers, ask them to bring their cars in to servicing stations, and have mechanics

all over the country or the world make the adjustments. The process could take a year and cost tens or even hundreds of millions.

Tesla took a stunningly different route. It beamed down a software update that addressed the problem. The entire process cost a few thousand dollars of programming time (rather than millions) and took seconds (rather than months) to put in place.

We are starting to see similar stories, with similarly radical drops in cost and time, in nearly every sector: banking, retail, energy, consumer products, real estate, agriculture, fashion, hospitality, and more. Across the board, a sudden surge in speed and drop in the cost of delivering value are challenging incumbent organizations—large and small—to keep up.

Digitization Is Changing the Game . . .

You can fill an entire library with research, articles, and books on the transformational impact digitization is having. What first began with ecommerce is now restructuring entire industries. We used to buy a car because of its physical aspects (motor, wheels, chassis), and now a growing portion of the value we are paying for is software. We used to purchase typewriters (the keys, drum, case), but now pay mostly for word-processing software. We used to pay for physical books, but as of 2016 ebooks command 49 percent of the market. Everywhere we look, the physical is becoming digital.

Why does this matter? Ray Kurzweil, who, among other things, leads Google's efforts in artificial intelligence, machine learning, and language processing, has shown that when artifacts become digital, then something he calls the Law of Accelerating Returns is activated.[11] The artifact's performance per cost begins improving at an exponential rate. The implications of this are so profound that most organizations are struggling to deal with them.

The implications of the pending "digital revolution" are profound and well detailed in books like those of Kurzweil or *Exponential Organizations* by Salim Ismail,[12] Kurtzweil's colleague at Singularity University. To simplify, perhaps oversimplify, their thesis: a shift to digital is leading us into a world of exponential improvement in cost performance, accelerating the pace of change, and challenging and pushing hierarchical organizations to the limit as they increasingly struggle to keep pace.

. . . and Dramatically Lowering Costs

We see evidence of this exponential drop in costs across a variety of areas.

- In 2000, for example, the first human genome was sequenced. The effort cost $2.7 billion. Today improvements in computing and measurement have driven that cost down to less than $1,000.
- The toy drone that I—I mean Santa—gave my son for Christmas this year cost $20 on Amazon.com. Five years ago it would have cost $700.
- In 1977, one kilowatt of solar power cost $75; today it is 75 cents.
- A traditional artificial appendage costs $5,000–$50,000 to produce. Today, organizations like Po (www.po.com.py) print them on 3-D printers for about $1,000.

Companies that embrace the digital, asset-light, idea-intensive revolution achieve radically lower cost bases and put themselves on the path of exponential cost improvement.

Why does this matter? Because it is driving their competitors into complexity.

Companies that fail to take advantage of the acceleration and lower costs that digitization brings face a terrible burden: they must increasingly compete with complexity. There are two reasons for this.

First, their competitors move more quickly. They adjust their product offering, pricing, distribution, and marketing messages weekly rather than annually. It is no longer practical to anticipate their big moves at the beginning of the year or to wait until the end of the year to decide how to react.

Second, there are simply more competitors. As the information component of products and services grows and the cost drops, the "barriers to entry," as Michael Porter named them, fall. Organizations have to either adapt to a faster-moving, less predictable competitive environment or fall behind. Most organizations are struggling to evolve.

And here is the crux of the matter: to manage it all, organizations will need to reorganize. This puts internal innovators at the very center of the action, with unparalleled opportunities.

Hierarchy Cannot Keep Pace

Acceleration is thrusting traditional organizations rapidly toward a dilemma. Most of them are still primarily run as centrally planned economies. A central authority decides where capital and talent should be deployed; sets salaries; defines how much businesses should pay for internal support like IT, HR, or finance; and so on. When new information is received ("the average salary of database engineers is rising"), it is passed up the hierarchy through memos and meetings, and a decision is made ("let's increase our salaries for database engineers by saving money somewhere else") and then implemented (new salary bands are set, raises given, recruiting materials updated).

Gary Hamel has been studying the cost of bureaucracy for decades and concludes that while the world has changed dramatically, we continue to hold on to an outdated operating model—the bureaucracy—that companies will need to abandon if they are to survive.

We know how central planning worked out for economies. We are likely to see a similar bifurcation now with companies. Organizations that adapt their model, that abandon the centralized approach, will survive. Those too slow to adapt risk dying.

As we will see in chapter 10, an answer is emerging. Forward-looking organizations are adopting a new, more agile organizing principle. They are evolving into platforms in which employees have the freedom to spot opportunities, act on them, and rally the resources to pursue them. In other words, we are entering a world that will thrust the internal innovator back into the central role of innovation.

A Final Word: The Financial and Human Problem

In summary, then, the data all point to the fact that internal innovators have been and continue to be critical drivers of innovation. We owe much of the modern world—from mobile phones to the internet, from MRIs to stents—to their creativity and persistence. Furthermore, all the evidence suggests they are playing an ever more critical role in shaping the future. We should be celebrating them, honoring them, and encouraging them. Yet too often we persist with the myth that entrepreneurs are the innovators that most matter.

This disconnect between the stories we like to tell and reality comes at a cost. One enormous cost is worker disengagement. More than 80 percent of employees in the United States and most other developed countries are disengaged at work,[13] meaning eight of ten workers spend their work hours just trying to get through the day.

This disengagement costs the U.S. economy about $450 billion per year in lost productivity.[14] That is more than the revenues of Amazon, Boeing, GE, and Google combined. It is more than all U.S. companies spend on R&D every year.

And that's not all. Beyond economics, this is a major humanitarian problem. Disengagement at work has been shown to link to anxiety, depression, and damaged family relationships.

I believe that a major cause of this disengagement stems from the fact that most employees feel their creativity is being suppressed. Is it any wonder so many have lost their sense of purpose or passion? Imagine the growth we could fertilize if we could reignite that passion. Imagine what we could accomplish as a society if we could reinvigorate that sense of purpose.

CHAPTER TWO

Six Attributes and Seven Barriers

WHAT DOES SUCCESS look like?

It's tempting to imagine, watching Mark Zuckerberg stride out on stage in jeans and a gray T-shirt, or Jeff Bezos with his clean-shaven head and shades, that top innovators have a certain style about them, and that how they look is an outward manifestation of inner qualities, some sort of clue to success.

Relax. You don't have to start wearing hoodies and ripped jeans. To succeed as an internal innovator, you do not need to look, speak, or act like an entrepreneur. In fact, doing so is quite likely to put you on the wrong track. Some of the qualities that make entrepreneurs successful may actually work to the detriment of internal innovators.

It's Not the Same as Entrepreneurism

Don't make the mistake of thinking that internal innovators are just entrepreneurs drawing a paycheck from someone else. The challenge that they face—that you will face—is different, in quite significant ways.

- You have two jobs, not one. In all likelihood you will have to maintain ongoing management activities while simultaneously pursuing something new.
- You have one investor, not forty. Entrepreneurs typically pitch their idea to forty or more investors before finding a funder that fits the idea. You have just one funder—your employer—and must find the idea that fits that funder. This means you need to invest a lot of time in understanding what kind of ideas your employer will support, sort through them for the best option, and get your pitch just right. To say this another way: while entrepreneurs seek supporters for their idea, internal innovators seek ideas for their supporters.
- While entrepreneurs often lead the effort from the moment of conception to realization as a profitable business, internal innovators are rarely involved from start to finish. More often, they advance the effort and then pass off responsibility. Entrepreneurs run a marathon; you will probably run one leg of a relay race and then pass the baton.
- While entrepreneurs launch ideas quickly but struggle to scale, internal innovators struggle to launch but can scale with speed. Getting an idea approved takes more work from within a large organization, but once you get it going, it can grow far more quickly.

So what can we say instead about internal innovators, and about the qualities that make them successful? There are two questions to explore: Is there a pattern to how they work? And are there personal attributes they all share?

The Core Process

As to the first question, there is a core process that defines the internal innovator. It starts with the notion, validated by research, that first and foremost they are people who seize opportunities. They do so by doing four things well (see figure 2.1):[1]

1. They discover new opportunities.
2. They evaluate and choose which opportunities to exploit.

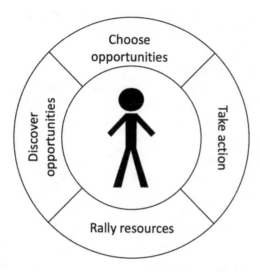

Figure 2.1 The internal innovation process.

3. They take autonomous action to move on those opportunities.
4. They mobilize resources while operating within a dispersed environment; that is, they are able to find the capital and talents needed to pursue an opportunity and rally those resources even if they do not have direct influence over their course.

In the chapters that follow, you will see those four process elements play out over and over. As we examine exactly what steps you need to take to bring your innovative idea to reality, and as we learn the stories of successful innovators in many industries, you will see that every one of them rests on the foundation of that core process.

But we need to consider a more fundamental question: What kind of person does it take to do those four things well? What are successful innovators like, and can their qualities be learned and emulated?

Six Vital Attributes

It's easy to understand the frequent blurring of the lines between entrepreneurs and internal innovators. They do have some things in common. But they are different in more—and more important—ways.

Traditional entrepreneurs are distinguished by three critical attributes:[2]

- Innovativeness: the practice of exploring novel approaches and solutions rather than following accepted ways of doing things
- Market awareness: awareness of the external environment (competitors, customers, and industry) combined with a drive to help the company win
- Proactivity: a propensity to act before one is told to act, to "lean in," to act autonomously

In simpler terms, we can say they are innovative, market aware, and proactive. Does that sound like anyone you know?

It probably comes as no surprise that research shows internal innovators share those three qualities as well. But the same body of research shows they also exhibit three other characteristics that differentiate them from entrepreneurs and make them uniquely qualified to take on the challenge:

- Strategic approach to risk
- Political acumen
- Motivation

To bolster your chances of success, you need to consider carefully the extent to which you embrace these characteristics.

Calculated Risk

Common public perception is that innovators are unabashed risk seekers. In pursuit of something new, they're willing to risk capital, career, or both. This perception is not wrong. It has been well established that, on average, entrepreneurs have a much higher risk tolerance. Elon Musk, after selling PayPal, invested nearly all of his wealth to launch SpaceX. Ted Turner gambled his company numerous times as he built his media empire. And we admire them for it.

Internal innovators think differently. They may appear to take high-risk gambles, but actually they are very deliberate about when and how to do so. They excel at calculating risk and then making thoughtful bets.

To see this in action, meet George Pyne. A few years after graduating from Brown University, where he was captain of the football team and an All–Ivy League and All–New England player, he found himself working in Atlanta for the real estate development firm Portman. In 1994, when the Super Bowl was coming to Atlanta, the former football star saw an unexpected opportunity. He came up with the idea of converting one of Portman's commercial properties into a hospitality space for NFL players, and he negotiated a deal with the NFL Players Association whereby three hundred players and VIPs would gather at the space before the Super Bowl. It was such a success that he convinced Portman to form a new division called AMC Events to manage and market sports-related properties.

A year later Pyne joined NASCAR, one of AMC Events's clients, as head of business development. While there, he structured numerous opportunities that would deliver NASCAR high rewards at relatively low risk, including a $750 million sponsorship of the NASCAR Nextel Cup Series in 2004, a $4.5 billion television rights deal in 2005, and investments by one hundred Fortune 500 companies. He helped NASCAR to become one of the most recognized sports brands in the United States and to build a $2 billion licensing business on that brand.

George Pyne believes that a key to his success is something he learned from Ted Forstmann, his mentor and the billionaire former CEO of IMG: the importance of taking carefully calculated risks. "Ted showed me that while other people thought he took big risks, he actually was careful to avoid them. He would engineer a deal in which he was protected on the downside but would capture a lot of the upside. Regardless of what happened, he was likely to win. Only when he had finished engineering the deal did he bet heavily on that deal. I learned that's what you need to do."[3]

Internal innovators approach risk differently for another reason. Even if you are comfortable with risk, your company may not be. And since you are risking your employer's capital, not your own, it's your company's risk profile that matters. That capital is usually backed by more conservative sources. Stock market investors tend to want growth without risk. Their risk aversion drives through the board into the company's top team and throughout the organization. (How to understand your company's investors' risk tolerance will be discussed further in chapter 4.)

How do internal innovators overcome the intrinsic risk aversion of their company? They can try to remove it by, say, transforming the company's ownership structure. But it's more realistic, and far easier, to find creative ways to de-risk your bets. Just as George Pyne learned from Forstmann, you must figure out how to engineer ideas to maximize your upside while protecting your downside.

Political Acumen

Remember that while entrepreneurs may shop their ideas to, on average, forty investors before getting funding, internal innovators really have only one option—their employer. So, winning support depends less on the quality of your pitch than on the political work performed before the pitch to understand and align interests.

In a breakthrough study of what they call serial innovators, researchers Raymond L. Price, Abbie Griffin, Bruce A. Vojak, Nathan Hoffmann, and Holli Burgon conducted in-depth interviews with nearly one hundred internal innovators. They found the key trait that separated successful internal innovators from frustrated ones was that they viewed the political challenge simply as part of the problem-solving process.

Here's how they describe the successful approach:

> Serial innovators described themselves as consciously "crossing the bridge" from having a naïve view of the organization's political machinations to becoming willing to engage the organization polit-ically using their talent, creativity, and persistence. Their political actions usually emanate from a foundation of trust and respect, which must be built over time and across people in multiple func-tions at multiple levels of the organization. Then they apply a wide variety of political influence actions to help move the organization. They actively engage people across their organization. They position the product and the project in the context of the organization in a way that others could see the value and benefits. Then, they use both soft and hard influence actions to help others move with them. Politics, almost, become a natural part of what they do in order to ensure that their innovations reach the market and address the customer needs they so thoroughly understand.[4]

Your internal innovation journey, then, will look less like banging down the doors of funders and more like carefully navigating a complex, interconnected network of internal stakeholders. Hoby Darling—the Nike executive who led Nike+, the company's digital business behind the Nike Fuelband, arguably the product that proved the mass market for wearable sports technology—put it to me this way: "When you work for a large company you need to spend a lot of time lining up the cannons, but when they go off, they go off with a big bang."[5]

We will dive more deeply into the implications of this in chapter 9, but for now, appreciate that your challenge as an internal innovator is to design a solution that will work in a system that has multiple stakeholders and is continuously evolving. Success depends not only on whether the market will embrace your idea but also on whether you can synchronize your idea with the motivations of internal stakeholders.

You will also have to balance between incongruent systems of rules: what is formally allowed and what is best for the company. This will force you to deal with unique ethical choices.[6] Think of it this way: If you're pursuing something that you know your organization would benefit from but would require a change in an existing policy or procedure, how do you move forward? Internal innovators often have to step outside of the norms and bend or even break rules, but they are very clear that they do so for the benefit of the organization.

Intrinsic Motivation

One source of tension that continually pops up is compensation. Internal innovators often express frustration that they could be making more money if they were building their own businesses and driving their innovation independently. "I am torn," one told me, "because I used to be an entrepreneur and I know that if I were doing this on my own there would be a significant potential payout for me. Because I'm doing it here, it's not clear that my effort will be recognized or rewarded. I may get a bonus or a pay raise but it will never be comparable to what the payoff would be if I did it on my own."

But when I asked why he didn't just quit and go out on his own, he candidly admitted that doing so would come at considerable risk. He didn't want to "eat ramen noodles every night" or put his family's financial security at risk. He made a conscious choice that he was

going to forgo the potential payoff in exchange for a more predictable career path. His supervisor, who heads the internal venturing group, said that whenever he gets into discussions about compensation, he reminds his internal innovators that "they are not incurring nearly as much risk as they would have were they to do it on their own. What you get to do here is build an exciting career."

As we will see shortly, even the best internal innovators face significant barriers at every step of the way. These barriers can be so discouraging that some people simply give up. Others keep going, finding a way around or through those barriers. What motivates them to persist?

There are several answers, as documented by numerous research studies. They may be driven by the opportunity to leverage the scale of the organization and create something new that they could potentially become the manager of, thereby accelerating their career path.[7] They may be moved by the sense of purpose that comes from building something new.[8] They may want to serve the greater cause of their leader or organization.

Sometimes it's all of the above, or a combination. But whatever their underlying motivation, all great internal innovators are passionate. They proactively drive and independently think to pursue their idea. They tend to serve a higher purpose, perhaps even greater than their CEO. They seem to serve an understanding of what their organization stands for and seek out opportunities to help their organization fulfill its potential in the world, even if people around them initially say no. "My boss may not get it," one told me, "but when I know it's right I see it's my job to help leadership see the possibility as well."

If we pull together all six attributes, we see that they map neatly onto the internal innovation process. Each characteristic helps you advance through a key step along the internal innovation journey, as shown in figure 2.2.

The Root of Success

You would think that today's business organizations, knowing full well that the global economic landscape in which they perpetually struggle to compete demands innovation, would make it easy for employees to pursue new ideas. I've come to believe that most organizations want to make it easy, but they get in their own way. Without intentionally

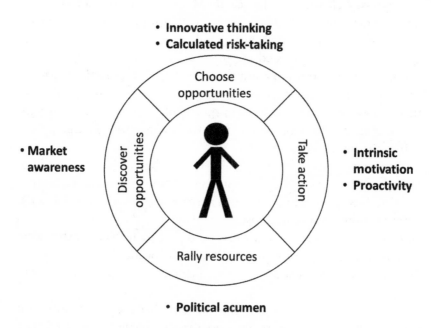

Figure 2.2 Attributes of successful internal innovators.

doing so, organizations erect barriers to innovation. Let's visit two examples, with two very different outcomes.

In a workshop we conducted for a Fortune 500 logistics firm, managers came up with the idea that they could operate a seaport. Doing so would leverage their logistics expertise, their assets (primarily a large fleet of trucks), and their industry relationships. But nothing happened after the workshop, mostly because one of the senior leaders thought that for security reasons the U.S. government was unlikely to allow outsourcing a seaport to a private company. A year or so after the company decided not to move on the idea, the port they had studied was outsourced to a private company—a *different* private company.

Now perhaps seaport operations was not a business line the company should have entered. But what frustrates me is that the company did not even consider it; no one made a phone call to inquire about federal regulations or worked on a business plan. Instead, they chose to abandon the idea simply because someone with influence thought it not worth the effort.

Contrast that with another client who came up with an idea for a new business strategy that her company might pursue. This company is a leading retirement fund firm. While most of the assets they manage for retirees are invested in public stocks and bonds and must fit within strict guidelines to ensure that they don't expose their customers to too much risk, they also manage tens of billions of dollars of their own assets. Those assets can be put to work more creatively, so the fund managers make private investments in startups, large private companies, and real estate.

Our client (out of confidentiality I'll call her Helen) had an idea. Since her employer had gotten quite good at managing more complicated and risky private investments, perhaps they could start doing the same for other, nonretiree customers. They could collect capital from large institutions and manage those funds in parallel to what they were already doing with their own capital. This meant they would move into the space dominated by firms like Blackrock or KKR—a bold step, to be sure.

You probably won't be surprised to hear that Helen was met with the same kind of unease that the logistics company team faced. But instead of shelving the idea, she persisted patiently for several years, systematically building political support, testing the assumptions, finding ways around the barriers placed in her path. Slowly the company opened up to the idea. Today it is one of the largest asset managers in the world with more than $800 billion of assets under management as of 2018.[9]

What is the difference between these two stories? How did Helen guide her idea to fruition when the logistics company team could not?

Overcoming Barriers

To answer these questions, I started interviewing internal innovators, asking each of them, "What, in your experience, are the biggest barriers to driving an innovation from within?" Three years and over 100 interviews later, I had learned a great deal. Then, to go deeper, I interviewed innovation experts such as Bharat Anand (Harvard), Steve Blank, George Day (Wharton), John Hagel (Deloitte's Center for the Edge and Singularity University), Gary Hamel (London Business School), Roger Martin (Rotman School of Management, University

of Toronto), and Rita McGrath (Columbia) to capture their points of view.

Once I had collated all their answers, I realized that they clustered into seven clear groupings. Together, the employees and the innovation experts repeatedly mentioned these seven barriers as the most common challenges to internal innovation. I also realized that if we turn those seven barriers around and look at the obverse, we see solutions. Overcoming barriers requires certain skills and personal qualities, all of which are common to successful internal innovators.

I realized something else too. Successful innovators understand that, while any one of the seven barriers can crop up at any time, there is usually a natural flow to the sequence of events, a sequence that outlines a pathway of innovation. Their ability to recognize and control that sequence, to the greatest extent possible, plays a big role in their ultimate success.

The following list reflects that natural sequence of the most common barriers and their solutions. You'll see that I have given them names that form an acronym (IN-OVATE), which I hope will make them easy to remember.

1. **Intent:** Facing early obstacles, many would-be internal innovators abandon their original intent. They eventually simply give up looking for chances to innovate. Successful innovators dig deep to keep their intention alive and, as a result, are more likely to spot innovation opportunities.

2. **Need:** Most employees do not understand what kinds of innovations their organizations need. Want proof? Fewer than 55 percent of middle managers can name even two of their company's top strategic priorities.[10] So, even if someone is inspired to look for new ideas, they look in the wrong places and then propose ideas of little strategic value. Successful innovators take the time to learn about the critical market forces affecting their company, understand what their organization cares about, and sense unmet customer needs.

3. **Options:** Would-be internal innovators often grow frustrated because they become fixated too early on a few innovative ideas—or even worse, just one. It's much more strategic to continually generate a flow of new ideas and manage them like a portfolio of options.

4. **_V_alue blockers:** It is commonly accepted that innovative ideas are inconsistent with, and therefore disruptive to, a company's current business model. The organization appears to raise value blockers that inhibit an appropriate new business model from forming around the new idea. Successful innovators find clever ways to engineer their ideas so that rather than conflicting, they enhance the company's standing.

5. **_A_ct:** Established organizations tend to ask employees to prove an idea will work before giving them permission to take action. This puts would-be internal innovators in a fatal catch-22: they can't take action, so they can't prove their idea will work, so they can't take action. Yet most new ideas are better suited to the opposite approach: taking action in order to prove the idea. Successful innovators devise ways to do just that.

6. **_T_eam:** Corporations hamper internal innovation by the nature of their structure. They use siloed hierarchies, act slowly, and value results over learning. Successful innovators recognize that pursuing new ideas often requires the opposite; they pull together a cross-silo team that runs at a rapid pace and is geared toward learning, rather than delivering results.

7. **_E_nvironment:** Getting support for new ideas is politically complicated because the leadership behavior, types of talent, organizational structures, and cultural norms that help established organizations sustain their core operations also tend to hinder internal innovativeness. Successful internal innovators figure out how to create "islands of freedom" from which they can access the talent, structures, cultural norms, and leadership support that will support their attempts at innovation.

A Final Word

In the next seven chapters, I tackle each of these barriers and show how new, emerging strategic concepts and methods can help you prevail over them. My goal is to help you learn to recognize where you are on the IN-OVATE path, predict which barrier is most likely to put a brake on your effort next, and pull out the appropriate tool so you can accelerate your path to success—not just for your sake, or that of your organization, but for all of us. The world needs you.

CHAPTER THREE

Intent

Choosing to See and Seize Opportunities

The most difficult thing is the decision to act;
the rest is merely tenacity.
—AMELIA EARHART

YOU MAY NOT know that you know her. But if you or your children were ever spooked by *Goosebumps*, entertained by The Baby-Sitters Club, or had your mind bent by Animorphs, you have Jean Feiwel to thank. Currently senior vice president at Macmillan Publishers, she has been behind the scenes creating the imprints and platforms that brought Harry Potter and Captain Underpants to the world.

But unlike many prolific editors, Jean's creativity has expanded beyond bookends. Throughout her career, she has challenged traditional publishing business models. Her most recent innovation is Swoon Reads, which today is the leading crowd-sourced platform to help undiscovered romance writers refine their manuscripts and find their audience. It has been lauded in the industry press as an uncommon example of an established publishing company introducing the kind of innovation we usually expect from Silicon Valley. CNN called it "a new way to hear what readers want," *Publishers Weekly* has called it a "pioneering publishing model," and the *New York Times* says it "is upending the traditional discovery process."[1]

I have chosen her story to illustrate the IN-OVATE model because it is so thoroughly representative of the process successful internal innovators seem to follow. It did not come out of an R&D lab or a corporate-sponsored innovation group. It is built on technology, but it's not the kind of technology story we so often hear. It was born out of the passion of an unlikely internal innovator who sensed a need and intuitively managed the process to navigate a solution through the sprawling bureaucracy of a 175-year-old corporation.

Jean is the middle child of an eclectic family of teachers, designers, and computer programmers who found her passion for literature and free thinking at Sarah Lawrence College. When she interviewed for a job at Avon Books, she failed the typing test. But her would-be boss at Avon saw that she "had a great reading background, loved books, and could talk intelligently about them," as Jean told me, and took a chance on her. She rose quickly to senior editor at the age of twenty-eight and was asked to build Avon's children's book business.

But Jean soon ran up against the dilemma many internal innovators confront. Sometimes your organization's leaders say they want innovation when in reality they are uncomfortable diverging from the status quo. Jean left Avon for Scholastic.

Scholastic afforded her more freedom to innovate. They were interested in expanding from textbooks to general-interest books that could serve book clubs. That required a new rhythm of publication, long series of books, a blend between a book and a magazine. Jean structured such a program, *Ginny's Babysitting Job*, and it sold very well in their book clubs year after year and was the inspiration for Ann Martin's *The Babysitter's Club*.

As her stature in the industry grew, other publishers began courting her. They wanted her to innovate for them as she had for Scholastic. She eventually left Scholastic "not of my own choosing," as she told me, after being at the company for twenty-two years and being the architect for their trade publishing program. She joined Macmillan, which seemed to be an organization that "encouraged entrepreneurship and innovation." They didn't hand her spreadsheets with targets; instead, they gave her the latitude to "make it great, make it wonderful." And that mandate eventually produced something entirely, stunningly new to the publishing world.

———————

The path to innovation begins when someone sees an opportunity and takes action on it. Finding opportunities is not hard; they surround us. The difficulty is that most people fail to recognize them or, if they do, choose not to move on them. There could be any number of reasons for this, but the most common one is this: somehow they never take the first step. Jeff Bezos says, "Invention requires a long-term willingness to be misunderstood."[2] Most employees have heard "no" more often than they can stomach, so they have simply given up trying.

The first necessity, the first step on the path, is what I have called "intent." I chose this word as it alludes to "entrepreneurial intention," a concept well established in entrepreneurship theory, which I refer to later in this chapter. It could just as easily be called "commitment," "determination," "tenacity," "resolve," or "perseverance."

Stepping into the Kitchen

Kat Cole is the chief operating officer and president of Focus Brands, a conglomerate that owns numerous restaurant brands, including Schlotzsky's, Carvel, Cinnabon, Moe's Southwest Grill, McAlister's Deli, and Auntie Anne's. Before that, she was the CEO of Cinnabon, which sells branded baked goods through 1,200 stores in forty-eight countries.

Kat started her career as a waitress serving chicken wings and beer at a Hooters restaurant in Jacksonville, Florida. Her mother was a single parent struggling to support three kids, so Kat had to work full time.

Her impressive rise from waitress to CEO can be traced back to a single incident that happened while she was still at Hooters. The cooks at the store had decided to walk out. The remaining staff responded in two ways. Many staff members, figuring there was no food to serve, took off their aprons and went home. Cole and several others walked into the kitchen and began to cook. "You could see the divide immediately," she shared in an interview with Knowledge@Wharton.[3]

That divide neatly illustrates the moment at which someone decides whether to act like an internal entrepreneur or like a conventional employee. When faced with an unexpected challenge or opportunity, do you step into the kitchen or go home?

Defying the Boss to Serve the Company
and the World

Chuck House was an engineer at HP in the early 1960s, working on a project to build large-scale electrostatic displays. He described these to me as a "big TV connected to a computer."

When David Packard visited House's lab, he didn't like House's project at all and told him that he didn't want to see it in the lab when he returned next year. Of course Packard meant he wanted to kill the project. But House chose a different interpretation. He took this to mean that the project had to be launching in less than a year.

On his own time, during the holidays, he took a prototype to potential buyers and returned with orders. His boss at the R&D lab was furious, saying, "I thought I told you to kill this thing." To which House replied, "No, sir. You said when you came back, you didn't want to see this in the lab. It isn't. It's in production."

By making an unconventional choice—to "go into the kitchen" so to speak—House laid the foundation of a technological revolution. His technology became the first commercially available computer display. Had House not made this choice, we would not have seen Neil Armstrong land on the moon.

Two decades later, HP awarded House the "Medal of Defiance," which was "awarded in recognition of extraordinary contempt and defiance beyond the normal call of engineering duty. . . . Charles H. House, using all means available—principally pen, tongue, and airplane to extol an unrecognized technical contribution, planted the seeds for a new market."[4]

Seeing and Seizing Opportunities

When I started digging into how intention works, I thought its role would be straightforward: someone sees an opportunity and either acts or decides to let it pass because the person doesn't want to seize it. In other words, that person either possesses or lacks intent. But I discovered the influence of intention is far more profound and pervasive that you might think.

Seeing Opportunities

In a fascinating study, Richard Wiseman,[5] a psychologist at the University of Hertfordshire, studied two groups of people: those who considered themselves lucky and those who considered themselves unlucky. He asked each to look through a newspaper and report how many photographs were inside. On average, unlucky people took two minutes to come up with their count and lucky people took seconds. What was the difference?

On the second page of the newspaper was a message: "Stop counting—There are 43 photographs in this newspaper." The message took up half the page and was written in large type, so no one should have missed it. Yet unlucky people tended to overlook it.

His research, encompassing this study and others, concluded that "lucky people generate their own good fortune via four basic principles. They are skilled at creating and noticing chance opportunities, make lucky decisions by listening to their intuition, create self-fulfilling prophesies via positive expectations, and adopt a resilient attitude that transforms bad luck into good."[6]

It is as if lucky people step into a situation with the intention of finding luck—so they find it. Those without such an intention fail to see opportunity even when it is staring them in the face.

Lee Pilsbury was born with intent. Fresh out of the hospitality management program at Cornell University, Lee had found himself working as an assistant manager at a Marriott hotel in Houston. Shell was relocating its headquarters from New York to a new building several blocks from his hotel. So when Lee met the Shell executive responsible for managing the relocation, he immediately spotted an opportunity.

He offered Shell a nightly rate of $24 per room, whether single or double. Shell booked the hotel for its employees. Lee was proud he had brought such a significant deal to the company after only a few months on the job, so he was shocked when his manager told him he had made a mistake.

The Marriott's rates at the time were $19 a night for a single and $21 a night for a double, the manager told him. There were cards on every door clearly stating that the maximum rate for every room was $21. Lee was told to go back to Shell and revoke the deal.

Instead, Lee spent the weekend personally changing every card on every door. His boss reluctantly accepted Lee's idea. Lee's intent drove him to lead innumerable innovations within Marriot, such as guaranteed late check-in and 30-minute room service delivery, propelling a rapid career rise. He went on to become the executive vice president for Marriott International and to found one of the largest hospitality private equity firms.[7]

Seizing Opportunities

Even if you recognize an opportunity, the lack of intention will make you unlikely to move on it. Shaun Neff's decision to act on an opportunity sowed the seeds for what has become one of the most exciting activewear brands in the world, sold in thousands of shops in more than forty-five countries, with an impressive list of corporate partners such as Disney, *The Simpsons*, Nickelodeon, and Richard Sherman, and celebrity collaborators such as Snoop Dogg, deadmau5, Wiz Khalifa, Mac Miller, Kate Upton, and Scarlett Johansson. Even my own twelve-year-old aspiring snowboarder reaches for his Neff beanies before hitting the slopes.

While still a freshman at Brigham Young University, Shaun set a goal of building a global activewear brand centered around snowboard culture. His best path to achieving this, he decided, was Neff-branded T-shirts. He gained some traction pasting stickers on signs around town, toting around a backpack of T-shirts to show buyers at snowboard shops, and wooing local influencers. But his efforts were falling short of his aspirations. For his brand to break out, he concluded, he needed nationally renowned snowboarders to wear his shirts.

Shaun counted numerous competitive snowboarders as friends. But when he asked them to wear his shirts, the most successful ones declined. They would love to help him out, but they were under exclusive contracts with other brands.

Shaun was frustrated but determined. So one day he asked several of his professional snowboarder friends if he could take a look at their contracts. That night he stayed up late, studying the contracts, looking for a way out of his dilemma. Suddenly he realized that none of the contracts mentioned headgear. So he decided, literally overnight, to abandon his T-shirt business and become a headgear company.

Time was not in his favor. There was a tournament coming up in just a few days, not enough lead time to manufacture his branded headwear. So he went to the dollar store, bought a few white beanies, and wrote "Neff" on them with a black Sharpie. He convinced several competitors to wear his Neff hat at the competition.

At the end of the tournament, two of the medalists standing on the podium were prominently wearing "Neff" beanies. For Shaun, it was a magical moment. "The heavens opened . . . I am no longer Neff clothing; I'm Neff Headwear."[8]

You will see this same pattern repeated at the beginning of many great innovations. Kendra Scott started a hat store, but when customers started asking for her jewelry more often than hats, she decided she was a jewelry store. Today her company operates more than seventy-five stores throughout the United States and is valued at more than $1 billion.[9] Chuck House at HP, and Elliott Berman at Exxon and other internal innovators we will meet in later chapters all experienced the same pattern. When a roadblock presented itself, they held strong to their intention, found an opportunity, and moved quickly to seize it.

When you hold fast to your intention to innovate, you are more likely to see and seize opportunities. It's critical, therefore, to identify and erase whatever may be dimming your intention. If you feel your intention lacks power—if you are thinking "I'd like to innovate when I get the chance," instead of "I am passionately committed to changing the world"—research suggests that one of three kinds of beliefs may be at play.

Three Blockers of Intention

You can't cross the sea merely by standing and staring at the water.
—RABINDRANATH TAGORE

What is going to stop you from taking the initial action that will put you on the path to innovating from within? What is stopping your people from seeing and acting on the opportunities around them?

The research points to a clear answer.

Alan Carsrud and Malin Brännback, two of my mentors and thesis advisers, are leading experts on the topic of entrepreneurial intention.

The topic is fascinating and complex, certainly worthy of deeper study, but here I will attempt to summarize what you need to know.

Intention precedes the recognition of opportunities and the taking of action to pursue those opportunities. Let's say that again: Intention comes first; all else follows. If you have ever found yourself either missing an opportunity you should have recognized or holding back from taking action on an opportunity when you should have, you were probably stopped because your internal dialogue was having one of three conversations: it won't work, you can't do it, or it's not socially acceptable.

Academics use slightly more formal descriptors.[10]

- **Behavioral beliefs:** whether you believe that the actions that would be required would result in a desirable outcome. You are asking yourself "Would this work?" and answering yes or no.
- **Control beliefs:** whether you believe that you are capable of taking the actions that would achieve the outcome—that you can accomplish the task, that you have the self-efficacy required.[11] You are asking yourself "Am I capable?" and answering yes or no.
- **Normative beliefs:** how you believe other people will react if you take the actions necessary, and the degree to which that influences you. You are asking "What would my colleagues or friends or mother say?"

Five Ways to Overcome Blockers

Rather than constantly questioning and challenging our beliefs and being willing to think differently about the opportunities that are out there, we withdraw into what we've done before. And in a world that's rapidly changing, that's a formula for vulnerability.

—JOHN HAGEL III

Over the years working with teams of innovators, I've come to appreciate how profound this framework is. Here is a five-step process that has proven quite effective at removing whatever beliefs may be holding you or your people back.

Step 1: Diagnose

First, identify what stops you from taking action. To do this, try to picture yourself inside a movie. Imagine that you are presented with an opportunity to innovate, but in the end you decide to pass. Maybe you have been invited to join an ad hoc team working on a new initiative. Perhaps you have discovered an unmet customer need and thought, "We should do something about that." Maybe you have come up with a new way to improve a process within your organization. Whatever specific scenario fits your life, in your movie you feel a moment of excitement, but then you decide not to pursue the possibility.

Now think about what you were telling yourself when you decided to pass. Which of the following sets of statements, which I have pulled from my interviews, sound closest to your internal dialogue?

Behavioral Beliefs ("This won't work.")

- They will never listen to me.
- You just can't innovate in the company.
- We are too stuck in our ways.
- We move too slowly.
- It's too hard.
- It's unlikely to succeed.
- I can't be sure it will work.

Control Beliefs ("I am not capable.")

- I don't have what it takes.
- I'm not an entrepreneur; I'm not innovative.
- I don't know enough; I lack the technical knowledge.
- I'm not that kind of person.
- Who am I to think I could do this?
- I don't have the right mind-set.
- I'm not the kind of person willing to take the risk.

Normative Beliefs ("People won't approve.")

- What would people say?
- I would look weird.

- My colleagues or friends would laugh.
- This could hurt my career.
- What would happen if I failed?
- This could be embarrassing.
- That is not the kind of thing that people like me do.

Step 2: Be Willing to Choose Your Beliefs

> Everything we hear is an opinion, not a fact.
> Everything we see is a perspective, not the truth.
>
> —MARCUS AURELIUS

Once you realize which types of unhelpful beliefs are at work, it's time to start replacing them. It helps to recognize that beliefs are not necessarily true. They are rules humans adopt to help explain what has happened in the past and to give us the sense of security that we know what will happen in the future. Beliefs often seem to be true because they can become self-fulfilling. If you believe something is impossible, you will attempt it and fail, thereby proving that it is impossible.

Dr. Amanda Foo-Ryland (formerly Amanda Mortimer), a performance coach based in Portugal and New Zealand, has coached executives throughout the world on dismantling unhelpful beliefs— what in Neuro Linguistic Programming (NLP) are called "limiting beliefs." She is an expert in NLP, hypnotherapy, and timeline therapy, and has been one of my personal coaches for a number of years. She puts it this way:

> The first thing to establish is that our beliefs, whether they're limiting or empowering, aren't the truth. They're just things we think. They *feel* real to us. Other people have different beliefs, which feel real to them. None of these beliefs are objectively true.
>
> Limiting beliefs are the things you believe about yourself that limit your abilities, and especially your ability to make the most of the opportunities that come your way. Sometimes we're aware of these negative beliefs, while at other times we're not because they're unconscious. They may be founded or unfounded. But limitations are actually a product of the mind. In reality there are no limitations on a person. Anything can be done if you put your mind to it.[12]

To loosen your attachment to unhelpful beliefs, be willing to consider, if only for the next thirty minutes, that the belief(s) you identified in step 1 above may not be true. Can you find any examples in the past of someone proving this belief is not true? Has anyone ever done something that contradicts the belief? Rarely do our beliefs hold true 100 percent of the time.

Step 3: Feel the Cost

Foo-Ryland has created a process that enables clients to start deconstructing beliefs. It helps to work with a coach, but you can do it on your own as well. It not only clarifies the limiting belief; it also demolishes the destructive thought pattern. She calls it the Sherlock Holmes Technique, because you become something like a "detective" of your thoughts—you're observing yourself as closely as Sherlock would, and as objectively. Try it for forty-eight hours, and I think you will notice your behavior and outcomes change for the better. All you need is a notebook and a sense of playfulness.

1. Every time you have a thought about taking an innovative action, ask yourself, "What is it I believe about myself that caused me to think that?" Notice what comes up for you and write it down in your notebook.
2. Every time you feel bad, ask yourself, "What do I believe about myself that caused me to feel that?" Notice what comes up for you and make a note of this.
3. Each time you do either one, physically move yourself away from where you were sitting or standing and in this new position ask the question again (What is it I believe about myself that caused me to think that? or What do I believe about myself that caused me to feel that?). Ask in a playful way, as if you have caught the limiting belief by surprise.
4. At the end of your forty-eight hours, look at your list and ask yourself two questions about each item on it:
   • What has been the cost of having this belief?
   • What will be the cost of living in this belief for the next five years?

When calculating "cost," think about the monetary value of your time and energy, and put a real dollar value on it. Think also about

the emotional costs—to your relationships, to your sense of fulfil-ment, to your career, to your capacity to have an impact in the world.

Step 4: Assess the Payoff

Of course, a fair assessment of a belief involves payoffs as well as costs. Ask yourself, "What is the benefit to me of holding onto this belief?" Does it reduce your risk? Does it help you avoid embarrassment?

Often this payoff is something you are not comfortable admit-ting to yourself. For example, if you are being limited by behavioral beliefs ("This won't work"), your payoff may be that you don't have to admit you are simply too scared to try. This one is widespread, as leading management thinker Dr. Pankaj Ghemawat, points out: " 'The system made me do it' is the perfect cop-out for today's man-agers." If you are limited by control beliefs ("I am not capable"), you may be avoiding taking full responsibility. If you are limited by normative beliefs ("People won't approve"), your payoff may be that you avoid the jealous eye of others who see you succeeding at something they were too scared to try themselves.

Step 5: Choose a New Belief

> Life can be much broader once you discover one simple fact:
> everything around you that you call life was made up by people that were
> no smarter than you and you can change it, you can influence it,
> you can build your own things that other people can use.
> Once you learn that, you'll never be the same again.
> —STEVE JOBS

Finally, think of a new belief you might use instead. Don't neces-sarily choose something that feels like a directly opposite belief. For example, if your belief is "I don't have what it takes," don't pick "I do have what it takes." Instead consider "I have fun inno-vating" or "I am a passionate person" or "I am driven to have an impact on the world." Imagine how your life would be in five years, and then in ten years, if you lived this new belief. What would your career look like—your level of fulfillment, the impact on people around you, the role model you set for your children, your customers, your level of energy, your health, and so forth?

Using the Sherlock Holmes Technique, "catch yourself" living in this new belief. Congratulate yourself. The more the new belief runs, the stronger it becomes, just as the limiting belief did.

Once you have chosen a belief that leads you to the future you want, you will find that the old belief starts fading and the new one starts taking hold. You will notice opportunities you didn't see before and take actions you would not have considered before. You will start exploring the world with an intention to innovate and affect what you care about.

A Final Word

We must do our work for its own sake,
not for fortune or attention or applause.
—STEVEN PRESSFIELD[13]

As Jean's story from the publishing world illustrates, great internal innovators don't enter new situations content to merely keep doing things right. They carry with them the intent to do things differently and better. Their innovations come not from one-off sparks of insight but from an ongoing drive to look for and pursue new opportunities.

If that does not describe how you, or your people, are wired, there is something you can do about it. You just need to activate the intention to innovate.

Without an intention to innovate, we tend to overlook opportunities and avoid taking actions to pursue those opportunities. If your intention is missing or restrained, this is likely because you believe it won't work, believe you're not capable, or believe it's not socially acceptable. But if you identify the belief holding you back, and then deconstruct and replace it, you will naturally create the intention to innovate. You will start seeing and acting on new possibilities.

Moving forward with clear-eyed intent, Jean Feiwel began to create something the book-publishing world had never seen.

CHAPTER FOUR

Need

Knowing Where to Look

Everything can always be done better than it is being done.
—HENRY FORD

PART OF JEAN'S job as an editor in Macmillan's children's group was to recruit promising authors—but her pitch seemed to be getting tougher. More and more, authors seemed to be interested in self-publishing, sidestepping traditional publishing companies altogether.

One day, Jean opened *USA Today* and saw five self-published titles on the bestseller list. What's going on here?" she wondered. "Why are they on the list?" She read three of them and found "loads of issues with structure and grammar . . . and it didn't matter." They were still selling.

Additionally, she observed that old titles were reappearing on bestseller lists. For example, *Ginnie's Baby-Sitting Business* by Catherine Woolley, originally published in 1969, would hit the list every couple of years and sell hundreds of thousands of copies.

Something was changing. A growing segment of readers seemed not to care about the high-quality, fresh titles that traditional publishers thought were the key to market success.

When Jean tried to recruit a few self-published authors, she was surprised to hear they were less than enthusiastic about being traditionally

published. Then, in what (in retrospect) seems like a turning point, Jean read a manuscript by a young writer named Colleen Hoover. It was a little rough around the edges, but so raw and authentic that Jean "couldn't put it down." She wanted to publish it. Colleen, to Jean's surprise, responded, "What do I need you for?" That question lodged in Jean's head. "What *do* they need us for?" she asked herself.

At that moment, Jean recognized an emerging market need. "The system was broken," she realized. "We needed to go beyond the system."

In the workshop where I first met Jean and her team, we explored several emerging trends and their impact on the publishing industry: digitization, ebooks, and self-publishing. That last trend—self-publishing—was at the top of everyone's mind. As we thought through the implications, it became clear to the fifteen people sitting around the boardroom table that the undeniable growth of self-publishing needed their wholehearted attention. More to the point, it needed action in response.

Jean's radar beeped. She had realized for some time that the company needed to address self-publishing; indeed, the beginning of an answer had already been building in her mind. But in that moment a door opened for her, because now the entire leadership team had simultaneously come to the same conclusion.

Therein lies an important lesson for all of us: Spotting a market need is not enough. That need must also match a strategic need for the company. Otherwise your organization is not likely to support pursuing it. When you understand what your company needs and, more precisely, what the company *recognizes* it needs, you can focus your search for innovation more strategically.

Like the drunk who looked for his keys in the parking lot (where even he knew they could not possibly be) because that's where the light was, too often we look where it's easy to look rather than stopping to consider which hunting grounds would produce the kinds of ideas our organizations want.

You wouldn't drill for oil or mine for diamonds by randomly picking a piece of land to which to apply your shovel. You would conduct some kind of survey to identify a site with a high probability of yielding something. You similarly risk wasting your time if you invest effort

in looking for ideas in areas your company doesn't view as important. You can dramatically improve your chances by directing your search in more fertile grounds, by seeking not just any idea your customers might want but also, of those possibilities, just the kinds of ideas your organization is likely to embrace.

How do you maximize your chances of finding ideas that make sense for your company and the market? How do you know where to look?

Knowing Where to Look

In 1959, a submarine surfaced off the coast of Florida and fired a guided cruise missile toward the shore. Luckily, this was not an enemy attack—the missile landed harmlessly at an air base in Jacksonville.

The missile's nose cone contained not weapons but mail: three thousand letters addressed to officials of the Eisenhower administration, from the president himself on down. The letters, signed by Arthur Summerfield, the U.S. postmaster general, introduced the U.S. government, and the navy in particular, to the first official "missile mail." In the letter, Summerfield predicted that "we will see missile mail developed to a significant degree before man has reached the moon." But eventually, the navy viewed his idea as a public relations gimmick with costs too high to warrant its insignificant benefits. We got to the moon, but we never got missile mail.

Get used to this: The failure rate for internal innovators is high. A macro study conducted by Strategyn, an innovation consulting firm, found that on average only 17 percent of innovation efforts succeed.[1] For every innovation adopted, we can find ten or more missile mails that are rejected. This is one instance where entrepreneurs have an advantage: When one funder rejects their idea, they have forty other doors to knock on. You only have one, so you have to be smart about it.

One internal innovator put it this way: "It's like baseball. I learned that baseball teams don't just scout players, they scout umpires. They study what strike zones different umpires have. Some are wider and some more narrow. Some higher and some lower. If you want to throw a strike, you have to know what your umpire's strike zone is."

Similarly, you'll want to know what your organization's strike zone is before you pitch an idea.

What your company will embrace may not be immediately obvious. Amazon Web Services, for example, seemed to be a significant break away from Amazon.com's core business of ecommerce. Yet it was embraced by the company and its partners, turning into a $17 billion business in just eight years.

Or consider Google. By its third year of operation, Google had become the leader in online search, overtaking internet powerhouses like Yahoo! and Alta Vista. Google could have gone on forever, doing very nicely as the leading search provider, but then Sheryl Sandberg joined the company and saw something different. Almost immediately she understood Google's strategic potential and, more importantly, the path needed to realize that potential. She volunteered to oversee a team of four Googlers in order to develop what was then called the AdWords program, selling small text advertisements next to search results. It did not take long before AdWords was making money.

Sandberg then started working on something bigger. A new initiative, AdSense, would place advertisements directly onto external sites, with Google earning a commission on their sales. Linking paid advertising to search results was a game changer for Google. AdSense positioned Google at the center of online commerce. Revenues soared. As online advertising revenue grew, so did Google's. The profit fueled new products, which further strengthened Google's share of online activity, setting Google on a cycle of growth. In 2001, when Sandberg joined the company, Google's ad revenue had been $70 million; by 2008, when she left to join Facebook, it had grown to $21 billion.[2]

How did Sandberg spot the strategic potential in AdWords and AdSense? By making a big-picture survey of the landscape, which enabled her to see what others could not see, and then applying a clear-eyed, strategic analysis of possibilities.

At McKinsey we called this adopting the "top-management perspective," which means that you step up and think like your CEO. You understand not only what it takes to succeed in your own role, but also why your job matters to your team, and why *that* matters to your group, and why *that* matters to your company, and

why *that* matters to the world. Because you see the full picture, you can spot the best places to look for the ideas that your organization will embrace. This, research shows, reduces the risk of your ideas' being rejected.[3]

The internal innovators I interviewed and the research I studied offered a plethora of advice and framework for addressing this challenge of knowing where to look. I have summarized that into a set of tools you can use to direct your search more strategically.

The Strategy Pyramid

Many companies conceive of their strategy as a pyramid. At the top are elements of the strategy that change rarely, if at all. At the bottom are the elements that must adjust often to deal with changes in the market. Taking the time to understand the layers of your company's pyramid is time well spent.

Purpose or Mission

Every well-run organization holds at the very top of the pyramid some overarching purpose. You may see it referred to as the "core purpose" or "mission." Whatever your organization calls it, it defines what your organization should do (things that support the purpose) and should not do (things that do not support the purpose).

Sheryl Sandberg left Amazon to join Google because of the company's purpose: "to make the world's information freely available." Southwest Airlines' purpose is "to give people the freedom to fly." Amazon's is to be "Earth's most customer-centric company." Alibaba.com's is to "make it easy to do business anywhere." Johnson & Johnson exists to "alleviate pain and suffering"; Disney lives to "create happiness."[4]

I have used those examples of core purpose because they are easy to grasp. That is not always the case. Many organizations, in my experience, have more complicated purposes or pursue purposes that fail to inspire employees and customers. For example, Barnes & Noble's mission at the time of this writing is "to operate the best specialty retail business in America, regardless of the product we sell. Because the product we sell is books, our aspirations must be consistent with the promise and the ideals of the volumes which line our shelves."

Whatever your organization's core purpose is, it's worth using it as the starting point for your idea search. Here are some practical ways to clarify your organization's mission:

- Look it up in your annual report.
- See what the mission was in the past, all the way back to the company's original founding.
- Interview five colleagues and/or managers and ask them what they think the mission is.
- Interview five customers to understand what need they seek to meet when they use your product or service, and why they prefer your offer over others.

Long-Term Strategic Intent

Create your future from your future, not your past.

—WERNER ERHARD

Your purpose is something you pursue every day, yet may never fully attain. By contrast, your strategic intent is a vision of something, usually an outcome or state, that you will one day realize, even if it takes a long time.

At the time of this writing, for example, Cisco's stated vision is "to deliver a highly secure, intelligent platform for digital business." Mastercard's vision is to realize "a world beyond cash." These succinct statements may not immediately make sense to you, but to Cisco and Mastercard employees they speak volumes.

To assess your organization's vision, you can follow steps similar to those you use to clarify your mission:

- Read your annual report.
- Ask colleagues and managers what they think the vision is.
- Listen to quarterly earnings calls to see what your CEO says the vision is.
- Ask what future state of the world would be achieved if your organization experiences success over the next five to ten years.

Trends

Your organization may be bombarded with numerous signals and market changes and need to make sense of them. Ideally, your leadership has converged on a common view of the trends that matter and painted a picture of a potential future state, showing how your long-term strategic intent fits into that picture.

Microsoft, for example, defines its key trends this way: "We believe a new technology paradigm is emerging that manifests itself through an intelligent cloud and an intelligent edge where computing is more distributed, AI drives insights and acts on the user's behalf, and user experiences span devices with a user's available data and information." Cisco puts it this way: "As our customers add billions of new connections to their enterprises, we believe the network is becoming more critical than ever. We believe that our customers are looking for intelligent networks that provide meaningful business value through automation, security, and analytics."

Identifying a few particularly relevant trends, as these two examples illustrate, removes the clutter. Smart organizations can then merge those trends to paint a comprehensive view of the future state in which they must compete.

To pinpoint the trends that matter, it helps to start with your formal strategy statement. If you're lucky, you will find them clearly laid out there. But you can also:

- Look up conferences related to your industry and review the breakout sessions that are part of the agendas.
- Attend industry conferences and listen to what people in your industry are concerned about.
- Search articles that have up-to-date thoughts about the top trends affecting your industry. They may have titles that promise "the top trends impacting [your industry] today," or something similar. Such third-party lists are often more insightful than leadership lists; they are typically more objective. I do this whenever I am preparing to deliver a speech inside a new industry.
- Talk to colleagues or friends in other companies in your industry and ask them what they think is important.

Near-Term Strategic Goals

A long-term strategic intent is a vision of something that will take time to reach. It requires phases or steps. Your near-term strategic intent describes the phase or steps your organization is undertaking *now*. It answers the question "Where must we be in the near term to know we are on track to achieving the long-term intent?" Typically, we hope to achieve near-term goals in one to three years.

If you look through your company's annual report, investor presentations, and budget presentations, you will likely find four types of near-term goals:

- Financial goals, such as "to increase revenue growth to 10 percent annually" or "to achieve zero long-term debt"
- Customer goals, such as "to achieve a 95 percent customer-satisfaction rate" or "to introduce seven new products into the market"
- Operational goals, such as "to improve efficiency by 10 percent" or "to improve our acquisition success rate"
- Organizational goals, such as "to become a more agile organization" or "to develop a culture of collaboration"

This framework was first introduced by Robert Kaplan and David Norton in the early 1990s and has continued to influence how organizations set strategic goals.

Your organization may have scattered the expression of these goals throughout various internal documents and across functions. Compiling them may take some detective work on your part, but would give you insights into the overall workings of your organization that few people in company have. To do this:

- Ask functional leaders (e.g., HR, IT, operations, sales, marketing, regional divisions, brands) to share their strategic plans with you.
- Ask your manager for the strategic plan or budgets of your group or division.
- Attend or read the transcripts of town halls or internal conferences in which divisional leaders share their plans.
- Search through your internal blog, if you have one, for insights.

Strategic Priorities

The next layer in your strategic pyramid may be the most important: your organization's strategic priorities. These are simple themes or "thrusts" that clarify what your organization is focusing on now and for the next one to three years. They are what your organization has decided are the most important ways to achieve your near-term goals.

When I was diagnosed with high cholesterol, my doctor told me to do two things: take red yeast rice supplements and go on a specific eating plan, the South Beach Diet. That diet, in turn, had very simple instructions: during the first week, eat absolutely no carbohydrates.

In the whirlwind of my days, it's easy to mindlessly pick up a hamburger when I get hungry. Had the doctor's instructions been more complicated, I probably would have eaten a hamburger. But because the instructions were so simple, concise, and clear ("take red yeast rice every day and don't eat carbohydrates"), I was able to stop myself from putting the hamburger into my mouth or leaving my house without having taken my pills.

Strategy works the same way. In order for strategy to translate into action, it needs to be simple enough that people can align their behaviors. Unfortunately, most strategies are far too complex to remember, let alone to keep in mind during a business day. But somewhere, formally or informally, there exists a set of priorities that your organization deems important.

Mastercard, for example, is currently very clear on its priorities: grow, diversify, and build. At nearly every earnings call, executives repeat the same mantra. Cisco's current strategy states it this way: "Our strategic priorities include accelerating our pace of innovation, increasing the value of the network, and delivering technology the way our customers want to consume it."

Each of your company's strategic priorities captures a number of initiatives. If you link your project to those priorities, you are more likely to get buy-in for your ideas.

Alignment Priorities

Finally, in order to implement its strategy, your organization is always undertaking several alignment initiatives, defined as efforts to ensure you have the resources, capabilities, and practices needed to

operationalize your corporate strategy. These initiatives often go over-looked or underappreciated by employees and mid-level managers. So if you understand them and look for innovations that will advance them, you have a chance to stand out.

Academic research has numerous frameworks, philosophies, and checklists for assessing what alignment efforts any particular organization is undergoing. At my company, we compiled several of them into a simple checklist of eight dimensions:

1. **Key Performance Indicators (KPIs):** Your company may be adjusting its system for measuring and managing performance. How can you help them do that better, faster, more simply?
2. **Resources:** Your organization may be shifting resources from one area to another. What ideas do you have for facilitating this rebalancing?
3. **Configuration:** Your company's strategy likely requires adjustments to organizational structure—who reports to whom, how groups are defined, etc. What opportunities do you see to improve your organizational configuration?
4. **Policies and procedures:** Internal innovators often cite this as a point of frustration and opportunity. What ideas can you propose for improving your policies and procedures so you can better execute your strategy?
5. **Leadership:** How your leadership team members interact with each other and with the next level down can have a profound impact on your organization's success. This is a touchy area to get involved in, but think about what ideas you could diplomatically suggest to improve your leadership team's effectiveness at implementing your strategy.
6. **Staff and talent:** Your organization will need to hire and fire staff members and shift sources of talent. What ideas do you have to help your firm access the talent it needs to win?
7. **Skills and capabilities:** When your company's strategy shifts, you often need to begin building new skills and capabilities in your organization. How can you help your organization build the skills and capabilities its strategy demands?
8. **Culture:** The norms, habits, and values that your organization shares comprise its culture. When strategy changes, culture must follow suit. What cultural characteristics does your strategy demand, and what ideas do you have to help ease the shift?

An Idea That Opened Possibilities at Red Hat

Doing the detective work and assembling a picture of your strategy that is as precise as possible can make the difference between toiling in frustration and living the life of a successful innovator who affects your organization and the world. Consider Marina Zhurakhinskaya.

From a young age she was drawn to computers. She often visited her mom's office and played games on the computers there. No surprise, then, that she joined a programming club in the eighth grade. When the family emigrated from their native Ukraine to the United States, Marina chose programming as her college major. It was, she says, "a profession that matched my abilities, provided financial security, and did not require perfect proficiency in English."[5]

Her second job after graduating was with Red Hat, the innovative company that has been a pioneer in the "open source" movement, essentially taking a community-powered approach to building technologies for enterprises. Organizations and individuals can freely use and collaborate on open-source technologies. Working in such a context gave her the freedom to bring her passion for programming to another community she has passion for.

Marina was working as a developer on the GNOME Project, which builds an easy-to-use desktop for the GNU/Linux operating systems. She found few other women contributing to the project, so when the board of a nonprofit supporting the project, the GNOME Foundation, approached Marina for help getting more women involved with the project, the mission immediately spoke to her. She says, "I loved my job. I loved how connected I felt to the community. Open source has this additional appeal that you feel you are contributing to the world and I wanted more women to have access to this."

In 2010, Marina started an effort to support women in applying for Google Summer of Code with GNOME. In this program, college students from around the world apply to spend the summer working on an open-source coding project with mentors from open-source communities and financial support from Google. While many men were applying to work with GNOME, few women were doing so. Despite Marina's efforts, only about six of the eighty-three applicants to GNOME were women.

Later in 2010, in true "open organization" style, Marina led the creation of the Outreach Program for Women, which supported women contributing to GNOME with paid, mentored internships. She built a community of GNOME contributors, many of them from Red Hat, who mentored women in the program.

The program Marina started proved so successful that the GNOME Foundation expanded it to support multiple free and open-source software communities offering internships to women, trans men, and genderqueer people. That effort quickly outgrew the GNOME Foundation and was transferred to Software Freedom Conservancy, which provides a nonprofit home and infrastructure for numerous free and open-source software projects. During that transition, the program was renamed to Outreachy and expanded to offer internships to people from groups underrepresented in technology in the United States, such as African Americans and Latinos.

Marina had a passion for expanding this community even further and for working to promote diversity and inclusion in open source in other ways. She wanted to focus on this full-time, but she still had a full-time role working on an engineering team at Red Hat.

So she thought about how she could turn this passion into a new full-time job. She wanted this project to be her core job, not just a side project. This meant getting buy-in for such a role at Red Hat and moving to a different team. She brought the idea to a senior leader at Red Hat, who suggested that she create a proposal outlining what such a role would entail and all the ways in which the company could benefit.

In 2015, she did just that—thinking through Red Hat's mission and strategy, its priorities and challenges—and a number of clear, compelling benefits emerged. If she engineered her proposed role correctly, it could very clearly support Red Hat's strategic success.

1. **Purpose:** Her effort to increase the diversity of the open-source community aligned beautifully with Red Hat's mission "to be the catalyst in communities of customers, contributors, and partners creating better technology the open source way."
2. **Long-term intent:** Red Hat was growing quickly, and this role could help expand the community of people familiar with working in a collaborative open-source environment that Red Hat could engage as employees, collaborators, partners, and customers, which could fuel continued growth.

3. **Alignment initiatives:** Employee engagement was a key alignment priority for Red Hat, and Outreachy could help. It could
strengthen engagement and retention of current employees by
giving Red Hatters, as Red Hat employees are called, an opportunity to directly affect diversity in their open-source communities
through mentoring. Additionally, supporting Marina and other
employees in organizing and mentoring for the program would
be another way for Red Hat to demonstrate its commitment to
promoting diversity and inclusion in open-source communities.

Company leaders quickly saw that Marina had demonstrated how
her idea fit Red Hat's strategy, and they agreed to create a new position that allowed Marina to continue working on Outreachy and other
diversity and inclusion initiatives as her formal role. As of August
2018, Outreachy has supported close to five hundred people from
underrepresented backgrounds in gaining experience in open source,
nearly a fifth of them mentored by Red Hatters.

More Tools for Focusing Your Search

Beyond the strategy pyramid, internal innovators I interviewed empha-
sized several other tools they used effectively to understand their company's strategic needs:

- Capabilities
- Strategic orientation
- Investor goals
- Time horizon
- Market/user need

Capabilities

Most companies define themselves by their industry. If you sell dog
food, you prioritize dog food ideas. If you sell beauty care, you look
for beauty ideas.

An effective way to uncover new innovation opportunities is to
take a different point of view. Our research shows that most successful companies today define themselves less often by their industry and

more often by a unique capability, unrelated to their industry, that they can apply in new areas. Indeed, many of the most impactful corporate innovations over the past ten years have sprung out of this way of thinking.

- Amazon Web Services was not an ecommerce idea, but rather leveraged Amazon's skill managing technology.
- Google's AdSense was not a search product, but rather leveraged Google's unique ability to understand what customers are looking for to help advertisers.
- Slack, the team communication tool with more than eight million daily users as of the time of this writing, was an internal communications tool commercialized by the gaming company Glitch.

In every case, the innovators who pursued the idea would not have done so had they limited their energies to their company's industry. Consider Hoby Darling, a Nike executive who led the company to explore territory beyond sneakers.

When Hoby assessed the opportunity to lead Nike's electronics business, he could have shied away. Nike, after all, is known for athletic footwear and apparel. Why would it think it could compete with electronic giants? As Hoby explained to me, he saw the company's core advantage differently. He recognized that what made Nike great was its unique ability to understand, and meet, the needs of everyday athletes.

Nike's campus is filled with top athletes who come in to try new products the company is developing. The company's designers spend hours with clipboards in hand, watching these athletes play basketball, tennis, and other sports, as a means of tracking unmet needs. Hoby understood that this unique ability to draw insights made Nike the natural innovator to introduce one of the first athletic wearable devices.

The device was so profitable that it sold out twice when it opened for preorder in the United States. In fact, one consumer on Twitter tracked the Fuelband preorder time as not more than four minutes before its inventory ran out. Though Nike eventually decided to discontinue the Fuelband, industry insiders believe Nike's rapid initial success inspired Apple to launch the Apple Watch and helped convince Fitbit, Samsung, and Garmin to take wearable devices seriously.

By ignoring your industry and orienting yourself instead to your company's capabilities, you can open up exciting opportunities. These capabilities can be tangible (e.g., your company has machinery that allows it to produce something others cannot) or intangible (e.g., a brand, intellectual property, or unique culture). Regardless, to be valuable, the capability your idea leverages will only be worth something if two things are true:

1. The capability allows you to achieve superior performance on an attribute that your customer or user actually cares about.
2. It is so scarce or hard to duplicate that if your idea succeeds, competitors will have trouble replicating your success.

Ask yourself: What are my organization's unique capabilities (not as defined by its industry) that can be leveraged to make an idea work?

Strategic Orientation

Every organization evolves to develop a particular strategic orientation. While you need to be good enough at everything, in order to survive over the long term, you need to become outstanding at one thing. Michael Treacy and Fred Wiersema first proposed this idea in their 1995 bestseller *The Discipline of Market Leaders*. We have found this concept to be powerful in enabling innovators to rapidly separate promising ideas from bad ones. Treacy and Wiersema proposed three types of orientations (they call them disciplines),[6] to which we like to add one more:

- **Product orientation:** If your company focuses on winning by producing the best product, you have a product orientation. Think of BMW, which builds the "ultimate driving machine," or Samsung, which adds new features to its products so quickly competitors have difficulty keeping up. Product-oriented companies seek to push the boundaries of product performance, they value research and development, and product designers carry considerable power. Such companies encourage innovation and accept risk as a path to leadership.

- **Process orientation:** If your company competes primarily through the efficiency and precision of its operations, you have a process orientation. Think of Walmart or McDonald's, which daily pursue opportunities to wring cost and waste out of their operations. Such companies tend to be cost-conscious, have involved measurement systems, adopt rigorous quality- and cost-control approaches, and train people to be as efficient and cost-effective as possible.

- **Customer orientation:** If your company competes primarily on the strength of its connection with customers, if it prides itself on knowing customer teams even better than customers do themselves, then you have a customer orientation. Nike wins by understanding its customer better than the competition. Apple does the same. Amazon similarly seeks to win by understanding the customer more effectively, but in their case through data rather than personal observation. Customer-orientation companies obsess over knowing their customers in detail, view success as depending on predicting customer needs early, and adopt business practices that encourage deep customer insight.

- **People orientation:** If your company competes primarily on the basis of your people, if you focus on culture and recruitment, you have a people orientation. Zappos is a great example of such a company. It obsesses over culture and is famous for adopting unusual people policies. For example, about a week after being hired, Zappos employees are offered $2,000 to quit, the idea being that every employee who stays is there because he or she want to be, not out of obligation. In consulting, Deloitte has long been known as a leader in orienting itself toward its people. McKinsey and Goldman Sachs are known for being able to recruit top-tier talent. People-oriented companies have strong cultures (which makes them a great a place to work for those who fit, but an undesirable place for those who don't), adopt unique people policies, and invest heavily in people development.

If you are clear about your organization's orientation, you can focus your innovation search in the areas that play toward it. Ask yourself: Given our past success, which strategic orientation—product, process, customer, or people—has been at the heart of our success?

Investor Goals

To better understand which kinds of ideas your organization will support, take a higher-order perspective. Recognize that while customers ultimately will be the judges of whether your company thrives or struggles, in the near term your investors' demands may matter even more.

Pressure from investors flows down through board members to your leadership team and then down the line. Your CEO is likely fretting daily about what investors will ask. So think like a CEO. Seek to understand what your investors are demanding; this will help you make better-informed choices about which types of innovations to pursue. Generally, your investors will cluster into one of four categories:

Value investors seek to buy stock at a price below what it is truly worth (its intrinsic value), trusting that the market will eventually appreciate the company's worth. Warren Buffett is the archetype of the value investor. We have worked with multiple companies owned by Buffett's Berkshire Hathaway, and they tend to prefer innovation ideas that:

- Do not involve significant risk.
- Do not promise huge growth potential.
- Generate immediate cash flow.

Income investors are interested in cash flow. They prefer you give them cash left over at the end of the year as dividends rather than investing in projects with uncertain and longer-term returns. In such environments, you will likely find leadership shying away from ideas that require big up-front investments in favor of innovations that fund themselves. You won't get far proposing a new factory; instead, propose to outsource manufacturing. Rather than build technology, find a technology partner.

Growth investors are the opposite of income investors. They are pressuring your CEO to reinvest profits to fuel faster growth. They expect you to invest whatever you do earn in new growth initiatives. They don't need cash now; they want a future payoff. For example,

Amazon investors have cared little that the company, for most of its history, until the time of this writing, has not delivered profits. An investor base dominated by growth investors is looking for ideas with future payoff, even if the idea may require some investment up front. In a meeting with a team seeking to launch a mining business within a company that knew little about mining, I was at first shocked that they were planning to build a massive mining operation, until I realized their investor base was asking the company to prove they had big, long-term investment opportunities to fuel future growth.

There are other types of investors, of course. New York Life is a mutual company, meaning that its policyholders actually own the organization. As a result, their executives and internal innovators, in my experience, are continually oriented toward innovations that serve policyholders. The Co-Operators, a leading insurance firm in Canada, is structured as a cooperative, so their innovations must benefit a countrywide network of members. REI, the outdoor apparel retailer, is also a cooperative, owned by its customers. As a card-carrying loyalty member, you receive a dividend each year to use on purchases. One of our clients is a B corporation, requiring it to embrace innovations that serve the environment and workers before profits.

Many of the internal innovators I interviewed had an intuitive sense of their investors' goals and steered their search accordingly. Here are some tips from them, to help you assess your organization's investor goals.

- Consider your corporate structure. Are you a traditional corporation or a cooperative, for example?
- Look at which investment funds own shares in your firm, then research their investment goals. For example, the funds invested in your company may have the words "growth," "value," or "income" in their title.
- Look at investment blogs liked seekingalpha.com or motleyfool.com to see what investors are saying about your company.

Time Horizon

Finally, you want to understand your organization's time horizon. Knowing ahead of time how far in the future your organization is looking can save considerable heartache later on. At my workshops, I always ask participants what they see as the most persistent barrier to internal innovation; without fail, "short-term thinking" is always in the top five. I'm not suggesting you abandon long-term pursuits. But if you clarify in the beginning what time horizon will excite your leadership, you can start making some clever, strategic choices.

At the end of a two-day innovation brainstorm during which thirty managers worked passionately to generate more than two hundred growth ideas, they were ready to pitch to senior management. Through a flurry of Post-it notes and flip-chart diagrams, seven big ideas emerged that participants were sure would deliver major impact on the company's future.

But as the teams pitched their ideas in a "shark-tank" format, the executive judges grew noticeably uncomfortable. It soon came out that the leaders wanted ideas that delivered a financial impact within ninety days. Had we clarified this ahead of time, we could have easily avoided this disheartening moment.

Several frameworks are available to distinguish time horizons. From two of our favorites—the Three Horizons of Growth[7] and the Three Boxes[8]—we pulled together elements that collectively give you four potential time horizons within which to look for ideas:

- **Abandon:** abandoning practices, systems, and businesses that are no longer serving the organization. What could your organization abandon?
- **Core:** ideas for protecting and expanding the core business, including improving efficiency, fixing broken processes, improving core products, evolving policies, or increasing penetration into existing customers. How could your organization strengthen its core business?
- **New:** ideas for adding new value on top of the core business, including expanding into new customer segments or geographies, finding new uses for existing technologies, expanding younger

products and services that are not yet scaled. What opportunities might generate new value?

- **Options:** ideas that create "option value"—something that may or may not turn out to be valuable in the future but requires you to take action now. What actions could your organization take today to create "option value," even if the true potential of those actions cannot be accurately calculated right now?

To assess which horizon(s) your organization is most interested in now, you can:

- Gather recent initiatives your organization has launched and ask into which category (abandon, core, new, or options) they fit.
- Interview managers and senior leaders. They are likely to already be aware of where the organization wants to focus.
- Look at the strategic priorities you identified earlier, in your strategic pyramid; these will likely give you a clue as to what is important to your organization right now.

Market/User Need

An innovation, to be effective, has to be simple and it has to be focused. It should do only one thing, otherwise, it confuses. If it is not simple, it won't work. . . . It should be focused on a specific need that it satisfies, on a specific end result that it produces.

—PETER DRUCKER[9]

The tips presented here will help you build an informed assessment of what your organization needs. When you marry that with clarity on a specific need of your customer or your market and what you are passionate about, you can reveal a market need that your organization is uniquely qualified to meet. Kevin Systrom, cofounder of Instagram, put it this way: "Building new things requires that we step back, understand what inspires us, and match that with what the world needs."[10]

Ten years ago, understanding what the market needed involved extensive top-down market research, surveys, and data analysis. But over the past decade, a more human-centered approach has emerged. Inspired by the human-centered design approach (more to come in chapter 7) popularized by Apple, IDEO, and Silicon Valley more generally, companies are finding that the most important insights come from getting out of the office and talking to customers.

George Day of Wharton points out that leaders are often separated from customers by so many layers that they no longer understand what the market needs. This disconnect creates an opportunity for you to close it by doing your own firsthand market research.

Tom Chi, former head of Google X, advocates picking up the phone to speak to a customer within minutes of having an idea. Debra Brackeen, the chief innovation officer of CSAA, forces her people to "get out of the office, talk to customers, talk to agents." When they return from doing this kind of research, she told me, "They realize there is no substitute for it." Steve Blank advocates getting "out of the office." Stop guessing what users want (whether those users be customers or internal to your company) and talk to them or, even better, observe them firsthand. George Day has a simple formula: force yourself to have in-depth conversations with at least two customers your company has lost.

Few people have more experience at gathering valuable customer insights than Tomer Sharon, senior user experience (UX) researcher at Google. He summarizes his approach with seven tips:

1. Ask yourself why you are conducting the interview before you start. What are you trying to learn?
2. Watch out for the phenomenon called "rationalization." If you ask people why they did something, they have a tendency to give you an answer they think is socially acceptable instead of revealing what they were actually thinking.
3. Look for the story. Ask about stories of things that happened (e.g., "Tell me about the time that . . ."), or better yet observe them ("Show me how you check your email.").

4. Ask follow-up questions like "What do you mean?" or "Why do you frown when you say that?"
5. Don't ask about the future, and avoid asking questions like "Would you use it? Would you pay for it? How much would you pay for it?"
6. Don't ask leading questions by inserting your opinion into the question. For example, remove "improved" from the question "Would you rather use the old one or this new improved one?"
7. Don't explain the question; ask it and let the silence settle in. Let them think and remember.

A Final Word

Many would-be internal innovators grow frustrated because their ideas are too rarely adopted. But often this is because they fail to understand what their organization and market really need. By investing the time to understand your company's strategy, then marrying that with first-hand customer research, you can develop a list of promising places to look for new ideas and become an unparalleled source of valuable innovations.

Jean would soon have an opportunity to link her insight to her company's strategic priorities. In a workshop my firm facilitated, her boss, Jon Yaged, head of Macmillan's children's division, gathered about fifteen of his top executives. Over the course of the day, we walked through a process to define their business unit's strategy. We discussed emerging threats, trends, and their long-term vision. Out of that conversation emerged a sense of clarity among everyone at the table that the growth of self-publishing was a major opportunity if they chose to take it, and a major threat if they did not.

Jean swung into action.

CHAPTER FIVE

Options

How to Generate Disruptive Ideas

There is nothing more dangerous than an idea
when it is the only one you have.
—EMILE CHARTIER

To have a good idea, you must first get a lot of ideas.
—THOMAS EDISON

IN THAT MACMILLAN conference room, sitting around a table
with fifteen of her peers, Jean Feiwel offered an idea. They had all
agreed the growth of self-publishing was unavoidable and clearly a key
strategic priority. But exactly how could they address it?

Jean laid the groundwork for her idea by pointing out the growing
popularity of crowd-funding models like Kickstarter. She proposed that
Macmillan could "take the elements of the Kickstarter model, extract
them, and translate them into a new space—publishing." It could be
like "*American Idol* meets publishing."

Jean outlined the rough structure of what she was then calling
"Romance 2.0," a model in which Macmillan would give aspiring
self-published authors a platform to find their audience and then let
the audience decide what is worth publishing. They should focus this
new model on the romance category, she argued, because romance
readers are particularly engaged in and passionate about the genre,
so it would be easier to build a community. The team loved the
concept.

Now, because we often trace the paths of an innovation back to its source, we tend to assume the idea was the only one the innovators had. But successful internal innovators like Jean are teeming with ideas.

In fact, generating new ideas has been central to Jean's job. She is always conceiving of new book concepts, angles, and series.

"I'm constantly thinking, we need a dog series where all the dogs are rescue animals. We need to go from very garden variety to bigger. But Swoon Reads was the first real business innovation idea. I am an innovator in that I don't look at something and figure out all the ways it's not going to happen. I have an inherent drive, trust, boredom of the way things are done," she explained. She knows that the low success rate of innovation requires a constant flow of new ideas. "You have to prove yourself every time. It is very much 'What have you done for me lately.' Yes, I have a certain amount of credibility now but unless you are independently wealthy there is no guarantee you are going to make it."[1]

It's very easy to fall in love with one idea that makes your heart sing. It could be your first idea, your best idea, your most revolutionary idea, your goofiest idea—the one you love above all others. It is also very dangerous and self-defeating. Too many people get so attached to their one big idea that if it fails, they are completely disheartened and give up. And the reality is that many of your ideas *will* fail. That's when you need to step right into the next great idea. The path to success is paved with a portfolio of multiple ideas.

In the previous chapter, you worked hard to identify strategic areas of need. Now it's time to brainstorm compelling ideas (emphasis on the plural: ideas) to fill those needs.

The FastPass

In the world of theme parks, Greg Hale is something of a rock star. He is famous for introducing one of the most exciting innovations to shape the theme-park business in recent decades: Disney's FastPass.

He is now the chief safety officer of Disney's theme-park business globally and chair of the International Association of Amusement Parks and Attractions (IAAPA).

Around 1999, Greg turned his attention to a mounting need. As ever more visitors poured into Disney's parks, the lines grew longer and longer. Guests were wasting increasing amounts of time in lines, time that could be spent enjoying the various shows, shops, and eateries in the park—which also meant that Disney was missing out on those potential dollars.

Boosted by his passion for wanting to give guests the best possible experience, Greg came up with an idea. What if they could offer guests a way to stand in line without having to physically be there? What if guests could virtually hold their place in a queue while they ate a delicious meal, purchased souvenirs, or took in a show?

So Greg came up with the FastPass, which you're most certainly familiar with if you've visited a Disney park in the last seventeen years. With the FastPass system, guests can scan their park tickets in a machine near the entrance to an attraction and receive a ticket that assigns a one-hour window for their return later in the day, when they can enter that attraction with little or no wait. "We actually went into the ride-control systems, looked at the capacity of every ride in real time, and have a computer system that knows that capacity and allocates a portion of the capacity to each FastPass issued," said Greg in an IAAPA article. "It took a very talented team." FastPass launched at Space Mountain on July 1, 1999, and it was an immediate success. "If guests had FastPasses at 7 o'clock that night, instead of leaving early, they'd stay for that FastPass," Greg said in the IAAPA article. "So the demand to roll this out skyrocketed. We couldn't implement this fast enough."[2]

The FastPass system is now in use at every Disney park around the world and sits at the center of Disney's award-winning mobile app, My Disney Experience.

That alone would earn Greg Hall of Fame status, if there were such a thing, but what often goes unnoticed in his story was that the FastPass was not his only innovation. It is but one of a string of innovations Greg has introduced throughout a rich career of invention.

Greg was an electrical engineer with a curious spirit when he interviewed for a position in Disney's engineering department almost thirty years ago. He was eager to see how things worked behind the scenes, so he applied for the job, figuring that even if he didn't get it, he would at least get a backstage tour.

But he got more than a peek into what makes the Happiest Place on Earth tick—he was offered a job overseeing the electrical- and controls-engineering department, and that started his search for new ways to innovate. He became a Disney "Imagineer," one of hundreds of Disney employees spread across the company's sprawling operations tasked with coming up with creative ways to enhance the business. Imagineers include architects, illustrators, engineers, show writers, lighting designers, and graphic designers.

Stepping into Greg's office in Orlando is like experiencing a museum of innovations. He has on display numerous inventions he has created, including devices to help improve accessibility for visitors with disabilities, employee training, and safety. As of the time of this writing, he holds eighty-two patents,[3] from a "system and method for wirelessly triggering portable devices" to a "configurable communication infrastructure for event spaces."[4] His FastPass invention was not a one-off idea—it was built on and draws from a series of innovations he has introduced over the years.

While a successful internal innovator may earn renown from one innovation, it is usually born out of a career of relentlessly chasing new ideas. The harsh truth is that many of your ideas will inevitably fail. By developing a portfolio of ideas, you have a greater chance of success, because you become more willing to abandon a flawed idea, knowing you have other, better ones in your pipeline.

A Framework for Building Your Portfolio of Ideas

A strategy that merely identifies a need is not a complete strategy. It must also include options for meeting that need. For example, you may know you need to lose weight, but walking around each day thinking "I need to lose ten pounds" is unlikely to get you to your goal. A better approach is to brainstorm a number of options for losing weight: eat less, stop eating carbs, run three times per week, sign up for a gym class that takes attendance—and then pick one or two of those options to initiate first. You will then attack your goal with clarity on what to pursue now *and* a backlog of options should those prove unfruitful.

My first client after leaving McKinsey and starting my own firm was Microsoft. Shannon Wallis, then head of learning and development for Microsoft's Latin American division, took a leap of faith and invited

us to run a strategic ideation workshop. Since then, Shannon has become a close friend and collaborator, and we have had the chance to work with innumerable product groups, sales teams, HR organizations, and customer-service divisions throughout the United States, Latin America, and Asia. Over the years, we estimate we have touched maybe two thousand people and through that effort produced maybe twenty thousand growth ideas.

We'd love to claim some role in planting the seeds that seem to be flowering now, as Microsoft evolves from a business driven by licensing desktop software into a modern technology leader that owns LinkedIn, Skype, and Xbox; runs one of the three largest cloud-software businesses in the world; and seems to be evolving into the kind of organization that is fueled by internal innovators of the future. But the truth is that all of those strategic ideation workshops and those twenty thousand ideas represent but a drop in the bucket of what it took to produce the strategic moves we are now seeing emerge. The volume of innovations needed to produce a true breakthrough is probably ten times larger than you think.

Over the past fifteen years of running strategic ideation workshops, we have gotten fairly good at understanding how to help people generate a large volume of strategic ideas.

To understand how to do this, it helps to consider that strategy is a conclusion to a conversation. The conclusions you arrive at matter because they determine the actions you will take and the possibilities you will pursue.

You have strategic conversations every day—in hallways, the banter before meetings, or impromptu phone calls. If you facilitate those conversations well, you increase the chances they will lead to breakthrough ideas.

Those conversations have patterns. Some lead to uninspired ideas, some to exciting breakthroughs. Any strategic discussion is composed of up to five kinds of conversations:

- You may be discussing what future you want. (Imagine)
- You may be assessing what issues to address. (Dissect)
- You may be brainstorming what options are available. (Expand)
- You may be deciding which options to pursue. (Analyze)
- You may be exploring how to get buy-in for the resulting ideas. (Sell)

Imagine–Dissect–Expand–Analyze–Sell spells "IDEAS." We have packaged the framework into this acronym to make it easy to remember, and thus easy to follow, for experience has shown that it will increase your chances of generating some truly innovative strategic options.

Over the past fifteen years, we have facilitated hundreds of strategic discussions. There is a lot I'm not good at, but with all that practice it would be hard for me not to have learned something about guiding strategic conversations. Here I will briefly cover the first four steps— I, D, E, and A—saving the final step, S, for a later chapter.

Imagine

To think differently about a problem or opportunity, it helps to start out by defining an "impossible" goal. By "impossible," I mean a goal that is unattainable by the solutions already in hand. In contrast, setting "possible" goals encourages an execution conversation. That is, you already have a solution that almost gets you there, so the easiest path seems to be to discuss how to tweak that existing solution to be a little bit better.

If you set a goal that is not attainable by ideas you already have, you force yourself and your team to start thinking differently. Greg Hale, for example, could have set a goal of shortening the lines outside of Disney's attractions. Or he could have imagined a future in which there were no lines at all. A goal of having no lines demanded new thinking.

An effective way to get your team to set an impossible goal is to work backward from the future. Just as great chess players envision checkmate and then work backward to plan what to do next, you step your team into the distant future, imagine an ideal outcome, then work backward to define what would have to be true in the near term to feel confident you are on the path to achieving your ideas. You can do this by following five steps:

1. **The mess.** Step out ten years into the future and imagine the "mess"—the undesirable but realistic future that would occur if you continued on your current path. At Disney, the "mess"

might have looked like this: "As the popularity of parks grows, the lines get longer and longer; guests grow frustrated and complain to their friends; the parks get a bad reputation; that reputation grows, until Disney loses its desirability as a destination."

2. **Long-term trends.** Still standing out ten years from now, think about the trends that will affect the future in which you will be operating. Think about new technologies (e.g., artificial intelligence, augmented reality), sociodemographic shifts (e.g., new generations of users and how their needs may be different), macroeconomic trends (e.g., interest rates, the emerging middle class in developing countries), and regulation.

3. **Long-term ideal.** Envision your ideal outcome ten years from now. If ten years feels too distant a period in which to plan, note that this reaction is precisely what makes it so powerful. Since competitors resist thinking that far out, there is less competition in the long term. Both Jeff Bezos and Elon Musk have explicitly underscored this point as central to their thinking process. What do you want to be true? What do you want customers/users to feel? What will people be saying about you? For Disney, this might be "There are no lines; guests are able to effortlessly step into attractions without a wait."

4. **Near-term ideal.** Then ask, in 18–36 months, what must be true for us to know, without a doubt, that we are on the path to realizing our long-term ideal? Since you have already committed yourself and your team emotionally to the long-term ideal, you now force them to go beyond what seems possible. You stop asking what's feasible and instead ask "What must we achieve?" For Disney, this might be "We have piloted a solution that entirely removes waiting for a portion of guests for the attractions in which we apply the solution."

5. **Strategic question.** Finally, you convert your near-term ideal into a strategic question. Simply rephrase it as a question. By placing a question mark at the end of your near-term ideal, you activate curiosity.

Dissect

Now that you have defined a seemingly impossible strategic question, you and your team will naturally start looking for answers. A word of caution: The tendency will be to look in the obvious places. Marketers

will naturally want to look at marketing ideas, salespeople at new sales tactics, and engineers at new product features.

To increase your chances of generating innovative options no one has thought of before, it helps to look where no one has looked before. Consider Nobel Peace Prize winner Muhammad Yunus. He and my mother both left Bangladesh to study in the United States and were activists in the Bangladeshi freedom movement of 1971. Later, as a professor at Chittagong College, he went on to introduce an innovation that would transform the lives of millions of the world's poor: microfinance.

When I interviewed Yunus I asked how he conceived of a strategy for combating poverty that no one, despite centuries of effort, had thought of before. He did it by looking in the less obvious places. While most efforts at alleviating poverty fixated on creating employment, Yunus observed that most poor people, in Bangladesh at least, had jobs. Indeed, they often had multiple jobs. Their problem was getting a sustainable wage for the jobs they performed. So he decided to attack the poverty problem from a different angle: financing. People with an idea for a small-scale business had the possibility of raising their family incomes, but they were unable to get traditional loans to start their business. That left them with two bad choices: borrow from loan sharks at exorbitant rates, or abandon the idea. Yunus's solution was a new kind of financial tool—microfinance, as it became known—which enabled these would-be entrepreneurs (many of them women) to take out very small loans at reasonable rates. With one simple idea, Yunus was able to break the cycle of poverty for millions of people.

Elon Musk similarly attacked the energy problem from a different direction. While most attention and investment have been directed to advancing greener sources of supply, such as solar, wind, and hydro-powered energy systems, Musk decided to focus on demand: liberating automobiles to accept electric power, rather than gasoline exclusively, essentially expanding demand for all sources of energy production. Solar farms, for example, can compete to deliver energy to a growing base of automobiles. His Solar City project seeks to have a similar effect on energy consumption in homes.

Here's your formula: before you fix on solutions, first dissect the problem into parts, assess which parts most people are working on, then focus on the overlooked leverage point.

Expand

You are now primed to brainstorm solutions. The more ideas you generate, the greater your chances of finding a truly innovative idea.

For the past two decades I have been studying the process by which human beings generate creative ideas. Multiple bodies of research point to the same answer. We don't generate innovative ideas by some lucky random chance, or through logic, but rather by applying patterns, or "strategic narratives" as I've come to call them. If you take a problem area you identified in the previous chapter (Need) and apply multiple patterns to it, you will inevitably start seeing uncommon solutions.

To explore this concept of "patterns," I looked through successful internal innovations of the past and grouped them into sets. Seven patterns emerge as promising pathways to finding innovative ideas.

1. **Make a small-scale advance.** Rather than attempting to dream up a large-scale innovation, identify a seemingly small pain-point that customers or users experience. Sometimes this is a pain-point they have come to accept as "just the way things are." Greg Hale at Disney, for example, addressed the issue that park guests had to wait in long lines. Sometimes this is a pain-point people have addressed with a workaround that you can codify into a permanent solution. The IKEA employee we met in chapter 1, for example, started off helping customers fit tables into their cars by removing the legs and then proposed this as a new way of doing business—to sell all furniture in flat-pack boxes. *What pain-point can you turn into an innovation?*
2. **Turn an internal capability into a business.** Andy Jassy convinced Amazon to turn its internal capability at managing technology into a service managing technology for other retailers and, eventually, for any kind of company. The resulting Amazon Web Services offering grew into a $17 billion business. *What internal capability can you turn into a business?*
3. **Do good.** Working to solve social problems is the source of inspiration for many internal innovations. Remember Heather Davis, whose Fruits of Employment program helps people with autism find meaningful work while solving a labor problem?

Or Marina Zhurakhinskaya from Red Hat who turned the need to empower more female coders into an ongoing program? Russ Gong was a consultant at Deloitte who wanted to create opportunities for junior consultants to get more international experience, so he convinced his firm to launch a rotational program that gives consultants opportunities to teach in developing countries. *How can you innovate by doing good in the world?*

4. **Find an unorthodox path.** We often get so used to delivering value in one way that we overlook opportunities to deliver it through different pathways. The Louvre museum, for example, delivers its experience through its landmark museum in Paris, but this limits its market to tourists willing and able to travel to France. It is now essentially franchising its model through a partnership with the Abu Dhabi government to open a museum in the Middle East. *What is the obvious path we have come to accept? What new, unexpected path have we not considered?*

5. **Apply an abandoned innovation.** Your organization has a junkyard filled with failed innovations. You can pick innovations out of the trash and apply them in new ways. The 3M Post-it note was born out of Arthur Fry's insight that a failed attempt to create a super-strong adhesive could be used instead to create a note that could stick temporarily to paper. Chuck House, the HP researcher we met in chapter 3, took a technology that was slated to be abandoned and turned it into a transformational new business line. *What has been abandoned that you could repurpose?*

6. **Coordinate the uncoordinated.** The growth of models like Airbnb and Uber point to the notion that we can now coordinate things (empty rooms, personal automobiles) that before we needed to control. You no longer need to own rooms, as a hotel does, to rent them out or to own cars, as a taxi company does, in order to offer rides. Carmen Medina was an analyst at the CIA who, post-9/11, convinced federal agencies to coordinate new ways of establishing a kind of cross-agency Wiki to share information.[5] *What is uncoordinated that you would like to coordinate?*

7. **Serve "super-users."** We often focus on customer segments that represent the largest portion of our market. But on the periphery, you will find "super-users" who are trying to use your product or service in new ways, pushing the limits of your offering. Look at what those users are asking for, and you'll

find clues to what you might offer next. Nike, for example, gets many of its innovation ideas by studying world-class athletes, literally inviting them to play on Nike's campus while designers watch. Garmen is, as of this writing, one of the world's largest manufacturers of wearable devices. Its lead was born out of the company's focus on serving hard-core outdoor adventurers who wanted to wear their GPS devices on their wrists. Had Garmen not served that market early on, even though the market was small, they likely would have missed the wearables craze when it hit. *What are your "super-users" asking for? What are their pain-points?*

In my experience, if you spend just seven minutes brainstorming each of these patterns, you will generate between thirty and one hundred ideas.

Analyze

[Circle your top five priorities.] Everything you didn't circle
just became your "avoid at all cost list."
—WARREN BUFFETT[6]

Finally, you will want to prioritize your ideas. As you do so, you may find you want to ignore the ones that are the most innovative. There is a logical reason for this. By definition, the most innovative ideas are departures from the past. They will be inconsistent with prevailing dogma and practices, so they are easy to discount. But you can avoid this through a simple three-step process.

1. **Sort your ideas on a 2×2 matrix—easy or difficult, high or low.** For each idea, assess whether it is easy or difficult to implement. Easy ideas will appear to be low-cost and simple, requiring little in the way of new capabilities. Then, for each idea, ask what its potential impact would be if you did successfully implement it. Would it have high or low impact? In assessing impact, consider the advice of innovation guru Professor Vijay Govindarajan: "We must think of innovation as doing a lot more for a lot less (money) for a lot more (people)."[7]

This gives you four groupings of ideas:

- **Difficult, low-impact ideas** are "wastes of time." Get rid of them.
- **Easy, low-impact ideas** are "tactics." Put them on a to-do list, then implement them when you have the time.
- **Easy, high-impact ideas** are "winning moves." These are the ideas one would think you should focus on. But we have found that the truly breakthrough ideas tend to fall into the fourth category.
- **Difficult, high-impact ideas** are "crazy ideas." They appear to be impossible, but if you could figure them out, they would have a major impact. Your breakthrough ideas are likely to reside here.

2. **Break down some "crazy" ideas.** We often assume an idea is "crazy" simply because it looks different, which is why so many great ideas die long before they reach the market. To avoid this reaction, simply pick one to three "crazy" ideas and follow Albert Einstein's advice: "It's not that I'm so smart; it's that I stay with problems longer." Force yourself and your team to sit with a seemingly impossible idea for ten minutes.

- List three big barriers that make the idea look crazy.
- For each barrier, brainstorm three ways to remove it. If you think it will cost too much, for example, you might write, "Partner with someone who has the money. Find a customer to fund it. Outsource to reduce the up-front cost."
- Then sit back and ask, "Does this idea still look crazy?" You will often find that what at first appeared to be an idea you came up with as a joke is actually worth exploring further.

3. **Document your idea portfolio.** Select about five innovative ideas you are committed to testing. Circle, highlight, or write them down in a notebook. One internal innovator I interviewed pastes a list on his office wall as a constant reminder of the innovations he is working on. Keep the 2×2 matrix with your full set of ideas on hand as well. This can become a useful backlog of innovations. Maintain a list of ideas you are working on, a list of those you have implemented, and a list of those you have ruled out. When you implement or rule one out, pull another innovation idea from your backlog and start activating it.

A Final Word

Many would-be internal innovators get frustrated because they myo-pically pursue just one idea. Instead, create a portfolio of options to work on. Do this by *Imagining* the ideal outcome, *Dissecting* the problem to focus on an unexpected part of the problem, *Expanding* your option set by brainstorming lots of potential innovations, and *Analyzing* the ideas by sorting and selecting a few options to pursue now.

Jean Feiwel is an idea machine. She tries new things, and when they don't work, she moves on to the next idea. But she left that first strat-egy meeting worrying that "Romance 2.0" was not going to happen unless she took it on herself. So the next day, Jean walked into her boss's office and announced, "I want to do this."

CHAPTER SIX

Value Blockers

Neutralizing "Corporate Antibodies"

THE OUTLINES OF Jean's idea had become clearer; she had even persuaded others of its potential. Then, as she thought through what it would take to make "Romance 2.0" happen, she saw an entanglement of issues. Since a significant segment of romance readers are often quite young, the site would host people under the age of eighteen, which could create legal liability. In addition, every publishing contract is unique, which wouldn't work for what she envisioned because they would want submitters of manuscripts to agree up front to publish with Macmillan if they won. Reviewers might turn nasty, saying bad things about an author's work. How would they convince the company to invest what could be hundreds of thousands of dollars in the platform? They would need a project manager with technology and marketing expertise, something the company lacked. A bigger question: Could they convince a 175-year-old publisher to consider shortcutting the traditional publishing process, taking out, or at least significantly diminishing, their role as purveyors of good literature?

Many aspiring internal innovators might view these roadblocks as a reason not to pursue an innovation. But successful internal innovators

view them more as puzzles to solve. Creating Swoon Reads would be, Jean Feiwel later said, "one of the toughest things I've done." But she would not be turned off by the challenge. "I am like the happy idiot. It's not that I don't see the problems that could happen, it's that I see more of the opportunity."

She would be proved right—largely because she astutely identified the biggest hurdle early on.

What Is a Value Blocker?

If you are to be successful with shepherding your innovation through your organization, it has to deliver value. How your idea will deliver value—how it should be sold, marketed, supported, priced, etc.—may be obvious to you and the colleagues helping you, and may even be clear to your company's leaders. But your organization, consciously or not, has a spider web of procedures, norms, and assumptions that flow from its current business model. These are often what frustrated would-be internal innovators call "corporate antibodies." They will block the value you are trying to deliver. If you fail to anticipate and neutralize them, and you will fail to realize your idea's potential. Many innovations flop simply because innovators skip the critical step of diagnosing and anticipating what could go wrong.

Consider McPizza. McDonald's market research uncovered something remarkable: people who eat at McDonald's also eat pizza! They also figured out how to bake pizzas in McDonald's stores. So the company, to great fanfare, launched McPizza. The idea failed for a simple but unpredicted reason. When consumers think of McDonald's, they think of hamburgers. It was too foreign for them to associate the brand with pizza.

Your idea may be a good one and yet still get blocked because it conflicts with some element of your company's existing business model. McPizza conflicted with the McDonald's brand (or, as we will call it later, its positioning). By predicting and neutralizing such issues, you can dramatically improve your idea's chance of success. The key is to assess your organization's business model, looking for potential points of conflict, and then to design your own business model to work around any conflict. In this chapter, we will guide you through how to do exactly that.

Business Models Matter

The business model you choose to put around your product is arguably more important than the product itself. Michael Feiner, former chief people officer of Pepsi and author of *The Feiner Points of Leadership*,[1] tells the story of the Pepsi snack business unit Frito-Lay, which had developed what they thought was the ultimate cookie. Taste tests, focus groups, and surveys proved it: Pepsi had a hit on their hands.

But their product—called Grandma's Cookies, a name that scored remarkably well in market tests—is relatively unknown today. Why? Because this breakthrough product did not line up well with Frito-Lay's business model.

To deliver Grandma's Cookies to stores, Feiner explained to me, Frito-Lay truck drivers would have to service a new aisle in the grocery store. They would have to march over from the snack aisle (where Frito-Lay's chips were stocked) to the cookie aisle. And they resisted doing this. To sell the cookies, Frito-Lay's sales force would have to sell to a different customer. Grocery-store managers who buy chips are different from those who buy cookies. The sales force would essentially have to start their sales process from scratch.

Grandma's Cookies were a failure—not because of a lack of customer desire or because of an inferior product, but simply because the Grandma's Cookies business model conflicted with Frito-Lay's existing one.

Each choice you make in designing your business model is critical. If you are careful to make the right choices, you can avoid the surprises that might thwart an otherwise promising idea.

In researching this book, I had the opportunity to interview Gordon Bell, the former head of Microsoft Research. A legend among technology researchers, Gordon has numerous patents and has seen perhaps as many technology innovations as anyone. He laid out a more nuanced explanation of why and when established organizations reject new innovations: "If it [the new innovation] is too close [to the current business model], it's going to get killed because it threatens to cannibalize the business, and if it's too far away nobody wants to back it. You try to find a min-max, not too hot but not too cold, and that is hard. You have to look at how close your products are to an existing product/sales channel."[2]

In a nutshell: You identify each potential area of conflict and then decide how to deal with it. And all of that is reflected in the business model you design for your idea. The key is to closely examine eight elements of your model (which we will delve into shortly) and make sure you have designed them in a way that customers (or users, if you are pursuing an internal innovation) will love, competitors will resist copying, and your organization will accept.

The Trick: Disrupt Without Disrupting

In 2004, George Day, a professor at the Wharton School of Business, noticed something strange happening. Corporations were pursuing few major breakthrough innovation projects, but they were launching more small, tangential ones. They were increasing their activity of what George calls "little i" innovations—small changes to existing products or continuous improvement efforts, such as adding features to your existing car. But they were reducing the rate at which they pursued "big I" innovations—initiatives that led the company into new markets or technologies.[3]

What he found was that companies were scared of pursuing "big I" innovations because they believed them to be too risky. So George set out to actually measure how much riskier they really are. He found that if you are trying to launch an innovation that targets a market (a core customer, say) that is entirely new to your company, using a product or technology that is also new to the company, you can expect to fail 75–95 percent of the time. But if you're introducing an innovation to an existing customer segment, using a product or technology that is the same as your company's current offerings, you can reduce your failure rate to only 25–40 percent. His conclusion was that to drive sustained growth, companies need to pursue a portfolio of ideas across the spectrum.

I'd like to take this insight and offer a slightly different conclusion: you can radically improve your idea's chance of success by pursuing an innovation that challenges the competition but is *not* disruptive to your core current business.

You can disrupt your competition without disrupting your business. And that is the best possible outcome.

Case in Point: Xbox

Unanticipated business-model conflict can easily kill off what seems like a no-brainer. We have already seen that happen with McPizza and Grandma's Cookies. But if you are strategic about anticipating and addressing future value blockers, you can turn ideas that on the surface look like they should fail into huge successes.

Xbox, for example, was far from an obvious innovation. Here was Microsoft, a brand not known for coolness, trying to launch a new product (their first gaming console) that required cool branding. Here was a software company attempting to manufacture hardware. Much could have gone wrong. But because the Xbox team thought through the value blockers, they made one key strategic move that boosted Xbox into success.

In 1999, on a flight home, Seamus Blackley was thinking about something he had just heard: Sony was going to launch a new PlayStation game console that was predicted to be so powerful, it would destroy PC gaming. A physicist who fell in love with gaming at a young age and, while working for DreamWorks Interactive, had produced a breakthrough video game based on *Jurassic Park*, Seamus felt distraught by the idea.

At the time, video games generally existed in two forms. One option was game-console games, played on hardware built by Nintendo or Sony. To fit this form, gaming companies had to develop specialized games that fit the tight controls of console makers. This gave them less freedom but potentially big audiences.

The other option was to develop games for the PC. This offered greater freedom, easier-to-use tools, and communities of other developers that supported each other's work. The trade-off was that since fewer gamers played on PCs, the market for the developer's game was considerably smaller. If Sony really did kill off the PC game business, it would leave PC game developers with an even smaller potential market.

Seamus believed that Microsoft was perfectly tailored to step in and take on Sony. They had the capital and technology talent to launch a game console that could compete head to head with the PlayStation. But it was a huge gamble. New customers, new developers, and new technology could easily mean higher than a 75 percent failure rate.

Instead, Seamus intuitively saw a different approach, one that would simultaneously differentiate Microsoft's console from that of the competition (making it *more* disruptive in the market) while doing it in a way that played to Microsoft's strengths, thereby making it *less* disruptive for the company. "We had the opportunity to make our own console," he explained, "something with the business potential of a game console but the tools, the support, and the power for artists of the PC and the sort of traditional off-line rendering community. And that was really a spark."

In other words, Microsoft would target a new end-user market—gamers—but stay close to its core community of PC game developers. Since a game console generally lives or dies based on the quality of its games—consoles that have the best games win—sticking to serving the PC game-developer community would not only make the Xbox a less disruptive effort for Microsoft, it would also turn Microsoft's strength with PC game developers into an impressive advantage to wield against Sony.

The rest of Seamus's journey was long. He gathered a small team, worked internal politics to build support, balanced day jobs with scaling a new business, and strategically separated key elements of the business model from Microsoft's core business—for starters.

The results have been remarkable. Because of Seamus's focused approach, what many believed to be a big, geeky business-software company now commands the largest online gaming community and sells the second most popular game console in the world, far ahead of number three.

The foundation for this success was laid when Seamus recognized that by playing to Microsoft's strengths—building high-quality tools that help developers build applications, designing for high-power systems like the PC, understanding and supporting developer communities—the company could introduce an offering that was less disruptive to its core business than it would be to competitors' businesses, should they try to copy the Xbox.[4]

Think of it this way: Your business model can either be disruptive to your competition or not. It can either be disruptive to your business or not. Breaking down your choices in this way gives you four options:

- **Copycat:** A new innovator appears on the scene with a new business model. The model is working, so you want to copy it.

You are a taxi company, and you decide to simply copy the Uber model. You are a traditional car company, and you decide you are going to launch a new business to compete directly with Tesla. You are essentially copying the success formula of someone else. That model is likely to be disruptive to your core business without offering much of a challenge to the competition, because the competition has already adopted the new model.

- **Business as usual:** If your idea for a new business model is not disruptive to you or your competition, it may produce short-term gains for your company. It may even be admired as innovative for a while, but the competition will be quick to copy it. On September 2, 1969, for example, Chemical Bank was the first bank to install an automatic teller machine (ATM) in the United States. It was hailed as a breakthrough—for a brief while. Within ten years, most major U.S. banks had done the same, and the ATM, while radically improving the lives of consumers, did little to alter the competitive position of banks.

- **Radical:** If your business model is both truly disruptive to the competition and also disruptive to yourself, then you are pursuing something radical. You probably should consider whether your company really is the right one to pursue the innovation. McDonald's, for example, launched Redbox, a business that operates DVD-rental kiosks primarily outside of grocery stores. It proved to be a successful innovation, but not one that McDonald's had any particular advantage in pursuing, which is why it was eventually spun off as an independent company.

- **Strategically disruptive:** This is where you ideally want to play. You want to design the business model behind your idea so that it complicates your competitors' ability to copy you while at the same time playing to your company's strengths, approaches, and business model. This is what the Xbox team was able to do.

How do you gear your business model so that it can disrupt the market without disrupting your business? The key is to analyze your business model across at least eight dimensions, anticipating where problems might arise and seeking clever opportunities to disrupt your competition without disrupting your own business.

Eight Dimensions to Untangle Your Business Model

You will find numerous schools of thought on what constitutes a business model. In my view, all the many descriptions are simply language tools that help us clarify things. We have found considerable success using a framework we call the "Eight P's." This model suggests you consider eight distinct but interrelated areas of your business.

- **Positioning:** who your core customer is and what position your brand holds in his/her mind
- **Product:** what you sell, including your core product/service and all ancillary products/services
- **Pricing:** how you price your product/service
- **Placement:** how you deliver your product/service (e.g., channels, store locations, distribution methods)
- **Promotion:** how you communicate to your core customer, including marketing, sales, public relations, and corporate communications
- **Process:** the internal processes that allow you to deliver on your value proposition
- **Physical experience:** the physical experience you create for your customers, including what they see, smell, hear, taste, and feel when interacting with your company and brand
- **People:** who you hire, how you organize them, and your culture

Let's break down each dimension and highlight the key considerations. We will spend more time on the first two, as they really set the direction for your business model.

Positioning

Great business models begin with sharp clarity on the positioning of their offering. They specifically make three clear choices:

1. Who your core customer is—and is not
2. What value you provide to them (or what possibility you help them achieve)
3. Which associations they have with your brand

If you can establish a strong, unique position across these three, every other element of your business model—how you price, distribute, market, etc.—can be equally unique. This is true whether your end user is a customer or an internal stakeholder. Even if you are in a support function—IT, legal, compliance—your innovation will have a business model, and that business model will have a core customer (the business partner using your internal service), a value proposition (the problem you help them solve), and a brand association (what they think of when they think of your department or service).

Consider Brendan Ripp. The son of Time Inc.'s CFO, Brendan grew up in the advertising business. So after college, he naturally felt a pull to advertising. After a year with the advertising agency J. Walter Thompson, Brendan joined his father at Time Inc. as a junior sales representative and "never looked back."[5]

When it comes to leveraging your employer's existing brand positioning to innovate new ones, few can claim a track record as impressive as Brendan's. He served as group publisher of the Sports Illustrated Group, where he led the development of nearly two dozen brand extensions, including a new film production unit, a college sports vertical, consumer events for Sports Illustrated Swimsuit, and most recently, the launch of SI Overtime, a branded content studio. Along the way, he also served as publisher of *Time*, *Fortune*, and *Money*. As of this writing, he leads sales and partnerships for Fox's *National Geographic*.

During Brendan's time with *Money*, a shift in market forced him to quickly rethink his strategy. One of his key advertisers announced they were cutting ad budgets overall and planning to move what was left entirely to digital properties. They were not alone; several other critical advertisers had similar plans. Yet *Money* had few digital products to offer. To make matters worse, advertisers no longer saw personal finance, *Money*'s historical category, as interesting.

Brendan realized something. "We needed to build something unique, never done before, that would appeal to both our readers as well as a new advertising base." If they didn't, *Money* would be in trouble. So he began looking for partnerships with other Time Inc. media brands to create entirely new platforms that could "break through the clutter" and allow advertisers to reach larger audiences.

Money convinced the leadership of *Real Simple*, a magazine and media property for women, to create a new print, digital, and video

series called "Money Management for the Time-Pressed" that would blend both audiences. The series proved a breakthrough. It became a feature on the *Today Show*, the most popular morning show, and Chevrolet jumped at the chance to pay $1 million to become a multiplatform sponsor. A partnership with *This Old House*, another Time Inc. business, enabled *Money* to open up an entirely new market: homeowners dealing with the financial issues related to home improvements.

Each combination of brands unlocked new customers, markets, and revenue. When Brendan took over as publisher of *Sports Illustrated*, for example, he persuaded the popular technology magazine *Wired* to partner in a new initiative at the intersection of science and sports. They quickly drew interest from two big advertisers—Gatorade and Microsoft. His editorial team could interview Gatorade scientists to highlight the work they are doing to enhance athletic performance. And Microsoft, a heavy advertiser of the National Football League, saw an opportunity to further deepen its exposure to the audience. It quickly signed on.

A successful business model begins with a unique positioning: (a) you target a different core customer than your competitors will want to service and/or (b) you promise a value proposition your competitors cannot or will not want to promise and/or (c) you link your brand to associations or attributes competitors will not be able to or want to emulate.

You need to fully recognize the notion that your positioning challenge is different from that of entrepreneurs, who typically start by asking "What does the market need?" If you start that way, you are likely to join the ranks of the disappointed, who complain, "I know this is the right positioning for my idea, but my company, the marketing team, won't let us take it."

Successful internal innovators take the opposite approach. They begin with the unique positioning assets their company already has—the core customers already loyal, value propositions already being delivered, and brands already known—and explore how they could combine or build on them. They look for the magical middle, where the position is both compelling to the market and one on which the organization is uniquely able to deliver.

How do you know when you have found the magical middle? Brendan says it will be obvious. The idea will make sense immediately. The positioning—customer, value proposition, brand—is so clear that you will hear something like "Of course! Why didn't we think of this before?!" *Money* for *Real Simple* women and *Wired* for Super Bowl enthusiasts are obvious—but only after someone thought of them.

Key questions:

- How can you pick a core customer or customers that your company already serves?
- What associations do customers already have with your company, products, or brand(s), and how could you use these to secure a powerful positioning for your idea?

Product/Service

Once you've chosen a unique positioning, it becomes easier to design an equally unique product. The more different your product is, the harder it is for your users to compare your offer to the alternatives, and the easier it becomes to charge more, sell more, or otherwise create value.

You want to differentiate your product. Every business owner knows that. But your notion of product differentiation needs a sharp focus. Since you are starting with more material—your company already possesses some unique capabilities, norms, and strengths to leverage—you will likely want to more assertively pursue attributes that your startup competitor will not.

THINK BEYOND THE CORE PRODUCT It helps to think expansively about what your product/service is. You want to consider the often overlooked related services that you offer as part of your core product. For example, a hotel does not just offer a bed for a night; it offers a portfolio of other elements that create a bundled experience—online registration, valet, porter service, check-in service, in-room Wi-Fi, cable, room service, etc.

These ancillary products/services generally fall into two categories:

- Facilitating: Products/services that help your customer access your core product/service, such as registration, scheduling, price listings, payment, and so forth.
- Augmenting: Products/services that enhance the value of your core product/service, such as customization, premium add-ons, and customer support.

How to Do It

We have found that by following four steps, you can systematically define a product/service that will be disruptive to competitors while also limiting the disruption to your organization.

1. **Brainstorm your full set of product/services.** Start out by brainstorming a full set of products/services that your customer (internal or external) wants or needs. Think about facilitating and augmenting products/services.
2. **Create a prioritized list of attributes.** Looking at the list of products/services, put together a prioritized list of the attributes that your core customer (as defined by your positioning) most cares about. Walmart, for example, is quite clear about what attributes of the shopping experience its core customer most values—low prices and selection across categories are at the top. And it knows which attributes its customer least values—ambiance and sales help are at the bottom. Look at your list of product/services (from step 1) to make sure you have covered all the important attributes.
3. **Identify business model issues.** For each attribute on your list (from step 2), ask yourself: Where might we run into issues (e.g., where our current approach will conflict with our success)? What would happen if we stuck to our current business model? Would it hurt us, or could it help us?
4. **Decide what you might want to accept, bend, or change.** Create three lists of attributes or elements of your product:
   - Which should I accept (e.g., because they are too hard to change or because doing it our way would create an advantage)?

- Which should I bend?
- Which should I change?

This process should give you a good idea of what flavor of product, or what mix of product attributes, has the potential to be disruptive in the marketplace (that is, something your core customers will love and your competitors will choose not to copy) and yet less disruptive to your organization.

Pricing

Many of the most successful business innovations of the past and present succeeded not because their product/service was superior (although, based on the preceding section, you may now have a truly unique product/service offering), but rather because they offered a different pricing structure.

Consider, for example:

- **Affinity:** MBNA decided to pay royalties to some large organizations for exclusive rights to offer credit cards to their members, and thereby shook up the business of issuing credit cards by introducing affinity clubs.
- **Service level:** Sprint surprised the competition by being one of the first to charge different rates for different levels of service.
- **Partial ownership:** NetJets (a private business-jet company) switched from charging per flight and instead decided to charge for a "partial ownership" right.
- **Subscription:** Today, companies like OneGo, Surf Air, and Jumpjet are offering unlimited flights between specific destinations in exchange for a subscription fee. The subscription model is being adopted across a broad spectrum of industries, from software (e.g., both Microsoft and Adobe have shifted to subscription models from license models) to food (e.g., HelloFresh and Blue Apron).
- **Freemium:** The "freemium" model, in which you offer a basic service for free and then charge for premium features, has contributed to the success of numerous business models, including those of LinkedIn, Skype, and Dropbox.

- **Leasing:** In the 1980s, Ford Motor Co. adopted the "leasing" model, in which drivers, rather than buying and owning a car, could get access to an automobile for a shorter time period for a monthly fee. This pricing innovation was quickly adopted by the industry, and today nearly 25 percent of new vehicles are leased rather than sold.[6]

- **Membership:** By asking customers to pay up front to get access to discounted services, you can transform their buying psychology. Consider Amazon Prime, for example: customers pay an annual membership fee in exchange for free two-day shipping and other benefits. As soon as someone pays the membership fee, their psychology changes; they want to extract as much value as possible from the fee, so they buy more. Discount retailer Costco creates a similar dynamic by selling annual memberships to their shopping club.

- **"Milk" pricing:** Grocery stores know that customers tend to judge the relative prices they pay in one chain versus another based on the price of milk. If they offer low milk prices, they can get customers in the door and create the perception that everything else they sell must be similarly competitively priced. This is also why the milk in your grocery store is located as far as possible from the front door, to force you to walk past as many shelves as possible.

- **Product to service:** Similar to the leasing or partial-ownership models, this approach shifts customers from buying products to buying services. Zipcar, for example, shook up the car-rental business by offering a car-sharing service that gave members access to cars when they needed them.

- **Community access:** Rather than directly charging for plumbing, roofing, landscaping, and other services, Angie's List decided to charge members for access to a community of customers who shared reviews. Angie later switched the model, making it free to customers and charging only contractors.

This is another area of difference from entrepreneurs. Entrepreneurs can start with a blank slate and create any pricing structure they think the market will likely adopt. Internal innovators must set a pricing structure from within an established organization. It is tempting to think of this as a limitation (it may be harder to convince leadership

to accept membership fees rather than the per-unit fees the business has grown up charging), but your size can equally become an advantage. The scale and assets your organization wields allow you to shift more easily into diverse pricing structures. While startups are motivated to collect revenue now, an established, resource-rich organization can more readily accept revenue later.

You want to explore interesting pricing models in order to move your business model into the "strategically disruptive" category. Don't simply jump in and copy what the newest, hottest innovator is doing. Think about cable companies who were derided as out of date when TiVo introduced the U.S. market to the DVR. Many wrote cable companies off as behind the times. Then cable companies suddenly woke up and started offering DVRs themselves. But instead of charging for the devices, as TiVo was doing, cable companies figured out they could give them away for free, simply installing them in the cable boxes they were already placing in customers' homes, because once those customers got a DVR, they tended to upgrade to a higher-priced cable package.[7]

Key questions:

- What is the accepted way of pricing your product/service?
- What would be the natural way that your organization would think of pricing this product/service?
- What interesting options do you see for changing the basis on which you price your product/service?
- Where will internal resistance to this new pricing model come from?

Placement

"Placement" is simply a way to put a "P" in front of the word "distribution" so that the "8P" model doesn't have to be "7P's and 1D." Think of it as how you deliver your product or service to your core customer. If your innovation is for external customers, your placement decision means things like where you place stores, whether you use kiosks, how you route trucks, the design of your logistics

system, and so on. If you are considering an internal innovation, your "placement" decisions include things like whether you interact with internal users face to face or digitally, whether they self-serve or you do the work for them, where your team members are located in the building, and so on.

Making a unique placement choice has been the central strategy behind numerous breakthrough companies. Think of Dell (go direct rather than through retailers), Walmart (place stores in rural rather than metropolitan areas), Southwest Airlines (fly point-to-point rather than through a hub), or Salesforce.com (deliver software via the cloud rather than install it on company servers).

The internal innovators I interviewed often cited distribution as a particularly vexing problem. The distribution norms of your organization have likely become ingrained over many years, as the Grandma's Cookies team discovered. The distribution assets that comprise your logistics chain—your distribution centers, trucks, inventory systems—required heavy investment that your organization will want to protect.

Based on the cases we have studied, your placement choice offers less flexibility than the other business-model choices. You can do one of three things:

- Accept your company's current distribution model.
- Create an entirely different model.
- Separate your product into parts.

Accepting the current distribution model would mean putting your product through the distribution chain, making it another item on the shelf of your warehouse, another box on your trucks. If you can design your model so this works well for the market and your customers, then you will have removed considerable risk of having your idea rejected.

Creating an entirely different channel would be to establish an entirely different business.

To separate your product into parts means to break down the services of your product and distribute some of them using the usual model and some of them using a new model.

Key questions:

- Thinking through your current distribution model, where might issues emerge?
- Should you accept the current distribution model, create an entirely new one, or separate your product into parts?

Promotion

Promotion involves everything you do to communicate your product/ service to prospects, customers, partners, and beyond. Specifically, it involves marketing, sales, corporate communications, and public relations.

When I asked internal innovators about their most serious barriers, "promotion" came up often. The challenges most often fell into two categories:

- **Marketing.** Your marketing department imposes strict brand guidelines that limit your flexibility; they take too long to approve advertising imagery, copy, and brand designs.
- **Sales Force.** Your sales force has a predisposition toward selling what they already know; it is hard to make them aware of the new innovation you want to offer, make them care enough to bring it up with customers, and incentivize them to sell it when they believe they can more easily sell what they already know.

MARKETING Regardless of the industry, the innovators I interviewed expressed frustration that often marketing moved too slowly, was too rigid, and was too limited in the scope of what they were willing or able to do.

This is true even if your innovation is an internal one. You are likely to find a corporate-communications group that will either energize and activate your effort or slow and water it down.

I have not found a silver bullet for dealing with marketing, but here are five tips shared by the innovators I talked with:

- **Develop friendships.** Take your marketing partners out for lunch, get to know them personally, so that when you need them, they will move more quickly on your request and give it special attention.
- **Engage early.** Knowing that lead times can be long and that your marketing department may have a backlog of work, engage them long before you need them to act. Your startup competitors may start thinking about marketing a few weeks before launch. You need to start long before that.
- **Co-create.** Let your marketing department help you create. Bring the idea to them when it's still in its infancy. Invite them to help design the business model with you. They will often help you address marketing barriers and opportunities ahead of time.
- **Know the rules.** Every established brand has carefully defined brand guidelines. Educate yourself on them. Try to work with them, rather than against them.
- **Create an informal marketing committee.** Since marketing decisions are increasingly merging with those of technology and operations, you might try this suggestion from one innovator I interviewed: Create an informal committee composed of allies in marketing, technology, and operations. Share your vision with them, and set a regular meeting rhythm, so they can efficiently provide you with cross-disciplinary guidance (see chapter 8).

SALES FORCE Another common barrier is convincing your sales force to support your innovation. One innovator in a pharmaceutical company had gotten approval to pursue a new business line. Although the technology was completely new, the target customer—the prospect that the sales force would visit—was the same. So it seemed natural to think that if the sales force is visiting the customer anyway, it should be fairly easy for them to start selling this new product line.

Unfortunately, the regional sales leaders did not all agree. Leadership in one region strongly supported the new venture; leadership in another did not. The results were as you would anticipate. Even though both regions had similar situations—same company, same core product,

same core customer, same new product—in the supportive region, the new offering was deemed a great success. In the less supportive region, it failed.

It is critical that you, as an internal innovator, think carefully about how you are going to engage your sales force. Success or failure may hinge on it.

We can break down this challenge by predicting where you may find issues, so you can address them ahead of time. One innovator I interviewed shared a well-structured, effective model.

1. **Target customers:** Who, specifically, is your sales force visiting? Just because they are visiting the same company that you want to target with your innovation does not mean they will be able to sell effectively to your target customer in that company. If they are visiting the purchasing manager and you want to sell to the CFO, as one of our clients recently attempted to do with an innovation, your sales force may not provide any advantage at all.

2. **Coverage and capacity:** Does your sales force have sufficient coverage (i.e., do you have salespeople touching enough target customers)? Does it have the capacity (enough time and resources) to effectively promote your innovation? If you know you need to talk to a thousand customers in order to get the initial sales that would indicate your innovation is a success, but your current sales force only has regular contact with five hundred customers, you will have a problem. Similarly, if you find your sales force is already overwhelmed, struggling to maintain their call and visit schedules, you are likely to face a bandwidth problem.

3. **Incentives and performance management:** By what metrics is your sales force measured, and how is their compensation calculated? For example, if your sales force is selling established products, their incentive structure may encourage them to increase "share of wallet" by focusing on selling more follow-on products to existing customers. You, by contrast, want them to sell new things and capture new customers. If they don't get as much credit for selling your new thing as they do for selling more of the old thing, you will face a problem.

4. **Sales tools:** Every well-run sales department has a tool kit that they arm salespeople with. It includes things like sales processes/checklists, sales scripts, product descriptions, and access

to support (such as experts who provide product details to help the salesperson close a sale). Because your innovation is new, your tools are likely to be less developed, so you want to invest in rapidly developing a few high-quality tools.

5. **Culture:** Finally, consider the rules and norms of your sales force. Does the culture value learning? If not, you may have trouble getting salespeople to spend the time to learn about the new offering. Does the culture encourage proactivity? This has been shown to be a critical driver of innovative organizations. If your sales force primarily responds to requests rather than proactively seeking to create opportunities, it will limit your innovation's chances.

The same holds true if you are driving an innovation for internal customers. You may not have a formal sales force, but there is some population of people who will be responsible for building buy-in for your innovation. Perhaps you want to introduce a new human-resource policy or a new technology interface. Who will be promoting this idea to the internal users? Do they already visit the target user? Do they have the coverage and capacity? Will they have the right incentives? Will you provide them with the tools they need? Does the culture motivate them to become advocates of the innovation?

Key questions:

- Have you done the things needed to build the level of collaboration and support you need from your marketing department?
- Have you developed friendships?
- Are you engaging early?
- Have you invited them to co-create with you?
- Do you clearly understand the rules?
- Have you created an informal marketing committee?
- Have you anticipated, and are you addressing, the sales-force barriers you are likely to face?
  - Target customers?
  - Coverage and capacity?
  - Incentives?
  - Tools?
  - Culture?

Process

During a break in a workshop with a leading consumer-products company, one of the participants, a senior member of the global marketing team, snagged me in the hallway and told me something I found shocking. "I think we have come up with a pretty breakthrough idea here, but there is a much more basic problem we face. It takes us weeks just to produce an invoice for one of our [retail] customers. Our small competitors take hours."

It shouldn't be this way, but it is. Because your company's business processes were developed over years, designed to create predictability and consistency, and engineered to optimize for efficiency over speed, your innovation is very likely to get caught on the thorns of the rules, checklists, and policies that are scattered throughout your organization. As with the other business-model elements, successful internal innovators learn how to circumvent the frustration by embracing, understanding, and predicting the obstacles—and then neutralizing them.

Operational structures are consistently identified as one of the most critical barriers to internal innovation.[8] Most of the research on removing those barriers is targeted at senior leadership; most suggestions for changing the internal structures are directed to the CEO and top team. The reality is, you will probably have limited influence over the processes. Indeed, many of the innovators I interviewed expressed little interest in trying. "I don't want to transform the company," one commented. "I just want to make this project happen."

If you decide you just want to better navigate the operational processes, rather than change them, you have a greater chance of prevailing.

So, which processes should you plan for?

In 1985, Harvard Business School professor Michael Porter introduced a breakthrough framework, now broadly known, called the "value chain."[9] Since it's more than three decades old now, you may be tempted to think of it as less effective. But it is a powerful checklist that, if followed systematically, can save your innovation from being blindsided down the line.

Porter suggests that any organization must perform certain activities in order to deliver a valuable product or service. He identifies nine sets of activities, in two categories: primary and supporting.

PRIMARY

- **Inbound logistics.** Anything your organization does to take in materials, inputs, parts, or inventory in order to produce your product/service.
- **Operations.** How your company manages the process of converting inputs (raw materials, labor, energy, etc.) into outputs (the product/service you deliver).
- **Outbound logistics.** Storing, moving, and delivering your product/service to customers or end users.
- **Marketing and sales.** We have covered this topic earlier in the chapter; take a second look specifically at the processes involved.
- **Service.** How your company helps keep its product/service working effectively after the customer buys it.

SUPPORTING

- **Procurement.** How your company acquires what it needs to operate from external sources.
- **Human-resource management.** This will be covered in more detail later in the chapter; here, look at the processes your company uses to hire, develop, and incentivize people.
- **Technology development.** Broadly speaking, this includes everything your organization does related to equipment, machinery, and information technology to help transform inputs into your final product/service.
- **Infrastructure.** This includes areas such as accounting, legal, finance, compliance, and general management.

As you work through these nine sets of activities, ask yourself two questions:

- What, if any, process issues will I face here?
- Is there an opportunity to create a "strategically disruptive" situation?

Physical Experience

This element has to do with what your core customers (whether external or internal) experience with their five senses when they interact with your innovation—what they see, hear, smell, taste, or feel. This dimension is overlooked in most business models, but that is a mistake. It can be enormously important, if only precisely because you and your competitors are likely to discount its importance.

Apple is a brilliant example. For decades they have invested more than any competitors on physical experience. They overinvest in package design, making sure the boxes have just the right color, weight, and texture. I've heard they even analyze the level of suction their boxes create when one opens them. They do all of this because they know that the physical experience they create for customers when they first unwrap their products creates a powerful brand association. One reason they launched the Apple Store was to have complete control of the environment in which their products are displayed.

Alaska Airlines, for another example, was lauded for being the first to introduce fingerprint identification into their check-in experience. They recognized the physical experience of fumbling with documents caused stress and frustration. Now travelers need only press their finger to a reader.

Key questions:

- In terms of the physical experience your core customers undergo as they interact with your company, brand, or product/service, what issues might your innovation face?
- How does this experience match, or not, with the physical experience your organization currently creates?
- What opportunities do you see to create a "strategically disruptive" opportunity?

People

We list this last not because it is least important but precisely for the opposite reason. Much of the most recent research on innovation has identified people-focused policies—who you hire, how you organize them, your incentive system, and your culture—as *the* most important factors in whether innovation efforts succeed or fail.[10]

Aetna, the 160-year-old health-care plan provider, earns about $60 billion per year primarily serving employers. In mid-2005, however, Laurie Brubaker recognized that the company was missing an opportunity. At the time, she was a senior vice president overseeing a few noncore markets like pharmacy and behavioral health. Nearly forty-five million people in the United States were uninsured, and another twenty million were underinsured. She felt that Aetna had an opportunity, and an obligation, to serve them. So she created a business plan showing how Aetna might sell health insurance to individuals.

Within two years, under her leadership, Aetna was offering its new individual health-care program to 250,000 members in thirty states. It became the second fastest growing business within the company. Brubaker had helped the company both make a profit and have a significant social impact, because many of the Aetna-insured individuals had previously gone uninsured.

But the innovation could easily have failed had she not thought carefully about the "people" dimension. She recognized that Aetna was good at producing the estimates of future medical costs needed to set the price of its policies by applying statistical methods to its corporate customer base. But accurately pricing policies for individuals would require an individual medical evaluation. That would necessitate a very different set of skills, including internet marketing so that the company could reach individuals.

To overcome this potential conflict, Brubaker assembled a team composed of two types of people: those who came from the core business, and a group of innovators who would represent the needs of the new business. This team helped fill capability gaps while also making sure they leveraged the "people" advantages.

To help ensure you are able to predict and prepare for potential "people" issues, as Brubaker did, search through four different areas of conflict/opportunity:[11]

1. **Tasks:** the specific activities implementing your innovation will require
2. **People:** the types of people your organization hires and develops (considering skills, personalities, etc.)
3. **Formal structure:** the organizational structure in which people work, including reporting, business units, incentives, and decision-making approaches
4. **Informal structure (culture):** the values, norms, and common behaviors prevalent within your organization

In each case, ask yourself two questions: Where might conflicts arise? What opportunity is there to create a "strategically disruptive" situation?

A Final Word

As a passionate, action-oriented innovator, you likely are eager to get going, to *do* something. While moving quickly to action may give you a sense of forward movement, the early momentum you build can easily smash against a conflict with your company's current business model. In frustration you may decide, "My company simply cannot innovate," and resign yourself to the conclusion that your organization should simply copy the business model of whoever the leading competitor is today. But this can only lead you to mediocrity.

To create something of truly transformative potential, explore how you can move your business model into "strategically disruptive" territory. Think through each element of the business model—positioning, product, pricing, placement, promotion, process, physical experience, and people. For each, assess where conflicts may arise and where opportunities exist, and then decide what you can accept, bend, or change in order to design a model that will disrupt your market without disrupting your business.

In appendix B, you will find a comprehensive checklist that will help you identify, and thereby neutralize, potential value blockers that could cripple your idea.

As you can imagine, the idea forming in Jean's mind would confront many potential value blockers. After all, the new venture would operate in ways that went against long-established publishing procedures. Even the very idea of letting readers give feedback on unfinished manuscripts was nothing short of radical. It raised all sorts of questions across many of the Eight P's:

- Positioning: The idea depended on romance writers and readers actively engaging on the platform.
- Pricing: Readers might refuse to pay for a book after they had had free access to its manuscript.
- Placement: Should they even distribute the titles that came out of this approach through bookstores?
- Promotion: The sales team might be apathetic to selling a new title when a version of it had already been available to the public online.
- Process: The crowd-sourcing of editorial feedback from readers might conflict with decades-old editing processes used by Macmillan and the industry overall.
- People: Did they have the requisite capabilities to build and manage a community of romance readers and writers? Did they have the technology skills they would need?

Thinking through the various points of potential conflict, Jean grew confident that the most immediate value blocker to address was a question of positioning: Did they pick the right core customer (the romance author and reader) for their innovation?

To assess this, they would have to run an experiment.

CHAPTER SEVEN

Act

Getting Permission to Experiment

It's not an experiment if you know it's going to work.
—JEFF BEZOS

TO GET HER innovation up and running, Jean could have prepared a business plan addressing all of the issues she knew would come—legal problems, the lack of technology capabilities, the need to introduce a radically different editorial process, and many more. In business school, we are taught that is the step that comes next. But instead, with her boss on board, Jean took a more modern approach.

"It used to be strategy-strategy-strategy-implement. Now by the time you implement, your strategy is outdated," her boss Jon Yaged explained. They decided to adopt an agile or scrum approach (more about those later) in which they asked, "What is the one thing I need to get done today?" They would conduct a low-cost experiment, learn from it, and adapt.

Of all the value blockers the idea would face, Jon and Jean believed that getting author and reader adoption was the most urgent. If they could prove that would-be self-published authors liked the idea and that romance readers would get engaged, they would have greater fodder to convince the company to implement the innovation. The

potential of the opportunity would make the legal, operational, talent, and process issues worth solving.

Unfortunately, most organizations expect the person with the idea to identify all possible areas of concern and solve them *before* giving permission to act. To proceed with a new idea, most innovators are told, in effect, to "prove it." This business-planning approach is so deeply ingrained that it has become reflexive and automatic.

We even have language to describe the dilemma. Established organizations are oriented toward a prove–plan–execute model. Internal innovators instead necessarily gravitate toward an act–learn–build model: take action, learn from it, and then build based on the last learning. It's ALB versus PPE.

The problem is that a PPE approach rarely works for truly innovative ideas because it's impossible to prove a truly new idea by analyzing existing data. You can't build out a financial projection if you do not yet know how users will react to your innovation. You need to create the data (how users will react). You can't look it up.

Sometimes You Have to Disobey the System

If a new idea requires experimentation to prove it will work, and if the system demands proof before the innovator is allowed to experiment, we have only two options for shattering this catch-22. Either the system must change, or the innovator must circumvent the system. Historically, innovators choose the latter, opting to operate in stealth mode.[1] If you've ever navigated London's subway system, or just about any modern subway system for that matter, you should thank Harry Beck for disobeying. Before 1934, the London Underground map showed a true geographical representation of the actual layout of the city. Stations in the city center were tightly crunched together on the map, and the distances between stations in outlying regions were shown as long blank spaces. The map was technically accurate and comprehensive—but almost impossible to read. Commuters hated it.

Harry Beck, then a draftsman working for the London Underground Signals Office, had a different idea. In his spare time, he began drafting a mock-up version of a simplified yet functional map: horizontal,

vertical, and forty-five-degree-angle lines with equally spaced dots denoting station stops and transfer points. He showed his map to management. No, they said, "too revolutionary."[2]

But Beck wouldn't take no for an answer. He revised the map, got a rejection, and incorporated the feedback into the next design. He considered each attempt an experiment to learn and improve his design.

Eventually, he convinced authorities to try his map with riders. The first print run of 300,000 copies was snapped up in a few days, and a million more copies were quickly printed. Today, his iconic map inspires subway maps around the world.

The moral of this story: when your company asks for proof, sometimes you have to disobey the system in order to experiment. That pattern is quite common among internal innovators. 3M's innovations, for example, are littered with stories of disobedience. When Arthur Fry, a 3M marketer, had his idea for the Post-it Note rejected, he made a batch of Post-its on his own and shared them with executive assistants in the company.

He first thought the product would serve as a paper bookmark. But as it turned out, the 3M executive assistants found entirely new uses for Fry's invention. They wrote reminders on the bookmarks and stuck them around the desk space. They wrote "sign here" on them and stuck them to documents needing their bosses' signatures.

Had Fry followed a PPE approach, his intended market—bookmarks—would have been too small to gain the interest of 3M. But by following an ALB approach, taking action on an experiment, he discovered an entirely new market. The Post-it Note quickly became the best-selling office product in the world. Even in today's digital world, more than fifty billion Post-it Notes are sold every year.

Learn by Doing

Fortunately, that internal innovator's dilemma—disobey my company's rules or do battle with the bureaucracy—has begun to change. In the past five to ten years, forward-looking organizations are realizing that the prove-it-do-it approach presents two critical issues.

First, they are recognizing an unassailable bit of logic: when an idea is novel, data that would prove its viability do not yet exist. Sometimes you just need to act and learn. For example, when HP developed the

first electronic calculator, market research promised little potential for the innovation. An entrenched competitor was already able to satisfy customer needs at a far superior price point: the slide rule. But instead of looking for proof, HP leadership decided to act. They approved the production of one thousand units, just to see how the market would react. Within a few years, HP was selling one thousand units *per day*.[3]

Second, in fast-paced environments, the cost of taking time out to do analysis can be significant. Wait too long, and you may lose your window to act. At McKinsey, we were taught to seek an "80 percent solution": conduct analysis until we were 80 percent confident we had the right answer. But former secretary of state and retired four-star general Colin Powell believes that in fast-moving, uncertain environments, waiting for 80 percent confidence is unreasonable and risky. He advocates a "40–70 rule." As soon as you have enough data to be 40 percent confident, then use your gut and act. If you have waited to be 70 percent confident, you have taken too long.

The difference between 80 percent and 40–70 percent confidence may seem abstract, but the implications are profound. For fifty years, corporations have held onto the idea that if they analyzed all the issues, they could move forward into the future with confidence. In a static world, this makes sense. In a dynamic one, the calculus changes. Perhaps this is why a new approach is taking hold. It is known by various names—lean, agile, scrum, and more—but the essence is the same: take action on a small experiment, learn, and improve your idea.

The Emergence of Agile

Agile, lean, whatever you call it, is such an important concept that it's worth taking a little time to understand its origins. Though many believe this idea is new, its roots stretch back several decades. Think of it as a confluence of three ideas: cycles of adaptation (instead of linear progressions), human-centered (instead of technology-centered) design, and agile development (instead of "waterfalls").

Cycles of Adaptation

In the mid-1970s, a fighter pilot named John Boyd proposed a radical new approach to warfare. Instead of viewing battles as linear

progressions, he suggested we should view them as loops in which each opponent cycles through four phases: observing the environment, orienting themselves to what is happening, deciding what to do, and acting. Then they repeat the process, starting with observing the results that their new decision produces.

This "OODA loop" (observe–orient–decide–act) has proven highly influential in shaping military strategy. It has also influenced a broad range of business domains, including business strategy, project management, operations, and manufacturing. Indeed, a direct link shows OODA as the seed that flowered into what we now call "lean."

Toyota's just-in-time manufacturing is a direct outgrowth of the OODA loop. Steve Blank, founder of the "Lean Startup" approach, said that while "the Customer Development Model with its iterative loops/pivots may sound like a new idea for entrepreneurs, it shares many features with a U.S. war-fighting strategy known as the 'OODA Loop.'" And Jeff Sutherland, the creator of "scrum," said, "Scrum is not an ideology. Scrum comes from fighter aviation and hardware manufacturing." Reid Hoffman, the founder of LinkedIn, said, "In Silicon Valley, the OODA loop of your decision-making is effectively what differentiates your ability to succeed."[4]

Finally, the OODA loop has also influenced how companies do strategic planning. The term "discovery-driven planning," introduced by Ian MacMillan and Rita McGrath in the 2000s, suggests that companies track leading indicators for their strategic ideas to learn whether the strategies are working. Instead of building a new business, for example, you identify the key uncertainties, launch a small initiative to track those uncertainties, and then invest more if the uncertainties indicate your idea is a good one.

Human-Centered Design

About the same time that Toyota was applying OODA to continuous improvement, architects and urban planners were embracing a concept that had been proposed a decade earlier called "satisficing" (a blend of "satisfy" and "suffice")—the idea that decision-making means exploring available alternatives until an acceptable threshold is reached. Instead of looking for an optimal solution, you are continually looking for a good-enough one.

This idea marks a departure from science toward design. While science seeks the truth, design seeks a solution.

Throughout the 1980s and 1990s, thanks in great part to a series of thinkers at Stanford University (most notably David Kelley, the founder of IDEO), this search for a solution evolved into what we now call design thinking, an underlying approach that has moved through several evolutions.

Designers began designing in collaboration with users: build something, let someone use it, and see if it works. They started involving users in the design process itself, in what came to be called user-centered design. They developed the approach further to explore the entire user journey, looking at what happened before and after the user interacted with what they were designing. Then came the next evolution, called human-centered design, which is where we are today.

My father, Klaus Krippendorff, is one of the leading advocates of human-centered design. He was trained at the Ulm School, a relatively new but highly influential design school in Germany to which many of the roots of design thinking can be traced. He and like-minded scholars argue that people do not interact with objects, but with the meaning they place on those objects, so an empathetic understanding of the emotional experience of users is critical. They also argue for a wide-angle perspective: looking not just at the user, but also at the network of stakeholders that might influence adoption.

Agile Development

In the mid- to late 1990s, software programmers began to abandon the old "waterfall" approach, in which you program in a sequence of work streams, one leading to the next. These programmers instead adopted a concept they called "agile," combining cyclical, continual improvement with human-centered design.

The agile methodology, in a nutshell, advocates for continuous planning, experimentation, and integration, moving through cycles of development, evaluation, and approval, on to the next level of development, and so forth. It quickly spread from the software world to a large community of followers in a wide swath of industries.

If we pull these three concepts together—cycles of adaptation, human-centered design, and agile—we see the key foundational elements of an approach to problem-solving that is now changing how we

think about strategy and innovation. It has expanded from technology and science to society and governance and, of course, to business.

An Agile Enterprise

Until recently, these three concepts have existed as separate ideas belonging to different, mostly unrelated domains (urban planning, warfare, software development, etc.). This has contributed to the myth that the agile approach works only in some domains—creative industries and small startups—and that it is contradictory to the fundamental orientation of large organizations. But forward-looking business leaders now recognize that this agile philosophy is far more versatile and applicable, and they are urging their companies to figure out ways to embrace it.

Numerous leading firms have formalized agile approaches in how they do business, including GE, Intuit, Qualcomm, Fidelity Investments, and ING.

Federal-Mogul, a 120-year-old auto-parts manufacturer that is one of our clients, has been able to effectively design agile/lead/design experiments. Using the approach suggested in this chapter, they have rethought how engineers within their client companies can participate in the design process. This new approach, now implemented globally, helps differentiate them from the competition.

A few points are worth repeating. First, whatever you call it, agile/lean/design thinking is not a novel concept; it has roots that are decades long.

Second, it is not just for technology or new products. You can use it to approach any organizational or strategic effort—a new philanthropic program, pricing structure, hiring approach, process improvement, marketing message, sourcing strategy, or reporting structure, to name just a few.

Third, it is not just for startups. A growing number of large companies are recognizing that this is a superior approach to designing strategy, especially in a faster-paced, more uncertain world that rewards speed and experimentation. Eric Ries, Steve Blank's former student and one of the most influential propagators of the "Lean Startup" movement, has now successfully applied the approach to numerous large, established organizations.[5]

Fourth, you do not need official blessing to begin applying this approach. Even if you do not (yet) have formal approval to work on developing a new idea, you can start experimenting in a lean/agile way.

All of this is good news for internal innovators, who often must work outside of their company's official innovation structure. It's difficult to get approval for a $400,000 beta launch. Getting a few thousand dollars and a few days of time to run a contained experiment is a whole lot easier.

In *The Innovator's Hypothesis*,[6] Michael Schrage advocates using small teams to collaboratively (and competitively) design and implement business experiments that will matter to senior leadership. I have used that approach with my clients with considerable success. To do this, gather teams of five people, have them develop five experiments, and give them $5,000 and five weeks (working two or three days a week) to conduct an experiment. By containing the experiment cost in this way, you might be able to operate without formal approval; certainly, you can get approval more easily.

Designing an Agile/Lean Experiment

Okay, you may be thinking, what next? I'm ready to do the kind of experiments you're talking about, but what exactly do I do? It's a question we get often at this point. They want solid, here's-how-to-go-about-it advice. Rather than invent something from scratch, we started with what already works.

We know, for starters, that most agile/lean approaches involve four cycles of experiments:

1. **Storyboard or text description:** You build, at no financial cost, something you can show to prospective users to see how they react.
2. **Minimum viable proposition (MVP):** You build a partial solution (e.g., a website with limited functionality) and actually try to sell the solution. This will give you a clearer sense of how potential customers will react.
3. **Beta version:** You then invest more money to build your beta product, something with more functionality but still not marketed as complete.
4. **Market version:** You finalize your solution and launch something your company can stand behind as complete.

Then we lined up several agile approaches from leading experts and mapped them against the paths that successful internal innovators had described to us. We found remarkable similarities, which I synthesized into a six-step model that will help you find your solutions more quickly and at a lower cost. You will see that this model echoes John Boyd's OODA loop, albeit in a somewhat different sequence:

1. Describe potential solutions. (Act)
2. Design a test. (Act)
3. Build. (Act)
4. Observe and gather data. (Observe)
5. Draw conclusions. (Orient)
6. Pivot or evolve. (Decide)

Think of these six steps as outlining *one* experiment cycle; from each cycle you will learn something new. If you are already close to a solution, maybe one cycle is all you need. But more likely, you'll need more. If your idea exists within your area of authority, you may be able to follow the process through all four cycles—four cycles, six steps each. But we have found that it's much more common that after the first two cycles you will need a formal business case to win approval to continue.

The key is to sequence your experiments so you start out risking very little, in terms of money and time, to learn as much as possible. When you finish one cycle, you decide whether to expand your investment and risk stepping out into the next cycle. Then, as you gain more confidence in your idea's potential value, you increase what you are willing to invest in the experiment.

Let's walk through all six steps together (figure 7.1). Remember, you may end up doing these six steps four times, through the four cycles. And you may find that the specifics of some of the steps will look different in the various cycles.

Step One: Describe Potential Solutions

You may already have a clear solution in mind, but before you commit to that vision, you'd be well served to develop several alternatives.

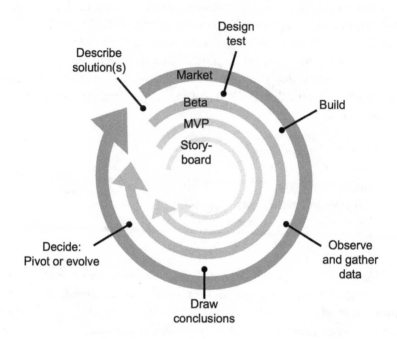

Figure 7.1 The experimentation process.

If you invest everything in just one solution and it turns out to be flawed, you'll have to start again from scratch. What's worse, you will have wasted precious time and money, and you might very well have demolished the corporate support you're going to need later. By testing multiple solutions simultaneously, you can arrive at a more optimal solution in less time.

In January 2010, Prescott Logan left his role as product manager of GE's Drivetrain Technologies business and took the job of building the Energy Storage division as its general manager. He and his team were provided with a well-thought-through business plan that laid out the needs and solutions that the division should be built around.

In the terminology of our framework, Prescott's team was given approval for a "market version." They had approval and funding to execute. Their next step was to build a factory, ramp up a sales force,

and launch the business. But they soon sensed that the plan contained considerable uncertainty. GE's battery technology had the potential to transform the industry, but that potential had not been tested. Were they about to jump off a cliff?

Prescott had seen a speech by Steve Blank and wondered if Steve's approach could help. So he sent Steve an email, out of the blue, asking for help. After some initial reluctance (his focus was entrepreneurship, not corporate innovation), Steve agreed to speak with Prescott. The prospect of exploring how lean/agile could work inside a huge organization like GE appealed to Steve, and he agreed to help.

As far as we can tell, this is the first instance of a large company formally adopting the Lean Startup methodology. Here's what happened.

Prescott's original business plan made a critical assumption: that intermediaries like Ericsson and Emerson Electric would underwrite the battery factory in exchange for the right to sell the batteries to their telecommunications customers. But it turned out neither Ericsson nor Emerson Electric was ready to do so until the market potential of the batteries was proven.

So, with coaching from Steve, Prescott's team decided to step back and run some tests. They ended up testing two solutions: a battery to provide backup power to data centers, and a battery to help telecom companies in rural areas of developing countries.

Step Two: Design a Test

The success of your solution depends on several assumptions being true. GE's version of the lean approach, which they call FastWorks, calls these assumptions "leaps of faith." McKinsey teaches its consultants to focus on "what must be true" for a hypothesis to work. So before you interact with your customer to test the concept, it is worth sitting down with your team to brainstorm about the assumptions inherent in the solutions you are testing. Ask, "What must be true for this to work?" or, more challenging yet, "What are we assuming is true?" You will quickly uncover a number of hidden assumptions.

For example, Prescott suggests looking out for three sets of assumptions:[7]

1. *Positioning.* Have you chosen a target customer that will adopt your innovation? Will they be able to get approval to buy it? Who will they need to get approval from? How long will approval take? How much are they willing to pay?
2. *Product.* Can you deliver on the product? Is it technically feasible? What will it cost to produce?
3. *Processes.* Will your internal processes support the concept? Can your accounting and customer-service processes move at the appropriate pace?

Remember the Eight P's from the last chapter? You'll recognize that Prescott's checklist focuses on three of the P's. It's well worth the time to walk through all of the P's, as you did earlier in the Value Blockers exercise, this time thinking not only about internal Value Blockers but about the broader market assumptions inherent in your idea. Then choose the most critical ones to test with an experiment right now. For each P, identify the key assumption (if one exists) that your innovation idea depends on, decide what metric you could use to test the validity of your assumption, and define the "success target" that would indicate that the assumption is sound. With that kind of clarity, you can strategically focus your experimentation efforts.

Step Three: Build

Next, you build something tangible that you can use to generate data to prove (or disprove) your assumptions. To keep your investment low, start small, perhaps with a storyboard or text narrative that describes the concept. You might create a PowerPoint presentation, with images that communicate to a potential customer what the product could do. Or you could design a mock-up of a marketing brochure. If you are testing a physical space, you might rent a room and set up furniture in the space. If you have the capability, you might create a three-dimensional depiction of the product using 3-D printing; or build a prototype using parts bought from a store.

There's a perfect example on your desk right now—the trackball mouse. When Apple got the idea and the technology for a computer

mouse from Xerox, they began designing their version. The Xerox technology required lasers to track the mouse movements, which made the mouse far too expensive for consumer application. Apple engineers, looking for lower-cost alternatives, had the idea of using a ball that would track movement against a flat surface. They could have designed a mouse with a high-tech ball, but instead they went to a pharmacy and bought a roll-on antiperspirant to build a mock-up.

It's remarkable how much information you can extract from would-be buyers simply by putting a conceptual piece in front of them and asking what they think. When a group of Chrysler managers were debating whether to launch a convertible version of the popular Sebring car, they proposed to CEO Lee Iacocca an expensive market-research effort involving focus groups and surveys. Lee suggested the team first take an existing Sebring, cut off its roof, and drive it around to see how people reacted.

For Prescott's first cycle (the "storyboard" in figure 7.1), his team pulled together data on the performance and specifications of their proposed battery: how quickly it would charge, how long it would last, and how much it would cost.

When you have completed the cycle for your storyboard, it is time to develop a minimum viable proposition (MVP). In the MVP cycle, you will build something that actually works, to see if you can generate sales.

The key word here is "minimum." For instance, you might build a website that performs some of the functions but not every single one. You might put together a program that requires you to perform manually things that will be automated in a future version. You might find a partner who for now will do some of the work that you may eventually do in-house. At GE, Prescott's team eventually built some batteries for telecom companies in rural, developing countries—but built only what they needed to run their test.

Steve Blank, who introduced the MVP concept[8] (he uses the term "minimum viable product"), defines it as something that delivers the minimum level of performance your user will need in order to make a purchase. It's critical, he emphasizes, because it accelerates the speed with which you learn.

If the MVP proves successful, in a later cycle you will create a beta version, with more features. You will test and improve the beta, and then formally launch the market version, ready for market.

Keeping the costs down during each cycle is particularly critical for internal innovators because you want to operate within certain thresholds where you need less authorization. Several internal innovators I interviewed told us they could fund projects unilaterally if expenses stayed below $10,000; once over $10,000, they needed their manager's approval.

Luckily, the cost of conducting experiments is dropping dramatically, thanks to new technology and the increasing ease with which you can gather data. Rietveld Architects LLP, for example, is well known throughout the United States and Europe for designing creative, energy-efficient spaces, both residential and commercial. Their typical process involves building numerous models, each increasing in detail and scale, to help clients visualize their designs. Like most architectural firms, they built these models by hand; it typically took two full-time employees two months. But a few years ago, they bought a 3-D printer, and today they can produce the same model with just a few hours of one employee's time.

Similarly, Manu Prakash, a professor of bioengineering at Stanford University, designed a microscope that anyone can build with everyday materials for less than a dollar. Using his template, schools in poor countries can print, cut, and fold, and thereby make microscopes available to students.

One of our clients headed an IT group that wanted to change the interface their internal clients used to make requests. Whereas in the past they would have stepped into a multimonth process—defining requirements, building, testing, piloting, and launching—they decided to adopt a more agile approach. They built a simple website that fed information to IT workers, who completed the missing tasks manually. With this, they were able to start measuring things like how many internal clients wanted to use such a system, what jobs they would use it for, and how likely they were to recommend the system to others, all in a matter of days rather than months and at a fraction of the cost.

Gone are the days in which you needed significant budget approvals to launch your test. You can tap affordable, short-term talent through portals like HourlyNerd.com and Upwork; get designers to create storyboards and sample videos at minimal cost through services like Fiverr.com or 99designs.com; produce samples for pennies using 3-D printing; and run small-batch manufacturing at a fraction of what it cost just five years ago from platforms like Alibaba.com.

Step Four: Observe and Gather Data

The next step is to get out of the office and put what you have built (your storyboard, MVP, or beta) in front of your key stakeholders: users, internal stakeholders, external partners, people who influence the buying process, or anyone else whose input you need to complete the test you designed in step three.

A manufacturer of custom picture frames, for example, had the idea of creating a kiosk for framing shops in which customers could see how their artwork would look in different types of frames. Two stakeholders were critical: users (people who buy picture frames) and the owners of the framing shops. Even though they had the kiosk and the software already built, they recognized that simply installing kiosks in stores would be unnecessarily costly. Instead, they could create a mock-up, show it to frame-shop owners at a conference they were organizing, and get their feedback. They asked questions like "What would this kiosk have to do for you to adopt it?" or "What are your concerns about putting this kiosk in your store?" A similar low-cost experiment with users would give them a much better idea what the adoption rate might be and what price they might be able to charge.

The goal is to learn as quickly and inexpensively as possible.

Talk to prospective customers with your storyboard or MVP in hand. Ask them to describe the need they would want to address with your solution. Ask them to outline when and where and why this need arises for them. Have them walk you through how and where they search for potential solutions. Ask them on what basis they compare their solution options and how they ultimately choose to purchase one, or (as is often the case) why they choose to do nothing.

Is this kind of interviewing new to you? Here's a technique you might find helpful. Pretend you are writing a play, and this will be a key scene. The scene opens with your prospective buyer talking to a colleague about a concern they both recognize. They brainstorm a couple of solutions, and eventually your name comes up. The buyer asks you to come in and chat. Now imagine, as lifelike as possible, how that conversation would go. What would you want to learn, and what might happen next?

In later cycles, as you develop your solution further, you will probably want to come up with other "discover" stories. But for

now, pick one that seems, based on your interviews, the most common. Really get into that story and understand the full context of what's happening with your customer: the psychology, the feelings, the circumstances.

It's also very valuable to learn how your customers react *after* they purchase your concept. Think of this as describing the story of them using your product or service.

Several models and experts suggest that the two most important parts of this story are the beginning and the end—the state they are in when they buy, and the state they are in when they have met their need. In between these two, you simply want to note any steps that you are fairly certain will happen. Knowing where your users start from and where you want them to end up will likely give you some great ideas for improving your proposed solution.

At this point, you do not need to be too detailed because you may still have several uncertainties about what your product or service actually is. What you are doing here is drafting out the key points in the story that move the client from a decision to purchase to a successful conclusion in which they have solved their problem.

Step Five: Draw Conclusions

When your team comes back from observation and data gathering, lay out everything you have learned. Look at everything as equally valuable; keep an open mind. This way you reduce the risk of information bias, which can occur when you latch onto one insight and overweight its conclusions.

Have a review meeting with your team. Look at the data. Draw conclusions for each area that you are testing. Synthesize these into an overarching conclusion that will take you to the final step in the cycle: whether to pivot or evolve.

Consider what happened with Procter & Gamble's Febreze product. It was built on cutting-edge technology that could eliminate odors from fabrics. But its launch—using P&G's traditional approach—was a failure, selling far fewer units than projected. To their credit, a P&G team took a new direction, to better understand the situation. They hired a researcher from Harvard Business School, got out of the office, and spoke to would-be users.

They learned that the problem lay in their positioning. Describing Febreze as a way to remove bad odors missed the mark because the users who lived with these odors had gotten so used to them they were no longer bothered. For example, they visited a woman who lived with nine cats. Though the researchers found the cat stench overpowering, the cats' owner hardly noticed it at all. Adopting an innovation begins when someone recognizes the pain or need your innovation promises to resolve. Would-be Febreze users simply didn't recognize a need.

Their second insight came from a woman in Phoenix who said, "It's nice, you know? Spraying feels like a little mini-celebration when I'm done with a room."

This led the team to adjust its messaging, filling ads with images of women (their core customer) spraying a room *after* they clean it, and smiling in celebration. With this small adjustment to the messaging (in the 8P framework, this is promotion), with no expensive changes to product or processes or business model, Febreze became one of P&G's most successful new-product launches.[9]

Step Six: Pivot or Evolve

The final step is to decide whether to pivot (change direction) or evolve (continue on your current path, increasing your investment while making improvements).

Business history is littered with success stories of ideas that made a surprising decision at this juncture.

Consider the Facebook "Like" button, which evolved out of a successful experiment. By the most recent count available (in 2010), it is clicked by more than seven million people every twenty minutes. Yet at first the project was considered cursed because it had failed multiple reviews by Mark Zuckerberg over a nearly two-year period. Then three Facebook employees—Jonathan Pines, Jared Morgenstern, and Soleio Cuervo—took up the challenge.

One of the company's biggest concerns was that allowing people to "like" pages might diminish their interest in leaving comments, a key indicator of user engagement. So the team designed an experiment. With the help of a Facebook data scientist named Itamar Rosenn, they set up the experiment, performed a few tests, and tracked data.

They found that the presence of a "Like" button actually increased the number of comments. The team won approval of the "Like" button and relatively quickly made it available to all Facebook users.[10]

Two further examples: Nintendo's famous Mario Brothers game was born out of a pivot. A development team at Nintendo was distraught when they lost the license rights to use the Popeye character in the game they had been developing specifically for him. So instead they created a new character they named "Mario." The Mario Brothers franchise, arguably today one of Nintendo's most important sources of competitive advantage, was born.

Wrigley, too, was born out of a pivot. A young man named William Wrigley moved to Chicago in the 1890s to sell soap and baking soda. As a marketing gimmick, he came up with the idea of giving away chewing gum with every purchase. When the chewing gum proved more popular than the soap and baking soda, he pivoted and started selling the gum. Today, the company that carries his last name generates more than $5 billion in annual revenue.[11]

To begin taking action on your idea, follow six steps:

1. Describe potential solutions, making sure to pick more than one.
2. Design a test by identifying the key assumptions that your innovation idea depends on, deciding what metric you could use to test the validity of your assumption, and defining the "success target" that would indicate that the assumption is sound.
3. Build a storyboard, minimum viable proposition (MVP), or beta.
4. Observe and gather data by getting out of the office and putting your storyboard, MVP, or beta in front of your key stakeholders to see how they react.
5. Draw conclusions for each area that you are testing by looking at and synthesizing the data.
6. Decide whether to pivot (change direction) or evolve (continue on your current path).

A Final Word

The traditional approach to innovation involves a well-established process: write a business plan, get approval, build a solution, and then launch it.

This is changing. Even within large organizations, we see this formal process giving way to an approach characterized by a series of experiments. "Agile/lean" is no longer the sole territory of high-tech entrepreneurs in blue jeans.

If you have an idea you want to pursue, this is very good news. It means that you can begin right now, by conducting small, inexpensive experiments for which you don't need formal approval. You will find that new technology makes it easier than ever to run small experiments. You'll also find a growing recognition that breaking your project down into smaller increments (the essence of agile) makes sense and is well received by colleagues.

Learning from your experiments is easier too. You can access data more easily, quickly, and inexpensively; for instance, you can measure website hits and average ratings in minutes rather than having to wait months to get prototypes into retail stores. Google Consumer Surveys, and research offerings built on Google's survey platform, allow you to conduct research for $2,000 that five years ago cost $50,000.

In sum, there is no reason to bet on untested beliefs. As Jeff Sutherland, author of *Scrum: The Art of Doing Twice the Work in Half the Time*,[12] urges, "Don't guess. Plan, Do, Decide, Act. Plan what you're going to do. Do it. Decide whether it did what you wanted. Act on that and change how you're doing things."

Jean and her team decided their first step would be to build a basic website that simulated what the final site would be like and put it in front of a group of people who represented the audience they thought they would attract. If that group liked it, then they would build a more robust site. This would be the lowest-cost approach they could think of to assess whether authors and readers would adopt the idea if launched.

Many people were surprised at the outcome. Jean Feiwel was not.

CHAPTER EIGHT

Team

Building an Agile Team

Learn from yesterday, live for today, hope for tomorrow.
The important thing is not to stop questioning.
—ALBERT EINSTEIN

JEAN KNEW SHE couldn't do it alone. She also knew the company would not give her a team unless she first proved the idea had potential. Classic catch-22: can't prove the idea without a team, can't get a team until the idea is proven. So she decided to hold a pizza party.

She sent out an email to staff, explaining her "Romance 2.0" idea and inviting anyone interested in getting involved to come to a particular room on a particular date. There would be pizza. "If two people showed up, I wouldn't do it," she said. If seven showed up, she would. But on that day, thirty Macmillan volunteers filled the room. And they weren't just editors. They were from marketing, sales, accounting, and operations. They were people who loved romance and were energized by the opportunity to work on something new, something that stretched beyond their day-to-day.

The group became a sort of shadow organization. They met every three weeks, for no more than an hour. They knew that if the meetings dragged on, people would stop coming. These were volunteers investing their extra time to advance the project. Everyone got a chance to speak. They talked a lot about what this could look like and decided

it might echo *American Idol*, with fans *and* the company having a say in who wins.

After every meeting, people were assigned follow-up homework. For example, three people had to work on a mission statement, others had to look at the cost to build a similar website, others would talk to legal about issues. Then these subgroups would meet on their own, and report back to the main meeting.

Her boss Jon was not involved in these meetings. At first, he was skeptical. He was worried about the money the project would take, but he thought it worth trying. "There was a lot of groundswell for this," he said, and so far the project was not costing the company extra money. "These people were not leaving at 5:00 p.m.; they were leaving at 7:00 p.m. They were engaged and empowered. They had an authority in that context that they didn't have in their day-to-day job." They were doing it because it was fun for them. Salespeople got to have editorial input, editorial people got to do marketing, Jon explained.

They ran through iterations of experiments, and with each iteration a new group would get involved. In their first experiment, they built a very basic site. To try it out, they invited about twenty people— bloggers and teenage writers, all romance fans—to assemble in a conference room. "This was the equivalent of pulling people off the street," Jean explained. In exchange for gift cards, with the Swoon Reads team watching, this informal focus group tried out the site's initial design and gave feedback.

The first experiment was encouraging, so they decided to expand to the next stage: a public launch of a beta site.

They issued a request for proposals to website-development firms and picked one that could build it for $150,000. But of course, it took longer than expected and cost more. The total amount spent on technology reached about $300,000 and would require a significant marketing investment. But by then momentum was building inter- nally, and the team had worked out many of the issues.

They launched the beta site in August 2013, just a year after the very first meeting on July 23, 2012. Jean thought that as soon as the site was launched there would be a hundred thousand manuscripts, but over the first six months, they only attracted a hundred.

They might have pulled the plug on the project at that point, but instead they decided to figure out what went wrong. The answer was

that they were not doing enough marketing and had no analytics to see what users were doing. The company wasn't ready yet to dedicate a full-time person to marketing and analytics, so they recruited three employees to pitch in their extra time to do the job. Then the manuscripts started accumulating.

They tested the idea of letting users pick the book covers, and found that readers loved the opportunity. So they incorporated the book cover design as a competition, and the impact was huge.

They thought it was critical that they have an ereader so that users could review books on their tablets. They built one using open-source software, but learned that their users actually preferred reading and editing on computers.

Eventually, the project grew so large that the team needed to evolve. They hired Lauren Scobell to serve as a full-time project manager, director of Swoon Reads. Lauren was then working in a digital agency as a product manager, but was a passionate book lover who had been trying to find a path into publishing. Through networking with people in the industry, she learned that Swoon Reads was looking for someone with just her skill set. After interviewing with Jean, she took over and began further developing the platform.

Lauren realized early on that romance lovers often don't consider themselves to be so. "You ask someone if they read romance and they often say no. Then you ask them what books they read and they are all romance books," Lauren explained. So Swoon Reads repositioned itself to include all of young adult (YA) fiction and redesigned its look and feel.

———————

You've designed the first experiment you want to conduct. Now it's time to take action, for which you need a team.

This immediately creates several complications, because the kind of team norms that lend themselves well to driving innovation will inevitably conflict with the norms of the more established parts of your organization. Those units are designed for repetition, efficiency, and reliability, while yours will be built for learning, adaptation, and flexibility.

GE's former CEO Jack Welch framed the challenge this way to me during a conference we presented at in Peru: "You've got to deliver on short-range commitments while you develop a long-range strategy and vision. The success depends on doing both. Its like walking and chewing gum."

Harvard professor and change-management guru John Kotter attacks the challenge in his book *Accelerate: Building Strategic Agility for a Faster-Moving World*, and writes in a related *Harvard Business Review* article:

> Any company that has made it past the start-up stage is optimized for efficiency rather than for strategic agility—the ability to capitalize on opportunities and dodge threats with speed and assurance. . . . But the old ways of setting and implementing strategy are failing us. We can't keep up with the pace of change, let alone get ahead of it.[1]

Internal innovators I interviewed repeatedly cited team formation as one of their most significant barriers. They specifically pointed to four critical challenges:

- **Assembling a great team.** It's difficult to pull together the perfect team because, as one internal innovator I interviewed put it, "You want the 'A' players, but their managers are less likely to let them join you because they are so valuable, and they are nervous to join because they worry that losing time on a risky project like yours could derail their careers."
- **Adopting flexible roles.** You will be best served by a cross-functional team in which members adopt flexible roles, but your organization has evolved into divisions of specialists. As Jeff Sutherland put it, "The fact is, when you look at the best teams—like the ones that existed at Toyota or 3M . . . or the ones at Google or Salesforce.com or Amazon today—there isn't this separation of roles."
- **Operating at a rapid pace.** Your team will function best when it operates at a rapid pace, with daily or at least weakly check-ins, but your organization is geared toward a more deliberate pace.
- **Managing expectations.** Instead of the prove–plan–execute approach (see chapter 7) that established organizations are more familiar with, in which you work out all the details before launching the innovation, you and your team will likely require an act–learn–build philosophy, in which you pick up one question, learn, formulate the next question, and repeat. The line between planning and execution blurs. In the early days, your goal will be to learn; later on, your goal will be to deliver results. This creates an issue because, if your organization is like most, leadership won't know how to gauge your progress in the early phases.

But here's the good news: these issues are surmountable. Indeed, we owe many of the most significant innovations in the world to small entrepreneurial teams that attracted great players, adopted flexible roles, moved at a rapid pace, and were able to manage expectations. Consider Redbox.

The Evolving Team That Built Redbox

In 2002, Greg Kaplan, a manager in McDonald's strategic and development team, had an idea. He was exploring ways to create an additional reason for customers to visit McDonald's stores, which would increase foot traffic, which presumably would lead to more hamburger sales. So he conducted an experiment.

He placed fifteen automated kiosks in the Washington metropolitan area. Four kiosks sold grocery products like milk, eggs, and sandwiches; the other eleven rented DVDs. Although the grocery kiosks were closer to McDonald's core business of serving food, they failed. The DVD kiosks, however, proved promising. So McDonald's decided to expand the program with a second experiment. They put six DVD kiosks in their Las Vegas restaurants, more in Washington, and over the next two years, extended the experiment by placing one hundred machines in the Denver area.

In 2003, McDonald's realized they needed to infuse the Redbox team with more entrepreneurial thinking and hired Mitch Lowe, a cofounder of Netflix. Lowe had attempted a similar service in 1982, launching a movie-vending company named Video Droid, which failed to take off. Lowe joined McDonald's first as a consultant, then became vice president of purchasing and operations and, in 2005, became chief operating officer. He took over from Greg as president of Redbox in 2009.

As vice president of purchasing and operations, Lowe focused first on proving the concept, testing, and learning. Then, as the questions the team sought to answer shifted from learning to executing, they realized they needed kiosk-operations expertise, so they partnered with kiosk operator Coinstar, selling them a 47.3 percent stake in the venture.

Lowe's team recognized that they couldn't slow their pace. If they did, Blockbuster might have time to copy the program. With a stronger DVD brand, deeper industry relationships, and lots of inventory, Blockbuster could have relatively easily beaten Redbox. They also

faced direct competition from a company called the New Release, which in 2007 had two thousand locations, primarily kiosks outside of grocery stores.

The Redbox team soon realized that, if they were to survive, they would have to move beyond generating foot traffic at restaurants. So, within months of signing the Coinstar deal, they set their sights on locking up the right to place DVD kiosks in supermarkets. They signed agreements with the Giant Food and Stop & Shop grocery store chains, then with Giant Eagle, Albertsons, SuperValu, and another half-dozen smaller supermarket chains over the next year. By 2007, McDonald's had more than tripled its kiosk count to three thousand locations, surpassing the New Release.

Thanks to the focused, fast-paced, entrepreneurial approach introduced by Kaplan and enhanced by Lowe, and thanks to an aggressive marketing campaign by Greg Waring, the company grew from one hundred locations to 4,500, and from $3 million to $30 million, in just thirty months.

The team's pace of learning and adapting allowed it to surpass its competition; challenge the dominant industry incumbent, Blockbuster (which eventually went bankrupt under the dual threat of Netflix and Redbox); outgrow the New Release (which eventually sold its kiosk business to Redbox in 2012); and continue to scale to a peak of 43,700 locations in 2012.[2]

It is tempting to think that this form of teamwork is appropriate for new products and services like Redbox, in which one can carve out autonomy, but less so for internal innovations. But even there, a fast-paced, dynamic team approach pays dividends. Let me introduce you to Don Hastings.

Unleashing the Leopards

Don Hastings, like most of the managers at the Lincoln Electric Company, was on edge. The company, an international conglomerate that sold machinery to large manufacturers, was facing a 40 percent plunge in sales. If they were like most corporations, they would have laid off employees to downscale the business and shrink losses. But Lincoln Electric prided itself on its commitment to a unique policy—lifetime employment. At Lincoln Electric, as long as you performed,

you would have your job for life. This policy was central to the company's culture, strategy, and purpose.

Pressure was building from investors to the board to abandon the policy. How else could Lincoln Electric survive the losses? To many, it would mean abandoning the company's soul, but what else could they do?

Hastings has a lifelong history of innovating in face of trouble. The idea of laying off workers "didn't sit right with me," he told me, so he decided to do something about it. He argued that the financial crisis the company was facing was essentially a problem of people allocation. Because of the sales decline, the company now had too many people on the manufacturing floor and too few people selling. So he came up with a clever program to build a new team of salespeople, recruited entirely from their army of manufacturing personnel.

He proposed recruiting volunteers from the manufacturing floor and training them to sell a new type of machine developed for a new market. This was unorthodox for two reasons. First, it was generally accepted that manufacturing floor personnel lacked the personality or skills to sell. Second, the market potential of the new machine they would be selling was untested. Lincoln Electric generally sold machines to large manufacturing plants, and this new machine would need to be sold to small shops.

Hastings was able to build enough internal support for the program to give it a try. He did this by implementing many of the features we will examine in this chapter. He focused people on a compelling mission they all cared about—saving the company and saving jobs. He gave the project a memorable name—"Leopard"—to symbolize how the manufacturing workers would change their spots and become salespeople.

Hastings sent out the request for volunteers, hoping that maybe fifty people would sign up. They got more than a hundred volunteers. Even Don's daughter Leslie, who was interning at the company, volunteered. They accepted sixty-eight of the volunteers and ran them through sales and product training. Within a few weeks the company had a new sales force, sixty-eight people strong, ready to hit the road and find new clients.

To get the "leopards" selling, Don also had to gain the trust of the regional sales managers to whom the leopards would report. He placed the leopards anywhere in the country a sales manager said they

wanted one. Soon sixty-eight new salespeople were blanketing the country "from California to Maine," knocking on the doors of small manufacturing shops. Back at headquarters, they held regular meetings to share feedback and incorporate it into the program.

The project worked. It generated new revenue, reduced manufacturing costs, and saved people's jobs. It's not too strong to say that Hastings also helped save the company. After a string of similar innovative ventures, he was eventually named CEO.[3]

Building an Effective Team in Seven Steps

As more organizations bump up against the challenge of activating internal innovation teams, numerous new solutions have emerged. In appendix C, I describe the most popular ones. We have tried several of them with clients, studied the efforts of organizations to implement them, and looked at the patterns by which successful innovation teams, like those of Redbox and the Leopard program, succeed. From this experience we have pinpointed seven critical steps to building an effective innovation team from within:

1. Remove organizational friction.
2. Assemble a cross-functional team.
3. Align around an important goal.
4. Use metrics and data to track the most important thing(s).
5. Build a scoreboard everyone can see.
6. Establish a rapid rhythm.
7. Generate positive velocity.

Step 1: Remove Organizational Friction

The first step is to diagnose where your organizational context will create issues for the team. Every organization is unique. Some impose multiple challenges, some none. Think through each of these and assess where issues might arise so you can preempt them.

- **Resources:** Al Shugart, founder of Seagate Technologies, once wrote, when describing the challenges of launching a startup, "Cash is more important than your mother." For your idea to take

hold, you need to ensure you will have the necessary resources. You will need both cash and time.

Only 11 percent of managers surveyed by Wharton professor George Day said that their company's strategy priorities have the resources they need for success.[4] The cash challenge for internal innovators means not only getting the budget you need, but establishing the internal political support to ensure that support will continue (we'll dive more deeply into this in the next chapter). Future funding may dry up if your primary advocates change roles, unreasonably high expectations for your innovation are not met, or the exciting "newness" of your endeavor dims. Redbox was initially funded by McDonald's Ventures LLC; its later partnership with Coinstar gave it access to new funding sources.

Time is another critical resource. Getting permission to dedicate 20 percent of your time to the project sounds great, but in reality it often just means you'll be working 20 percent extra. You'll do all you were doing before and spend nights and weekends on your pet project.

- ○ Have you secured the funding you need now?
- ○ Is there a risk they will pull funding later?
- ○ Will they give you the time or freedom you and your team need?

• **Rewards and expectations:** Because familiar managerial activities of the organization's core business are easier to measure than creative, innovative ones, they are easier to reward. So the incentives placed on you and your team are likely to encourage working on the core business and not on your new innovation. Unrealistic expectations have also been shown to be one of the key barriers to internal innovation. The company, used to operating with big numbers and scale, expects you to reach higher, faster than what is reasonable.

- ○ Will your team's incentive structure motivate scaling quickly?
- ○ Are the organization's expectations achievable?

• **Risk-taking:** It's one thing for leadership to tell you it's OK to fail; it's another for them to give a promotion, or even a second chance, to someone who does. Look for someone who has failed at an innovation initiative in the past. What happened to him or her? You are starting to explore here the potential limits that your organization's culture will have on your team's success.[5]

- ○ Is failure (really) an acceptable option?

- **Senior leadership support:** One internal innovator I interviewed warned against interpreting "the absence of 'no' for a 'yes.' " Senior leaders may say they support you, but how committed are they really? Have the leaders that are supporting you been behind other innovation initiatives? Have they maintained that support through tough times? Getting this right can help you avoid a dynamic many internal innovators have described as a "pendulum of support." Initially, you appear to enjoy the full backing of your organization; but later, interest wanes or priorities shift, and you find yourself without support.
  - Is your leadership support real and reliable?
  - Who, specifically, can you count on for sustained support?
  - What can you do to ensure your support endures?
- **Organizational freedom:** According to a study of eight thousand managers in more than 250 firms, 85 percent of respondents said they can rely on their bosses and 84 percent said they can rely on direct reports, but only 59 percent said they can rely on colleagues from other departments. In that same study, only 30 percent of managers said their organization can effectively shift funds across units to support strategy, and only 20 percent said their organization can do the same with people.[6] Achieving cooperation across departments and other silos is persistently difficult. If your innovation will require expertise, talent, and buy-in from power centers scattered throughout the organization, you must make sure you have put in place the relationships and commitments to actuate cross-silo cooperation.
  - What cooperation, talent, expertise, or other support will you require outside of your current silo or department?
  - Have you gotten the buy-in you need to ensure you can rely on this support?

Step 2: Assemble a Cross-Functional Team

A small body of determined spirits fired by an unquenchable faith in their mission can alter the course of history.

—MAHATMA GANDHI

John Kotter speaks of the importance of building a "guiding coalition" and enlisting a "voluntary army" of supporters who, collectively,

bring the skills and relationships you will need to get your innovation through. To implement "scrum," you form a team composed of a "scrum master," who leads the process, and a "product owner," who holds primary responsibility for the initiative, both supported by team members with specific expertise. Several innovation teams apply tools like wikis, telepresence, social-collaboration tools, and virtual reality to make it easy for staff dispersed throughout the organization to contribute efficiently to the common cause. Doing so can help leverage the power of the crowd, creating an internal staff-on-demand model akin to Upwork (for freelancers), 99designs (for designers), and Marketeeria (for marketing and PR talent).

What is the alchemy that produces the right kind of team? Numerous studies give us some fact-based guidance, pointing to a broad spectrum of potential attributes. Five factors appear to matter most:

1. **Variance in functional background (or job-relevant diversity):** The greater the diversity in the functional backgrounds of your team members, the more innovative they will be. You don't want a team dominated by marketers or engineers or salespeople; you want representation from a diversity of areas. Many innovation teams start with the functions their organization already has in place—an insurance firm we worked with wanted an actuary, a salesperson, and compliance, marketing, and human resource experts—but this is a mistake. Instead, the accelerated competitive environment encourages the opposite approach. Jeff Bezos calls this "working backward." Imagine what skills and capabilities you will need in the future to meet the customers' needs, and ensure you have those in place. That insurance company really needed consumer-data analysis (versus actuarial) and mergers-and-acquisitions experience to establish new partnerships.

2. **Average (mean) education level:** The higher the education level of your team—i.e., the greater the degree of formal education (it seems informal education also matters, but it is harder to measure, so no research I've found validates the importance of informal education)—the greater their innovativeness. In selecting your team, don't only look at diversity of experience, but also look for overall higher levels of education. Some researchers and innovators I've interviewed suggest that what really matters is that you have people who want to learn—that you establish

a learning culture within your team—and higher levels of education is an easily measurable indicator of that.

3. **Tenure:** In general, the lower the tenure of your members, the more effective they will be at introducing innovations. This is perhaps because, having spent less time in your organization, they have accepted fewer dogmas. They have less history to forget, which gives them greater freedom to pursue new things. Interestingly, age has less of an effect on team innovativeness. It is not so much about having a young team as it is about having a team that brings that rare combination of domain expertise and willingness to challenge accepted ways of doing things—starting with a "beginner's mind."

4. **Team size:** Larger teams tend to increase innovative output, but there is a limit to this. The studies analyzed teams of a certain size range; toward the top of the range, innovativeness increased. But very large teams have difficulty innovating. Bezos famously proposed the "two-pizza rule"—if you can't feed a team with two pizzas, it's too large. Various studies have tried to pinpoint the correct team size. At what size does the level of innovation peak? Overall, these studies agree that the ideal team size ranges between five and ten people.

5. **Goal interdependence:** When team members are bound by a common goal or mission or vision, they tend to be more innovative. They are both inspired and motivated to achieve something that is important, giving their effort meaning. But they also understand that they cannot do it on their own, that their success depends on others, which helps engender great teamwork. We will talk more about this in the next step of the process.

Balancing these factors takes some tinkering. Some are in conflict with each other. For example, greater variance (or diversity) in functional background would argue for a larger team, but ideal team size means pushing the team down to no more than ten. Ultimately, your team design should produce the right mix of functional backgrounds and include people who are learners (high educational level), unrestrained by accepted dogmas, and aligned behind a shared, compelling goal.

In one surprising insight, we found that the mythology of an internal entrepreneurial team that takes an innovation from concept to

market does not match what really happens. Innovation teams evolve over time, during each iteration of the experimentation cycle. As they make new discoveries and change design, their needs for expertise evolve, so new people step in and former members pass the baton.

Step 3: *Align Around an Important Goal*

In life, as in football, you won't go far unless you know
where the goalposts are.
—ARNOLD H. GLASOW

4DX, a popular team methodology introduced by Chris McChesney, Sean Covey, and Jim Huling in their book,[7] stresses the crucial nature of focusing on "wildly important goals." Nearly every effective innovation team model stresses the import of creating a simple, well-understood purpose that team members can get behind.

Research shows that once you have assembled a diverse team, the team's effectiveness will depend heavily on the presence of a shared goal. Interestingly, when there is less diversity among members of an organization, the presence of a shared vision has little effect on performance. But when you have a diverse team, the lack of a shared vision leads to dysfunction. People begin bickering over their differences rather than unifying behind their shared goal.[8] So if you pulled together a cross-functional team, as suggested in the second step, creating a shared mission becomes even more important.

It's also important to focus your team narrowly on one part of the goal at a time. In the scrum approach, for example, you focus the team on just one (or a few) priorities every week. Successful growth teams are also driven by focus. Brian Balfour—creator of Coelevate, founder and CEO of Reforge, and one of the leading proponents of a popular innovation-team approach called "growth teams"—puts it this way:

I've haphazardly given (and heard) the advice "you need to focus" many times in my career. On the surface I've always accepted it, but until recently I don't think I really understood it. Focus is a big part of my approach to growth, and how I build growth machines.

Focus gets misinterpreted a lot. It isn't about being short sighted. You need broader context to understand what and why you are doing something in the moment. It also isn't about sticking to the

same thing for a really long period of time. Achieving something great requires you to make smart iterations and changes based on lessons learned. . . . Maybe the best way to explain focus is simply this—zoom out, zoom in, zoom out.

Some individuals thrive on doing a lot of things at once. But they are the exception not the rule. A lot of startup founders are in this camp by nature. The mistake these founders make is to draw the conclusion that because they personally thrive on being unfocused, their company/organization will too.[9]

One particularly effective framework for building your team's commitment to a goal comes from Marc Benioff, the founder of Salesforce.com. Marc claims that the secret to the success of Salesforce.com—which grew past $1 billion in revenue in less than ten years, despite competition from much larger software firms, and which at the time of this writing produces more than $10 billion in revenue—is a "secret management process"[10] he developed called the V2MOM. This acronym stands for

- Vision: the outcome you want your initiative to achieve
- Value: why achieving this vision matters
- Metrics: what measures will indicate you have achieved your vision
- Obstacles: the barriers you will need to overcome to get there
- Measures: the actions you must take to get there

Here is how we have found it works best. You sit down with your team and spend a good two to three hours filling out a V2MOM template. Your agenda would go like this:

Vision: Discuss what it would look like to have achieved your goal. Think three to five years from now. Describe what impact you are having, what people are saying, what it looks and feels like to have achieved success. This will help clarify what your initiative is, and what it is not. It will bring to the surface hidden disconnects between what different people on your team believe you are up to. If you skip this step, you are likely to find that people are actually pushing slightly different visions. What they think to do, what actions they choose to pursue, will start diverging. The Vision discussion

prevents this. It helps ensure that all of the actions your team takes become aligned along one direction, for one purpose, one vision.

Value: Open a conversation about why this is valuable. This is a way to anchor your team in the conviction that "this is important." Think about why this is important to the company, but also why it is important to each of you individually and why it is important for the world. You are going to change the world. Why does the world benefit from the change you will cause? If you skip this step, you will find that your team lacks the conviction and passion to follow through when the initiative starts hitting obstacles.

Metrics: Get specific and define what measurable results you would need to reach to feel that you have achieved your vision. If you say you want to be the leading provider of a product or service, here you define precisely what that means: you have the largest market share, you are ranked number one on a specific industry ranking, you have more revenue than anyone else, or whatever. Define specifically how you will measure each element of the vision. This helps provide clarity to the team. There will be no vague, feel-good, pat-ourselves-on-the-back-just-for-having-tried rewards. You will know without a doubt whether you have made it or not. If you miss this step, you will find your team later lacks accountability because what they are pursuing is vague. Don't set more than three metrics.

Obstacles: Explore and prioritize the key obstacles you will face. It's powerful to discuss and define your obstacles now, before they appear, because when your team confronts them, they will not interpret them as reasons your idea is flawed. Instead they will think, "This is exactly what we thought would happen," and so feel they must be on the right path. List the three to five most important obstacles.

Measures: "Measures" really mean actions or activities. Here you break down the things that you should focus on now that will enable you to advance your idea most efficiently and rapidly. The idea here is to focus your team on the 20 percent of activities you should take now that would deliver 80 percent of the results.

The process of defining your V2MOM as a group should align everyone around a compelling, important shared goal. It should leave your team clear on what success looks like (vision and metrics), agreeing that achieving that goal is important (value), anticipating the barriers you will face (obstacles), and being ready to take the most important actions now (measures) to advance the idea.

Step 4: Use Metrics and Data to Track the Most Important Thing(s)

It's not enough to be busy; so are the ants.
The question is: what are we busy about?
—HENRY DAVID THOREAU

The "measures" in your V2MOM define the most important things your team should be working on now to advance toward your vision. The next step is to put metrics against each of these measures, divide them up among team members, and start tracking your progress with hard data.

Every innovation approach being adopted today advocates using metrics and data to track the most important things. Google, for example, applies an approach they call "objectives and key results" (OKRs). It plays particularly well to Google's philosophy because it provides data they can analyze. For example, a qualitative objective like "Transform user experience" is defined by three to four measurable "key objectives," such as "Interview ten users to identify most important pain points" and "Create a list of twenty most important best practices in user design." You may also have some results metrics such as "Customer-satisfaction score of users surveyed reaches nine." Week by week, your team members update their scores. If they have interviewed two users out of ten, they get 20 percent, and so forth. Every week, you collect the data and update your scoreboard. You then have rich historical data that you can analyze.

Balfour says that one of the key guiding principles of growth teams should be "Math and metrics don't lie, but they don't tell us everything." Scrum creator Jeff Sutherland believes that one key breakthrough was to start measuring "velocity." Each item the team works on has to be independent from other items and has to be actionable. It is then assigned a "definition of done," so that the team can actually measure when "done" is achieved. Velocity measures how quickly tasks get done.

There are three additional principles to keep in mind as you set your metrics.

The lead-versus-lag distinction. 4DX emphasizes the importance of acting on lead measures rather than lag measures. Lead measures

are ones your team can directly affect; lag measures are the results of the lead ones. How often your car breaks down is a lag measure. How often you service the car and change its oil is a lead measure. If you focus your team on lag measures, which are only indirectly influenced by their efforts, you may see a sense of hopelessness or at least a lack of focus. "Well, there are so many reasons that the car might break down; we can't control that." In addition, your performance when driving an innovation is often affected by factors outside of your control. Revenue may be influenced by the performance of other products. Costs may be heavily affected by how costs are allocated internally to other divisions and initiatives. Focus on what your team can control.

Independent parts. It also helps to break the work down into smaller pieces. When actor Will Smith was a young boy, his father made him and his brother build a huge brick wall. It took years. What Smith got out of that experience, what he thinks his father wanted to teach, was the power of taking on a big project, breaking it down into parts, and knocking them off "one brick at a time." Similarly, you are now breaking the big team objective down into parts, picking up one at a time, and focusing the team on that. If pieces depend on each other, then you find yourself staring at a block of interconnected bricks too large to act on quickly. Make sure every objective you choose to pursue in this cycle can be worked on independently of the others.

Learning, not only outcomes. Traditional key performance indicators (KPIs) used to manage the core business may not be appropriate for your challenge right now. The KPIs of your company—inventory turns, customer visits, etc.—are designed to manage outcomes or results. But innovations' outcomes are less predictable. During this experimentation phase, you want to focus on what will help your team learn and adapt.

Step 5: Build a Scoreboard Everyone Can See

When Jeff Sutherland started developing the scrum method, seeking to identify and systematize the things that made his teams hyperproductive, he found that one of the most important elements was having a visual display of the team's progress that was continually updated. In his case, he used—and scrum teams around the world continue

to use—a whiteboard with sticky notes showing what tasks are being worked on, what progress has been made, what has been completed, and what is on backlog.

It's universally acknowledged in thinking about innovation teams that every team member should always be able to know what the team's current score is. You can do this with dashboards updated weekly or daily. You can do it even more frequently, updating the scores in real time. Jet Blue's corporate control room in New York, for example, looks like a scene out of a spy movie, with screens tracking flights, weather patterns, and delays so teams can respond immediately to changes. Walmart tracks near-real-time sales by SKU so that if you are a designer, say, of a particular piece of clothing, you can see how quickly it is selling day by day, hour by hour.

Google takes scoreboard a step further. Every employee can see the OKRs for every other employee through an internal site. Since employees set their own OKRs, this becomes a powerful way of establishing accountability. You are saying, "This is what you can count on me for." It allows people to understand the interdependence between OKRs. They can see who is depending on them to deliver on their objectives and track the progress of people whose objectives their success depends on. Remember that "goal interdependence" is one of the most important determinants of high-performing innovation teams.

Step 6: Establish a Rapid Rhythm

I wrote much of this chapter from just outside of a beach house in Colombia during the Olympics. The rattle of palm trees overhead and sounds of wind blowing up from the ocean did not distract me from the task. But this "writing retreat" also happened to fall in the middle of the Olympics, and with the U.S. women's national soccer team playing Colombia's, I kept looking up, through the screened windows, to see the score. It makes little sense that I looked every few minutes. My knowledge of the score had no bearing on the outcome. And yet, I could not stop myself from checking.

That's the nature of games. They make us want to take part. Wharton professor Kevin Werbach has been studying exactly what makes games so engaging, and his field of study—gamification—helps explain the success of many of the most thriving businesses, movements, products, and teams. You have already installed, in the previous step, one

important gamification principle by creating a score that everyone can see. Now you want to put in place another principle: a rhythm of stages or rounds to build engagement and anticipation.

The quarterly rhythm common in most areas of your business will not engender the level of engagement you want. Instead, establish at least a weekly review, preferably daily. Verne Harnish—author of *Scaling Up*, founder of Gazelles, and the creator of a business-growth methodology being used by more than forty thousand growth businesses throughout the world—advocates a "daily huddle," lasting no more than thirty minutes, in which your team stands (rather than sits) to go through the numbers and discuss priorities for the day.

Consider a weekly or daily team review to achieve the following objectives:

- Update the scoreboard metrics.
- Review the score.
- Assess whether you are winning or losing.
- Capture and absorb lessons.
- Make adjustments.
- Remove blockages.

Meet Pat Pacious, president and CEO of Choice Hotels. He left a career at a large consulting firm to join Choice, one of the fastest-growing and most innovative lodging companies, and now the second-largest hotel chain in the world.[11] Choice's seventy-five-year history of industry firsts includes a telephone in every room, twenty-four-hour desk service, guaranteed reservations, and brand segmentation. The company has continued this legacy of innovation, developing the first global hotel iPhone application, the first internet-based property management system, a widely copied soft-brand concept, and a unique new model for vacation rental.

Although Choice is one of the largest chains, they are small relative to Pacious's past consulting clients because they franchise their branded properties and do not operate the hotels themselves. With Choice in this sweet spot—small enough to implement faster-paced, innovative change and large enough to do so at scale—Pacious decided to establish a team model that would drive innovation. I had the opportunity to talk with him about how he did it.[12]

He began by establishing a strategy review team that would meet every month—a faster rhythm than the more common quarterly schedule—and instilled hyperefficiency to make sure these meetings did not eat up too much time.

First, the strategy team defined a shared goal—together. After that, every meeting opened with repeating that goal to make sure they were not losing sight of what's important. Many companies use a framework in which meetings open with a discussion of *that meeting's* goals, but Pacious avoids this, because he believes it focuses too narrowly on tasks and the meeting itself, and removes people from the bigger picture.

Then Pacious took a drastic approach to smash down silos. He ended the practice of individual departmental meetings, choosing instead to integrate representatives from each group or department in the broader strategy meeting and establishing interdependence among stakeholders. For example, discussing something like customer journey, decision-makers could see how each department had to consider that one issue—and also the bigger picture. Previously, they had only understood their own roles, as they were only meeting with their own teams.

Finally, he reinforced three key norms at each meeting:

- Ask dumb questions (this is OK).
- Stick to the agenda at hand (no tangents).
- It's fine to say "I have nothing new to report" (this doesn't get you branded as a slacker).

Pacious said it took about six months of repetition to get everyone on board, but in slightly over half a year (two fiscal quarters), his team was operating more effectively than before he arrived. Revenue was ticking up. Goals were being met, and people understood the work of others, reducing friction among decision-makers.

Step 7: Generate Positive Velocity

The final step is to make sure you are generating a positive, empowering sense of momentum. We've all been in reporting sessions that people dreaded because they were behind and were about to be scolded by their manager and peers. When the reviews become a weekly "Why haven't you delivered?" conversation, you will sap your team's motivation, innovativeness, and commitment. Remember that a willingness to

accept failure is one of the most important drivers of innovation. This is why, in Google's OKR framework, individuals and teams aim for an 80 percent score instead of 100 percent. Demanding 100 percent performance can demotivate the team (rarely will they reach perfection) and encourage them to set less aggressive goals.

It is also important to generate and celebrate short-term wins. This gives people a sense of progress and accomplishment that builds confidence. It also signals to people outside the team that the effort is succeeding. All of this builds excitement and commitment, which in turn makes the team more likely to succeed going forward.

To summarize: Build an effective team for your innovation idea with these seven steps:

1. **Remove organizational friction:** Walk through the five points of organization friction (resources, rewards/expectations, risk-taking, senior leadership support, and organizational freedom), and identify what you must do to address, or at least anticipate, each one.
2. **Assemble a cross-functional team:** Pull together a team of between five and ten people with the right mix of functional backgrounds, who are learners (high educational level) and unrestrained by accepted dogmas (low tenure).
3. **Align around an important goal:** Complete a V2MOM to align the team passionately behind a compelling shared vision, with an understanding of what specifically qualifies as winning and what obstacles you will face.
4. **Use metrics and data to track the most important thing(s):** Decide which leading metrics your team should focus on.
5. **Build a scoreboard everyone can see:** Decide on a display for your team and individual metrics.
6. **Establish a rapid rhythm:** Agree on the frequency with which you will review your team's progress, and set an agenda for that meeting.
7. **Generate positive velocity:** Celebrate early wins; allow people to strive beyond what is easy by allowing for failure.

As with many of the internal innovations I've studied, Swoon Reads dispels the myth of the startup team—a hacker, a hustler, and a hipster—that builds and launches its vision from start to finish. With each cycle of experimentation, the Swoon Reads team evolved. As different skills were needed, new people were added, others passed the baton. But their passion and effort could have easily been squelched had Jean and the team not skillfully managed the overall corporate environment in which they had to operate.

CHAPTER NINE

Environment

Creating Islands of Freedom

The real damper on employee engagement is the soggy, cold blanket of
centralized authority. In most companies, power cascades downwards
from the CEO. Not only are employees disenfranchised from
most policy decisions, they lack even the power to rebel
against egocentric and tyrannical supervisors.

—GARY HAMEL

SWOON READS COULD easily have failed. Superficially, it may
seem that it succeeded because Jean was lucky to find herself inside an
organization that allowed for innovation freedom. She just happened
to work under a boss who would allow the groundswell of internal
passion for the idea to flourish.

But dig deeper and you will see Jean was quite clever in *creating*
the freedom she needed. First, the reason she chose to join Macmillan
in the first place, years earlier, was that it had a culture that fostered
innovation. Second, she didn't ask for funding too early; instead, she
assembled a cross-functional team at no cost to the company. She also
designed the idea in a way that minimized its dependence on many of
Macmillan's processes and procedures.

She drew her inspiration from Saturn, the automobile brand
launched inside GM as a "different kind of car company" that operated with substantial freedom from its parent. It used a different distribution network and built its own unique culture. She would tell
the Swoon Reads team that even though most were playing two
roles—their core job at Macmillan and their second job at Swoon

Reads—they should consider Swoon Reads as an independent group, separate from Macmillan. At Swoon Reads, hierarchy doesn't matter; you can play a role that matches your passion rather than your resume. That attracted a lot of dedicated, smart people.

Cleverly, she also positioned Swoon Reads not as an alternative to Macmillan's core business but as a vehicle to attract young readers and emerging authors. When your innovation becomes a complement rather than a disruptive threat, you are less likely to be rejected.

You may have done everything right until this point. You activated your intent, identified a strategic need, generated lots of exciting options, predicted the value blockers, designed just the right experiment to act on, and recruited an ideal team. But none of that means that your organization will immediately recognize the brilliance of your innovation idea. Generally speaking, the environments in which internal innovators operate are less than helpful, and often downright threatening.

Yet, as we saw in chapter 2, successful internal innovators see navigating the political headwinds as part of the problem-solving process. They do not expect immediate support. They know they will have to work through numerous noes to find someone willing to give them the yes they deserve.

They don't see rejection as a sign that innovating is impossible. Indeed, some of the internal innovators I interviewed say they see rejection as a sign that their ideas have potential. As one person said, "If people get the idea immediately, it probably is not that novel."

Consider some of these notable rejections:

- Harry Warner of Warner Brothers Pictures first rejected the idea of talking movies, saying, "Who the hell wants to hear actors talk?"[1]
- In 1920, David Sarnoff, an employee at RCA, urged his company to invest in radio. His managers responded, "The wireless music box has no imaginable commercial value. Who would pay for a message sent to nobody in particular?"[2]
- As an employee at Hewlett-Packard, Steve Wozniak proposed the design for what became the Apple computer five times. He was rejected five times.[3]

- When Fred Smith (the founder and CEO of FedEx) wrote a term paper proposing an overnight delivery system while an undergraduate at Yale, his professor gave him a C, explaining that while the concept seemed interesting, to earn a grade better than a C, his idea had to be feasible.[4]
- Walt Disney was fired by a newspaper editor for a lack of creativity.
- Impressionists had to arrange their own art exhibition because their works were routinely rejected by the Paris Salon.[5]
- Beethoven's teacher called him hopeless as a composer.[6]
- Vince Lombardi was rejected for coaching jobs because he "possesses minimal football knowledge and lacks motivation."[7]
- Robert Goddard, a rocket pioneer, endured rejection of his ideas by the scientific community. They all doubted a rocket could go into space and, even if it did, thought it would be of no value.[8]
- American poet E. E. Cummings had one manuscript rejected by fourteen publishers. Finally his mother paid to publish his book; Cummings dedicated the book to those fourteen publishers.[9]
- Western Union, in a story that might well be apocryphal, when offered the right to purchase Alexander Graham Bell's telephone, declined, saying "This 'telephone' has too many shortcomings to be seriously considered as a means of communication. The device is inherently of no value to us."[10]
- Decca Records rejected the Beatles, telling their manager that "guitar groups are on their way out" and "we don't like your boys' sound." Columbia Records also passed.[11]

When we launch a new product in the market and customers first reject it, we don't blame the customers. We rethink our marketing strategy to target early adopters and advocates who will give the innovation a chance. Similarly, getting an innovation idea adopted within an organization demands finding those spaces that are open to new ideas. John Hagel advises trying to innovate on the "edge" of an organization, and Clayton Christensen suggests doing so on the "fringes." You must find or create "islands of freedom" on which you and your team can go about the business of advancing the innovation.

To see this in action, meet Ken Kutaragi. By carefully creating islands of freedom within a global behemoth, he helped launch an innovation that revolutionized a market and redefined his company.

The Regular Employee Who Saved Sony

When he graduated from Tokyo's Denki Tsushin University in 1975 with a degree in electronic engineering, Ken was thrilled to get a job offer from the Sony Corporation. Sony was the world's leader in electronics (television was its number one product), but what really appealed to Ken was that the company had pioneered a system of meritocracy that recognized and rewarded talent and contributions from the rank and file.[12] In his first position at Sony, Ken did research on stereo sound and on liquid color displays (LCDs). Both are now common in television and computer monitors, but at the time this was cutting-edge research.

At home with his young family, Ken noticed that his daughter enjoyed playing the Nintendo Famicom video game. A tinkerer since childhood, he took the system apart and noted that the gaming console had a lot of room for technical improvement, especially the sound quality.[13]

Ken secretly went to work on a new sound system and proposed it to Nintendo. When the Sony bosses found out what he was doing, they were furious; they wanted him fired. But one person defended him and saw value in what he was doing: Noryo Ohga, Sony's chairman and CEO at the time. Ohga provided cover for Ken and even allowed him to collaborate with Nintendo on a project to create a CD-ROM player—dubbed the play station—to replace Nintendo's game-console cartridge system.

But the collaboration effort failed. Nintendo ended up walking away from the project in favor of a new partnership with Phillips Electronics, leaving Ken in the dust.

Recognizing this as a pivotal moment, Ken took the bold step of approaching CEO Ohga. Certain that a game console product had value to the company, Ken begged for another chance to work on it. He even went so far as to threaten to quit if not allowed to do so. Most of the Sony executives were skeptical of gaming and saw minimal future profit potential in it. But CEO Ohga again backed Ken, permitting him to work on the project and even moving him and his team to Sony Entertainment, away from the negative pressure of Sony's core electronics business.

Sony Entertainment had become well known for launching new musicians and other entertainment stars. Shigeo Maruyama, then head

of the division, had a talent for finding and nurturing "stars," a skill that carried beyond the artists Sony Entertainment developed. In a 2017 interview with a technology magazine, the seventy-six-year-old retired executive said:

> Stars are not followers. They are not people who do things because other people are doing them. People who become stars are those who see an opportunity and are the first to jump into that space. The people who jump in first need to be brave, and people who are brave have a distinctly . . . what is it . . . a strong heart. They usually don't have a lot of allies and because of that they're alone, but they're not afraid of being alone.[14]

Maruyama likened Kutaragi to a musical talent that needed a supportive and comfortable working environment in order to succeed.

Ken and his team worked in earnest, and eventually launched the PlayStation to worldwide success in 1995. It was the most advanced game console ever created, complete with 3-D graphics and far superior, realistic images and sound. Furthermore, it offered a CD-ROM to play the games contained on a disc, a much faster system than the cartridge-based console being sold by its biggest competitor, Nintendo.[15]

By 1997, Sony's game consoles had cornered more than 70 percent of the global market for video game systems and contributed more than 40 percent of Sony's profit.[16] Indeed, it can be argued that the PlayStation saved the company. By 2011, the company's revenues began a five-year-long decline. Apple and Samsung were beating out its mobile phones, the Sony Walkman was disrupted by the iPod and iPhone, its PC and laptop business was logging double-digit annual sales declines, and its television business was losing money. One of the few bright spots and profit generators was the PlayStation.

And Ken Kutaragi? He eventually rose to the helm of Sony as chairman of the board and then, until his retirement in 2013, president and CEO of Sony Computer Entertainment (SCE). In an interview in 2015, he reflected on his years with one of the biggest companies in the world. Asked about his motivation, he said, "I wanted to prove that even regular employees—no, especially regular company employees—could build a venture of this scale with superb technology, superb concepts, and superb colleagues."[17]

The Proven Drivers of Internal Innovation

To find or engineer "islands of freedom," it helps to understand the organizational drivers that will either encourage new ideas or rebuff them. When you understand these drivers, you can more skillfully pull the levers that will create the freedom you need.

Unfortunately, much of what has been written about the drivers of internal innovation reflect personal frustrations, based on emotion more than proof. To help you wade through the mass of folklore to identify what is known today as the truth, I looked through every piece of research I could find that shows a statistically significant correlation between a particular organizational driver and the level of internal innovativeness. Numerous researchers, particularly in the area of entrepreneurial orientation (EO), have diligently studied these drivers, highlighting factors such as management support, autonomy, rewards/reinforcement, time availability, and organizational boundaries.[18] I sought to cut through the clutter of opinion to get the facts. I only included drivers identified by researchers who could show they had studied enough data points and found a statistically meaningful connection. You will find some things here that are obvious, some that are surprising, and some that you would expect to see but do not.

Think of the drivers as being these four types:

1. **Talent:** If you can access the type of talent naturally adept at innovating, you will have a better chance of succeeding.
2. **Structure:** However, even if you have the right talent, if they must operate under structures that hinder their attempts, they will be ineffective.
3. **Culture:** Even with the right talent and empowering organizational structures in place, your team's efforts will be frustrated, and innovation is likely to fizzle out, if you do not also support them with the right culture.
4. **Leadership:** Finally, having the right talent in place, under the right structures, and supported by the right culture is still likely to produce only temporary success if you do not also find leadership that does the right things.

Figure 9.1 Drivers of internal innovation.

As illustrated in figure 9.1, this is an interconnected system. It offers no silver bullet. You are unlikely to find an ideal island in which talent, structures, culture, and leadership are all present and perfect, but you can use these levers to find, or create, greater levels of freedom. If you are seeking to increase the innovativeness of your team or organization, these drivers can help you diagnose what you need to change.

Talent

As described in chapter 2, research points to six attributes that compose the profile of successful internal innovators: innovative thinking, autonomy, market awareness, proactivity, calculated risks, intrinsic motivation (to innovate), and political acumen. As you think through which divisions or other areas of your organization your team will operate within, try to assess where you are most likely to find people with these characteristics. Is there a particular brand or product team, for example, or a region or division, in which you are more likely to find people with the right profile?

Structure

While the plethora of frustrations that people cite about the structural barriers to their efforts point to many causes, only four appear to have a proven impact:

- **Innovation resources:** the ability to access the resources (capital and time) needed to pursue innovation. To address this, some companies create innovation budgets and awards. 3M and Google famously give some workers 15 and 20 percent, respectively, of their time to allocate to new projects. EY, the big-four accounting firm, has created an innovation charge code so that employees can spend time pursuing innovation without its negatively affecting their billable hours.
- **Rewards:** incentive systems that reward innovation. One of most commonly cited barriers to innovation is reward systems that recognize only short-term returns. Many of the most innovative companies we have studied address the short-term nature of typical rewards with leading indicators of innovativeness, such as measuring experiments conducted, pilots attempted, cultural innovation assessments,[19] or the extent to which others in the organization view a team as innovative. Rewards need not be monetary (especially if people are intrinsically motivated). Indeed, one bank I interviewed found that monetary rewards were counterproductive. They had set up a financial reward for an innovation that ultimately failed. When they replaced the reward with recognition—a "leaderboard" that publicly tracked innovation activities—activity took off.
- **Allowance of risk-taking:** Do you get a promotion when an innovation attempt fails, or does it hurt your career? Seek out the areas within which you find examples of people taking risks and bouncing back from failure.
- **Organizational freedom:** As discussed in chapter 8, novel ideas often demand a cross-functional team with loosely defined roles. In some organizations, it is hard to tap the collaboration of people who fall outside of your reporting structure. Seek out spaces in which you have the freedom to work on projects outside the scope of your formal role.

Culture

Your organization as a whole may maintain certain cultural norms, but different areas will naturally develop their own subcultures. The cultural characteristics that correlate with higher levels of internal innovation correspond closely to the characteristics of innovative talent. Seek out, or seek to create, a culture or subculture that:

- celebrates innovative thinking and new approaches.
- encourages people to take action without asking for permission or waiting for direction.
- brings in ideas and insights about customers, competition, and market dynamics.
- allows for and even encourages calculated risk-taking.

Leadership

Many of the experts and internal innovators I interviewed said that "change needs to start at the top." While you may not have the formal power to change leadership behaviors, you can find leaders who do the right things to encourage innovation. There are four drivers to look for. Three of these correspond directly with the three groups of drivers above.

- **Prioritize innovation:** Look for leaders who put innovation projects toward the top of the agenda. A leading provider of animal pharmaceuticals decided to launch a new business based on genetics, both in the United States and in Europe. The U.S. leader accepted the new product line as part of the portfolio but did not consistently include an update on the project as part of his regular leadership team meetings. By contrast, the European leader did. Every meeting included an update on the progress of the project, even though its revenues were small compared to their core business. The new business took off in Europe but failed in the United States, not because customer needs or market dynamics were different but simply because leadership did not show it to be a priority.[20]
- **Attract and develop innovative talent:** Look for leaders who seek out and develop talent who fit the character of successful innovators.

- **Create organizational structures that encourage innovation:**
  Look for leadership that proactively seeks to enable or facilitate
  innovation—with resources, rewards, allowance of risk-taking, and
  organizational freedom—and removes structures that hinder it.
- **Curate culture:** Look for leaders who actively seek to identify
  those patterns of actions that help innovation while discouraging those that hinder it. Again, those norms are innovative
  thinking, autonomy and proactivity, market awareness, and
  risk-taking.

Elliott Berman, whom we met in chapter 1, created an island of
freedom. He first carved out a role as a researcher who was shielded
from cultural norms and structures that might have squelched his
work. This role also allowed him to recruit talent that was innovative
and intrinsically motivated. He convinced Exxon to let him operate
as an independent, fully owned subsidiary and then found a part of
the company—drilling-platform operations—that valued his innovation enough to let him continue to operate on an island of freedom.
When his runway within Exxon ran out, he created new islands of
freedom beyond the company's walls, first by finding a new user in
the U.S. Coast Guard, and eventually by carving out the business as
an independent company.

Six Characters

How do you find an island of freedom? Or, failing that, create one?
Ellen Auster, a professor of strategic management at the Schulich
School of Business at York University, laid out a framework for me.
She describes this framework in *Stragility: Excelling at Strategic
Changes*, which she coauthored with Lisa Hillenbrand.[21] She walked
me through how to apply this process to the specific challenge of
driving internal innovation.

In any organization, you will find six types of stakeholders
(individuals or groups):

1. **Early adopters:** stakeholders (internal or external) who are likely
   to be responsive to the innovation you have in mind. You want
   to identify these stakeholders early and start shaping your innovation in a way that will attract and benefit them.

2. **Advocates:** people with political power who are likely to promote your idea. Professor Rita McGrath at Columbia Business School calls them Sherpas. "These Sherpa people tend to be people with deep corporate experience, they tend to have a lot of ties and a lot of social capital, and they tend to get a kick out of nurturing of the new innovations."[22] Advocates may be external stakeholders: partners, regulators, or customers. Seth Godin, the marketing guru, calls this group of customers "sneezers" because they spread the word by telling others about your product. You want to identify these people early because they will be critical in opening up the political pathway for you. You can identify them by looking at past innovations and seeing who their advocates were or by asking "Who would benefit if this innovation succeeds?"

3. **Indifferent fence-sitters:** stakeholders who are open to your innovation but are so busy that they lack the time to get their heads around it. Internally, these may be staffs of the departments that will eventually support your innovation, but they don't see it as a priority today. Externally, these may be partners you will need to operate parts of your innovation or your secondary customers. You can ignore these stakeholders for now because they will get on board after they see early adopters doing so.

4. **Cautious fence-sitters:** stakeholders for whom your innovation does not quite fit, but they are not sure why. They may resist your idea because their colleagues and friends are against it. They may be partners and customers for whom your innovation is helpful but does not meet an immediate, burning need. For whatever reason, they are unlikely to get on board but are not engaged enough to really understand why. These stakeholders will only turn against your idea when they see skeptics (the next two kinds of stakeholders) activating, so you can ignore them initially.

5. **Positive skeptics:** stakeholders who have justifiable reasons to be concerned about the potential impact your innovation may have on the organization or the market. Internally, they may sit in compliance or legal departments. Externally, they may be regulators. You want to engage these people early, not only to win their support but also to understand their concerns and incorporate them into your innovation to improve it.

6. **Negative skeptics:** stakeholders who are worried that your idea may diminish their power or hurt their department. Sometimes they are going to resist the idea simply because they have had negative experiences with such ideas before. Going back to your value blockers (in chapter 6) may tell you who these people are internally. Externally, they may be competitors or other players who are mostly likely to lose out if your innovation succeeds. You are unlikely to convince these stakeholders. The best you can do is try to remove your dependence on them by, for example, avoiding placing your innovation under their hierarchy of authority.

The trick is, in Professor Auster's words, to "work the tails." Identify early adopters, advocates, and positive skeptics early so that you can consult them to build their support or extract their concerns. Identify negative skeptics early so that you can steer clear of them and do whatever possible to avoid attracting their attention too early. If you can sequence your interactions strategically, you have a far greater chance of succeeding.

How the American Stock Exchange Worked the Tails and Transformed an Industry

Few innovations have changed the investment industry as drastically as exchange-traded funds (ETFs). Their creation was based on a simple premise: What if you could combine the diversification of a mutual fund with the ability to trade it like a stock? Previously, the only way for an everyday investor to get into the stock market without great risk or expense was to either become an expert and carefully diversify a portfolio of well-researched, individual stocks, or pay a mutual-fund manager to do it.

The problem, of course, is that those mutual-fund managers come with expensive fees and, though they attempt to outperform the market, they rarely do so. In fact, they rarely match it. Study after study has shown that the vast majority of actively managed funds underperform market indices over the long term. In the past fifteen years alone, "the S&P 500 outperformed more than 92 percent of large-cap funds." Mutual-fund investors were paying stock-pickers to underperform the market, and those fees were eating into their returns even more.[23]

This all changed with the introduction of Standard and Poor's Depositary Receipts on January 29, 1993, and the wave of successful exchange-traded funds that followed it.

In the past twenty-five years, these funds—most of which hold specific assets to replicate investment indices—have diversified from baskets of stocks to assets from every possible investment sector and class, including bonds, commodities, and currencies. In addition to giving investors the novel ability to actively trade funds as they would securities, ETFs also enable holders to easily diversify while paying significantly lower fees and taxes compared to actively managed mutual funds. In essence, they have "democratized" the mutual-fund industry—while revolutionizing investing itself.

In 2017, ETFs accounted for 30 percent of all U.S. trading value, prompting the *Financial Times* to proclaim that "exchange traded funds are eating the US stock market."[24]

How did that happen?

An Unlikely Employee Innovator

In the mid-1980s, the American Stock Exchange (AMEX) was in trouble. AMEX was having "severe difficulties drawing enough business to be profitable" while "struggling to survive in the shadow of the New York Stock Exchange." The smaller exchange needed a new product, though it didn't have many resources to develop one.[25]

Nathan Most, an AMEX senior vice president for product development, who worked on the derivatives side of the exchange, "took things into his own hands" to try and devise "a product that he thought could make the AMEX some money."[26]

> [The AMEX] had a basic volume of about 20 million shares a day and it just stayed there, no matter what they did. They were spending all kinds of money to get new listings, but were unsuccessful. From our [derivatives] side, we needed a lot of money for the things we wanted to do and we couldn't get it. They kept telling us we weren't making enough profit. So I thought, well, maybe I could help the equity side and bring in some money. Well, here I see mutual funds just booming, gaining market fast, without being able to be traded. So I thought, well, why not?[27]

Most had an unusual background for a financial-products inno-vator. Born in 1914, he was a physicist by training who had con-ducted research on acoustic waves at the University of California, Los Angeles. Most put this knowledge to work for the U.S. Navy's submarine warfare effort in World War II, "cruising in danger-ous proximity to Japanese submarines." After the war, he trav-eled throughout Asia selling acoustical material to theaters before working in the cooking-oil industry. Most became executive vice president of Pacific Vegetable Oil in 1965 and eventually moved on to work as a commodities trader with the Pacific Commodities Exchange in 1974. By the time he began devising a new product to save the AMEX—where he'd started working in 1977—he was seventy-three years old.[28]

While devising the new product, Most posed two major questions:

- Could mutual funds be traded like stocks?[29]
- What if an index fund could be structured like commodities? Securities could be purchased like physical "inventory," housed in the financial equivalent of a "warehouse," and the "receipts" for that inventory divided and traded as shares.[30]

Most was operating in a more complex environment than a typical internal innovator. The financial-services industry is a complex web of stakeholders, including regulators, clearing firms, brokers, advisers, and fund managers.

Learning from Positive Detractors

To refine his idea, Most captured learning from positive detractors early on.

First, he looked at past attempts to launch ETFs to understand why they had failed. Arguably the first modern attempt at an ETF occurred in 1989. That year, Index Participation Shares (IPS), designed to closely mirror the S&P 500 index, began trading on the American Stock Exchange and the Philadelphia Stock Exchange. The product was popular, but its run was short-lived. A lawsuit by the Chicago Mercantile Exchange and the Commodity Futures Trading Commission (CFTC) challenged the sale of IPS because the fund

had "characteristics similar to futures contracts." The lawsuit successfully argued in federal court that IPS must be traded on a futures exchange regulated by the CFTC.[31] From this, Most learned that his new product would need to be seen as a different kind of asset, not as futures.

A second effort to create an equity-based index fund was introduced in Canada on March 9, 1990, when the Toronto Stock Exchange debuted the Toronto 35 Index Participation Fund (TIP). An exchange-traded fund that tracked the index, it is considered by many to be the world's first equity-like index fund. TIPs and a subsequent fund that tracked the TSE-100 were also popular with investors, but these original versions folded in 2000 "because their low expense ratios made them too costly for the exchange."[32] This meant that Most's new product would have to quickly reach sufficient volume to ensure enough revenue to support the product.

Most then felt out other positive detractors. When he broached his idea with mutual-fund experts and AMEX executives, he met resistance. He consulted with Vanguard Group founder and mutual-fund innovator Jack Bogle, who told him that mutual funds could not be traded frequently without "substantially increasing operating costs." The legal department at AMEX shot down the idea with a different set of reservations: they thought that the SEC would "never approve such securities."[33]

Eliminating these problems took three things: an innovative solution from Most, a crucial suggestion by the AMEX lawyers, and lucky timing.

To address the costs of trading, Most turned back to his commodities experience. Portfolios of stocks that mirrored an index would be deposited with a trustee, who would provide a receipt similar to a warehouse receipt used to track physical commodities. This receipt, which proved the existence of the inventory (stocks), would then be divided into units that traded like securities.

The next big contribution came from AMEX's legal department, which suggested using a unit investment trust (UIT) as the "warehouse" for the stocks. This structure addressed both problems. Because a UIT "required neither a board of directors nor corporate management," it would both incur fewer costs and face fewer regulatory hurdles.

Finding Advocates

Then, the third key appeared by pure luck: the stock-market crash of 1987. Most believes that because "the drop was so precipitous that there were no futures buyers to sell to," the SEC became more open to the idea of new instruments that could hedge huge market swings. A mutual fund that could be traded exactly like a stock fit the bill.[34] The SEC had become an advocate.

Once the basic structure was in place, Most partnered with a key internal advocate, Steven Bloom, AMEX vice president of product development, to run with the idea. With the pieces in place to create an "island of freedom"—a structure that turned the SEC into an advocate, a model that addressed the legal department's concern, and a "Sherpa" (Bloom) to provide coverage—Most assembled a team within AMEX and its eventual partner, State Street Bank, which served "as the trustee of this 'securities warehouse.'" Ivers Riley, the senior vice president of derivatives at AMEX, was also a major early contributor to the effort.

The AMEX and State Street team, soon joined by personnel from the specialist firm Spear, Leeds & Kellogg (SLK) and the law firm of Orrick, Herrington & Sutcliffe, created the architecture for the fund, pioneering the now commonplace tasks associated with stocking an ETF's "warehouse" of commodities. At the same time, they engaged in years of onerous but ultimately successful legal and bureaucratic negotiations with the SEC.[35]

The result was Standard and Poor's Depositary Receipts (SPDR, ticker symbol SPY), commonly known as "the Spider." Since its launch on January 29, 1993, it has become the most successful ETF in history while serving as the model for a transformational class of financial products.

Finding Early Adopters

Sensing the scale of the opportunity, AMEX's marketing and sales group became early adopters. The product launch was accompanied by a huge marketing effort, and the Spider traded more than

a million shares on its first day. The ETF's volume slowed to a crawl by the middle of 1993, however, trading as few as 17,000 shares in a single day. Most partnered with another early adopter, Jay Baker, vice president of options marketing at AMEX, to make a concerted sales push to right the ship, cold-calling institutional investors and trying to convince them to buy the fund.[36]

Avoiding Negative Detractors

It was obvious to Most and his team that mutual funds, which fed off large management fees, would have the most to lose from the success of ETFs. They wanted the ETF to fail. Baker remembers, "We criss-crossed the United States. At one point, I called the head of west coast distribution for a mutual-fund firm. He said, 'I like it, I own it and my firm is never, ever going to sell it. And to be honest, I hope you fail.'"

Baker says this was the moment he knew the fund was succeeding, because the traditional mutual-fund industry feared the democratization of its products.[37] They just needed to avoid the power of these negative detractors.

The speed of Bloom's and Baker's persistent marketing efforts helped rob mutual funds of an assertive response. A timely infusion of securities from Daiwa Securities Group in Japan also helped. "By the end of the summer [1993], SPY rarely saw a sub-100,000 trade day."[38]

Fence-Sitters Get on Board

Once indifferent fence-sitters hear the pull of adopters drown out the objections of detractors, they are likely to get on board. And like dominoes, cautious fence-sitters should follow suit. The ETF market continued to grow in the 1990s, and it experienced a huge expansion with the dot.com boom and the issuance of the Nasdaq-100 Index Tracking Stock (original ticker QQQ, still known as "Cubes") in 1999. The popularity of this technology fund boosted awareness of ETFs and "more than doubled" assets under management to $70 billion by the end of 2000. The growth rate continued: there were 102 ETFs by 2002, then almost a thousand by 2009, then more than 1,400 by 2011. By 2015, there were 1,800 ETFs "covering almost every conceivable market sector, niche and trading strategy."[39]

As of 2018, the Spider remains "the largest U.S. exchange-traded product with $292 billion in assets," though it competes with at least 105 different issuers of ETFs in a U.S. exchange-traded fund industry that now has $3.4 trillion in assets.[40]

"Not one of us expected it to grow to the magnitude that it has," said Joe Stefanelli, who headed AMEX's marketing and sales efforts for derivatives products while on the original team that developed the Spider.[41]

In 2001, Nathan Most wrote a matter-of-fact assessment of the product he had envisioned: "It is clear to me that the ETF design is only beginning its trading and investment penetration. Its design has made it a multipurpose instrument for many of an investor's needs."[42]

Most died at the age of ninety in 2004, leaving an immense legacy. He had invented a revolutionary financial product at an age when most people were long retired, and he was described by a friend as "active and lively, and bubbling with passion and great ideas up to his last days."[43]

Most's analysis of ETFs in 2001 was perfectly accurate but possibly understated, given the dominance achieved by the product in the seventeen years since his death. While numerous individuals were essential to the creation of Spider and the industry it spawned, this massive disruption stemmed from one big idea from an unlikely source—a former physicist and commodity trader's novel idea about structuring stock funds like warehouse inventory.

A Process to Create Your Island of Freedom

In our workshops and consulting, we have found that the following four steps can reveal key insights for creating your island of freedom. This exercise should not take more than an hour to complete.

1. **Brainstorm your key stakeholders.** Identify important internal and external stakeholders (these can be individuals or groups) across all six types: early adopters, advocates, indifferent fence-sitters, cautious fence-sitters, positive skeptics, and negative skeptics. Typically, you will identify seven to fifteen.

2. **Distinguish high power from low.** Group your stakeholders of each type into high-power (meaning that their actions can significantly help or hinder your success) or low-power (meaning their actions matter little).

3. **Strategize.** Explore how you can move low-power early adopters and advocates into higher-power ones by, for example, placing your innovation within their hierarchy of control. Explore how to shift high-power detractors (positive and negative) into lower-power positions by, for example, avoiding their hierarchy of control.

4. **Define your contact strategy.** Decide who you will contact first. For example, identify specific positive detractors and meet them to gather their concerns; create a short list of high-power advocates to win their support.

A Final Word

If the effort to build your island of freedom seems complex, think of it this way: Entrepreneurs spend as much as **50** percent of their time fundraising; your fundraising effort simply takes a political form. As Gary Hamel put it, "It's not unusual for a would-be entrepreneur to get turned down half a dozen times before finding a willing investor—yet in most companies, it takes only one 'nyet' to kill a project stone dead."[44]

Swoon Reads succeeded because the team was able to create its own "island of freedom" from within. Their "shadow organization" became formalized with Lauren's hiring as Swoon Reads director. Yet they have maintained flexibility, allowing employees from across the company to play part-time roles in the project while maintaining their day jobs. The success of Swoon Reads titles, the positive press, the ability of Swoon Reads to help other imprints in the company identify upcoming authors early, and the connections Swoon Reads is able to make with a new generation of readers have made the project a valued addition to the Macmillan enterprise, thereby providing the freedom it needs to continue growing.

CHAPTER TEN

For Leaders

How to Unleash Internal Innovation

The metaphor I often use—it's not the perfect one—is being a gardener.
I want to make sure that the irrigation and fences are working, that the
compost is alive, and that the plants are in roughly the right place,
but I don't tell the plants how to grow. I watch how the garden's
evolving. I may move things around, and I may prune here
and there. But it's not under my control.

—JOI ITO, DIRECTOR, MIT MEDIA LAB

THROUGHOUT THIS BOOK we've looked at innovation through
the eyes of the internal innovator. Whenever I present my findings to audiences, however, inevitably the question arises: "What
should I, as a leader, do to activate innovation from within?"
Whether you are at the very top of your organization, heading
a business unit, or leading a team, your success will increasingly
depend on your ability to strategically activate innovative behavior
among your people.

The Payoff

The payoff of activating internal innovation is huge. Research into
"entrepreneurial orientation" (EO) and "intrapreneurial intensity" (II)
shows that higher levels of internal entrepreneurialism drive faster
growth,[1] increase economic value added (EVA), and produce higher

returns (total return to shareholders, or TRS). You can measure your II by assessing two dimensions:

- **Frequency:** How frequently do your people pursue innovative opportunities (high, medium, or low)?
- **Degree:** To what degree do those pursuits show innovative thinking, involve risk-taking, and require proactivity (high, medium, or low)?

Doing this will show which of nine organizational profiles your organization currently fits. Figure 10.1 illustrates these profiles using brands of well-known companies. Note that we did not actually measure these corporate brands; we present them purely for illustrative purposes.

You may find yourself in the bottom left, a "business-model operator" like Walmart, which has achieved enormous success by operating its

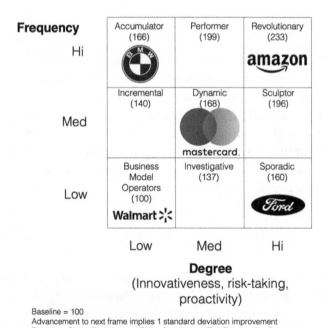

Figure 10.1 Organizational profiles.

core business model more effectively than its peers. Though today Walmart has launched innovations in an effort to occupy higher-order quadrants, its market-beating growth and profitability over the past decade have come primarily from effective business-model operation.

In the high-frequency, low-degree (top left quadrant) section you will find "accumulators" like BMW, which generates and accumulates new innovations into each new model of its cars. Keeping up with accumulators is tough because of the speed with which they innovate, but they rarely introduce new business models or enter new categories.

At the bottom right you will find "sporadic" innovators, illustrated by Ford. Every decade or two, they reinvent themselves and then run the new business model. Today, Ford is reinventing itself as a mobility company, to compete with Google, Tesla, and Uber. In the 1990s, at the height of the dot-com boom, it sought to reinvent itself as a technology company.

In the middle, you will find what academics call "dynamic" innovators, represented here by Mastercard. This is really a catchall for companies whose level of innovation spans various frequencies and degrees.

We often admire "revolutionary" innovators, like Amazon, that frequently introduce high-degree innovations—new categories, fee structures, lines of business. But we don't need to all perform at this level. Our research shows that you need only be a quadrant ahead of your peers. If you are working in technology, that may mean being "revolutionary." But if you are in retail or manufacturing, the bar is lower.

After identifying which quadrant you occupy now, you can decide which quadrant you want to be in. To get there, do you want to increase frequency (motiving employees to innovate more often), increase the degree of efforts (more innovative, more risk-taking, more proactive), or both?

The numbers in parentheses in figure 10.1 show what the effect might be on your stock price (more precisely, your TRS) if you were able to engineer a move to a higher-order quadrant. These figures are based on research that correlates the level of II with TRS. For example, if you are a business-model operator with a stock price of 100, simply increasing the frequency of innovative activity, without asking for more radical ideas, could deliver a stock price of 140.

This exercise gives you a sense of the potential payoff of unleashing greater employee-driven innovation. But the payoff is even bigger, because as people see others innovating, they are inspired to do so as well, and innovation is transmitted. Furthermore, research by McKinsey shows that investors place far more value on new revenue generated through internal innovation than on revenue you capture through acquisitions. To double your share price, for example, you would need to increase revenues by as much as 217 percent through acquisitions but only by 22–26 percent if you do so through internal innovation.[2]

So how do you increase II? First let's look at what *not* to do.

Clearing Away Theatrical Noise

Many organizations win press mentions for being innovative but fail to turn their innovations into value. I proposed in chapter 1 that for something to qualify as an innovation it should be (1) different, (2) adopted, and (3) valuable. By that definition, a company that does innovative things but fails to produce value from them is not effectively innovating. Unfortunately, the lists of "most innovative" companies are clogged with such firms. Following their example may deliver admiration but not results.

Rita McGrath and Steve Blank refer to what such companies do as "innovation theater." In Blank's words, "All too often, a corporate innovation initiative starts and ends with a board meeting mandate to the CEO followed by a series of memos to the staff, with lots of posters and one-day workshops. This typically creates 'innovation theater' but very little innovation."[3]

To help clear away the theatrical noise, we assembled a macro list of 367 companies that have appeared on two of the best-known "most innovative company" lists, from *Forbes* and *Fast Company*. We found they did not, in aggregate, perform better than companies that did not make the list. Making a "most innovative" list does not make you a better performer.

So we dug deeper, stripping away the companies that were deemed "innovative" but did not outperform their peers (see appendix D for detail on this analysis). Only thirteen companies qualify as effective innovators. (Note that while Asian firms are making impressive inroads

into most innovative lists, as evidenced by the inclusion below of Naver Corporation and Tencent, the lists remain quite U.S.-centric.)

- Amazon
- Apple
- Coloplast
- Regeneron Pharmaceuticals
- Illumina
- Incyte Corporation
- Mastercard
- Naver Corporation
- Netflix
- Starbucks
- Tencent
- Vertex Pharmaceuticals
- Visa

Looking at the innovation strategies of "innovative" companies that do not outperform their peers suggests four warnings:

Avoid the distraction of innovation theater. Innovative companies that do not outperform their peers heavily tout highly visible efforts to increase innovation. Their Silicon Valley–style incubation centers, internal business-plan competitions, and colorful open-office layouts offer physical evidence of their innovativeness; all of this attracts public attention, but proves insufficient to actually drive superior performance. Instead, as we will see shortly, real success derives from more significant, behind-the-scenes programs.

Don't limit yourself to products. Companies that make innovative lists but fail to outperform competitors seem to focus efforts on product-driven innovation, like research and development (R&D) and mergers and acquisitions (M&A). They tout figures such as patents filed and number of research labs. Such activity may be important, but on its own it is insufficient. Beyond a certain margin, you need to build a distinct capacity to continually innovate through institutional changes.

Don't overlook your scale. Innovative companies that fail to outperform often follow the leads of startups, launching copycat

innovations. But since startups, by necessity, build innovations in which scale is not important, a large organization following suit downplays its advantage of size. For example, in the small town of Gullingren, Sweden, two behemoths—construction conglomerate Skansa AB and furniture retailer IKEA—partnered to build ready-made rooms inside a robot-heavy factory. These rooms are later assembled like Lego houses at construction sites across northern Europe. Their joint venture, called BoKlok, reduces the cost of erecting fully furnished four-story residential buildings by 35 percent. As of 2018, they are producing 1,200 affordable houses per year. Just a few hours away, a small Swedish construction company tried the same model, but because they lacked the scale, they failed and shut down the factory. Don't copy startups—innovate in areas in which your scale creates an advantage.

Don't isolate. Innovative companies that fail to outperform talk often of isolating innovations in incubation labs and innovation centers. While such efforts are often necessary initially to reduce organizational friction (as mentioned in chapter 9), they come at a cost. Outperformers quickly integrate innovations into other products and services, which allows them to pool profits in ways smaller companies cannot. Apple's ecosystem of hardware, software, and services, for example, allows the company to undercut competitors in some areas and make up for the losses in others. Had Amazon managed its Echo smart speaker or Kindle reader as independent businesses, it would have lost the opportunity to give such hardware away at a cost that smaller competitors could not match, capturing value instead through content. Tencent was similarly able to beat the competition by combining the features of AOL, Facebook, Skype, Yahoo, Gmail, Norton, and Twitter into one app, which was only possible because of their practice of launching "micro-innovations" that they quickly test and incorporate into their core products.

Cultivating the Garden

It doesn't make sense to hire smart people and tell them what to do.
We hire smart people and they tell us what to do.
—STEVE JOBS

Breaking down the innovation programs of innovative, outperforming companies reveals clearly that they approach innovation expansively. Their more holistic approach seeks to elevate innovativeness broadly across the entire organization, creating a form of contained chaos. To borrow a Voltairesque metaphor from Joi Ito, the director of MIT Media Labs, they seek to cultivate a garden of innovation rather than simply grow more crops.

U.S. corporations invest more than $350 billion a year in innovation through R&D efforts, so it's easy to assume that such formal efforts propel innovation more than any other factor. But a 2018 study of 677 strategy leaders by CB Insights found that employees are actually a more important driver of innovation,[4] as shown in the study's "Top 10 Sources of Innovation":

1. Customers
2. Employees
3. Competitive intelligence
4. Supplier/vendors
5. Academic partners and/or scientific literature
6. Industry analysts
7. Accelerators & incubators
8. Corporate venture capital
9. External ideation consultants
10. Bankers & VCs

To outinnovate your competition, you must start cultivating innovation among your employees. Innovative outperforming firms do so by making distinctive choices across the four bundles of drivers outlined in chapter 9: leadership, structure, talent, and culture. Here are some interesting ideas culled from innovative outperformers that may inspire you. Note that I'm repeating a few points from chapters 3 and 9 in case you have not read them.

Leadership

When I started researching this book, I sought to prove that employees need not wait for leadership to give them permission to innovate, that they could trigger a transformation from the bottom up. But I've come to believe that for innovation to become systemic, you, as the

leader, need to take the initiative. This can be done by prioritizing innovation, cultivating the right talent, establishing supportive structures, and shaping culture. Here are some ideas for creating leadership that prioritizes innovation (we will cover ideas for talent, structures, and culture later in this chapter).

Facebook leadership prioritizes innovation by getting their hands dirty. Its executives, including Mark Zuckerberg, spend time working hands-on on new products and ideas. They emphasize "learning by making," understanding it's often hard to judge innovation ideas if they have not been involved in the process of developing them. They don't ask employees to present ideas through PowerPoint, but rather expect employees to prototype their ideas proactively.[5]

McGrath suggests a simple and effective way to ensuring you are prioritizing innovation: look at your meeting agenda. Check that somewhere toward the top you have carved out space to discuss innovation efforts, so they aren't squeezed off the table in your rush to end the meeting on time.

Netflix takes it a step further. Recognizing that innovation accelerates when leadership and employees engage in problem-solving rather than the progress-review ritual that dominates most meetings, they have rethought how board members interact with the company. They seek to create radical transparency between employees, leadership, and the board. Traditionally, boards engage in ritualistic quarterly reviews of well-rehearsed reports by the company's top team and handpicked employees. By contrast, Netflix invites board members to attend monthly staff meetings with the company's top seven leaders, quarterly executive staff meetings with the top ninety execs, and quarterly business reviews with the top five hundred employees. Board members are asked to observe but not influence or participate in discussions.

Netflix has also done away with PowerPoint presentations. Instead, board communications are shared online in thirty-page living documents. Executives and board members can ask for clarification, with supporting data and analysis included as links. As a result, board members are fully prepared before board meetings. They can jump right into problem-solving, and employees know they are heard.

It's not enough to prioritize innovation generally. You want your people to understand what types of innovation to pursue. In chapter 2, I mentioned that fewer than 55 percent of middle managers can name even two of their company's top strategic priorities.[6] Complex strategic plans propagate poorly, leaving employees confused. Instead, most of

the leaders of innovative outperformers present a compelling, succinct vision for innovation, showing how the future will be different and what role the organization will play in that future. At Mastercard, leadership drives for a "world beyond cash"; at Cisco it's an "intelligent web" (made possible when the internet of things, big data, and artificial intelligence collide); Naver (the South Korean online search company with nearly 75 percent of South Korean searches) seeks an "interconnected world where imagination becomes reality." Such pithy statements are concise enough to remember and repeat, yet unpack numerous implications of where employees should be looking for new ideas.

Finally, the rubber hits the road ultimately through the interactions you and your lieutenants have with staff, whether in hallways or in meetings. Do you inspire or thwart innovative behavior? Researchers have found that entrepreneurial leaders and traditional administrative managers differ in multiple ways. These differences are often rooted deeply and can take time for you to change. Some of the key differences are listed in table 10.1.

TABLE 10.1
Differences Between Administrative and Entrepreneurial Leaders

Administrative Leaders	Conceptual Dimension	Entrepreneurial Leaders
Driven by controlled resources	Your strategic orientation	Driven by perception of opportunity
A single stage, with complete commitment out of decision	How you commit resources	In stages, with minimal exposure at each stage
Hierarchy	Your management structure	Flat, with multiple informal networks
Based on responsibility and seniority	The basis on which you assign rewards	Based on value creation
Safe, slow, steady	The type of growth you seek	Rapid growth, with willingness to accept risk
Risk should be minimized	Risk orientation	Risk should be comparable to payoff potential
Coordinating	Your primary skill	Designing new organizational structures and processes

Source: Adapted from Odd Jarl Borch, Alain Fayolle, and Elisabet Ljunggren, *Entrepreneurship Research in Europe: Evolving Concepts and Processes* (Cheltenham, UK: Edward Elgar, 2011), 231.

Coaching your direct reports to shift their approach from administrative to entrepreneurial leadership is key to beginning a transformation toward an organization that unlocks internal innovation.

Cultivate Innovative Talent

Many employees, having felt the sword of bureaucracy too often, have stopped trying to innovate. They have abandoned their intent (see chapter 2). This contributes to the myth that innovation demands an entrepreneurial character. In fact, research shows that successful internal innovators exhibit behaviors that differ in remarkable ways from entrepreneurs. You don't need entrepreneurs. You need to cultivate internal innovators characterized by six vital attributes (see chapter 2 for more detail): using innovative thinking, being attuned to the customer and market, being proactive, taking calculated risks (not risk-seeking), having strong political acumen, and being intrinsically motivated to innovate (not driven by financial gain). Innovative outperforming companies do this in interesting ways.

To ensure that Amazon's new hires possess the attributes of innovative thinkers, Jeff Bezos say he likes to ask applicants he interviews to share an example of something they have invented. These may not be product inventions, but they are "lots of different kinds of inventions and I find that they are all super valuable." He is looking for people who "tend to be dissatisfied by a lot of the current ways. As they go about their daily experiences, they notice that little things are broken in the world and they want to fix them. Inventors have a divine discontent."[7] He looks for people who have a unique combination: not only enough expertise to invent in their domain, but also a willingness to attack opportunities with a "beginner's mind," as he calls it—a mind willing to attack challenges with novel approaches.

Several innovative outperformers create events to activate innovative behavior, giving employees pockets of freedom to innovate. This has the dual benefit of releasing employees from the burden of institutional bureaucracy, at least temporarily, and creating opportunities for them to exercise their innovative muscles. For example, Vertex Pharmaceuticals launched VOICE, "an internal, global innovation tournament that empowers all employees to develop ideas in response to 'game-changing' science and business challenges. Employees who

have their ideas selected go on to build cross-functional teams, develop refined proposals and execute their business plans." This effort has led to major research initiatives into new diseases, a 3-D printing lab, a mobile app to help Vertexians find one another, and a commuter bus program to reduce traffic congestion in Boston's Seaport District.[8] PPG, an innovative coatings company whose products cover everything from your mobile phone to your desk, launches innovation challenges in which teams from research centers across the globe compete to find solutions to common problems. They hold idea-sharing parties where researchers and salespeople interact to explore new uses for technologies. They manage their innovation funnel like a "bow tie"[9]—in from the left, a flow of many ideas narrowing down to a few that have enough potential to warrant launching, and out to the right, an expanding revenue flow that will come from new products as they scale.

To systemically encourage more autonomous action, Naver changed the name of its human-resources department to Better Workplace Support (BWS). It gave the role of recruiting employees to business units and redefined the role of BWS as providing information and convenience so business units and departments can recruit the personnel they need.

Another common tool to encourage intrinsic motivation adopted by many innovative outperformers is to abandon rigid performance reviews tied to specific key performance indicators (KPIs). This steers employees away from hitting narrow targets. For example, Netflix replaced performance reviews with more frequent and organic conversations between managers and employees about performance. Naver did away with role-based KPIs and targets entirely. Microsoft, General Electric, and Eli Lilly have done the same.

To foster market awareness, Starbucks hosts an internal platform called Workplace to enable employees to share insights. When a store manager posted he was selling twenty units a day of a product not on Starbuck's official menu, other managers took note, and within hours, many more shared that they too were selling twenty or thirty or forty a day. The product had been featured on Instagram. That evening, Starbucks's category marketing team caught on and, by the next morning, informed managers they had added the beverage to their official menu. What might have taken weeks took only twenty-four hours.[10]

Establish Supportive Structures

Leadership and talent cannot systematize innovation alone. To do so requires supportive organizational structures.

As described in chapter 2, to innovate, employees must have the freedom to take four steps:

1. Discover new opportunities
2. Evaluate and choose which opportunities to exploit
3. Take autonomous action to move on those opportunities
4. Mobilize resources to realize the opportunities

Unfortunately, your organizational structures create drag that restricts employees from taking these steps. As one interviewee put it, "We don't launch innovations . . . they escape." A study by Bain & Company found that the average company loses more than 25 percent of its productive power to such organizational drag.[11] And the problem may be getting more acute. Research by Gary Hamel shows that two-thirds of employees say bureaucracy has gotten worse in recent years.[12] Our macro-study of research on the topic shows a statistically significant link between your level of internal innovation and four organizational structural drivers:

- Innovation resources (money and employee time) to pursue innovations
- Rewards that encourage entrepreneurial behavior
- Allowance of risk-taking
- Organizational freedom

Innovation Resources

Most innovative companies, whether average performers or outperformers, implement the common practices of giving employees free time to work on special growth projects or organizing competitions in which the winners receive time and investment to pursue their ideas. Adobe received considerable press for its Kickbox program—literally

a box containing money (a $1,000 gift card employees can use to validate their idea), innovation tools and templates, caffeine (a Starbucks gift card), and sugar (a candy bar).[13] Michael Schrage's model of conducting a "5×5×5" experiment (giving 5 people $5,000 and 5 weeks) is popular among many of our clients. But such approaches, now broadly adopted, have become table stakes. Outperformers go beyond.

For example, Tencent not only tracks the ROI of its projects but also looks at values such as "perception as innovator" and respect from peers. Naver realized its reward system was discouraging innovative collaboration, so instead of linking employees' compensation to individual performance, it linked it to performance of their team. To afford designers the resources they need to think long-term, Apple's design teams, led by chief design officer Jony Ive, do not report to finance or manufacturing. They set their own budgets and are given the ability to ignore manufacturing practicalities. They circumvent budget hierarchy, reporting directly to the executive team.[14]

Rewards

Rewarding employees for innovation can take many forms. The most common is innovation competitions with linked financial awards. At Tencent, for example, employees proposing new ideas can win cash prizes—from five hundred yuan for redesigning an interface to one million yuan for more significant innovations.[15] But rewards need not be monetary. Activision Blizzard, for example, celebrates successes and accomplishments of employees and innovators in more creative ways. Their offices are filled with symbolic trophies like swords, ceremonial steins, rings, shields, and battle masks to mark an employee's efforts.

A dynamic we see in multiple innovative outperformers is spurring internal competition. The thrill of victory can motivate more powerfully than the promise of financial gain. Tencent's culture has been likened to a "shark womb," in reference to how some unborn sharks cannibalize their siblings to secure their own survival.[16] Amazon culls staff every year, creating an environment one former Amazon human-resources director described as "purposely Darwinian."[17]

Former Amazon employees I've interviewed complain about this practice, but it seems to drive innovation and profit growth.

Heier, the Chinese consumer-electronics and appliance manufacturer that has surged in recent years to reach $30 billion in revenue and $20 billion in profit, with eighty thousand employees, considers its employees to be "micro-entrepreneurs" who run three thousand "micro-businesses." Employees must pit their projects against other teams with similar ones. They must compete to secure projects, and then compete further to ensure that their projects succeed. This pushes them to be creative and innovative, and to use their resources wisely. As CEO Zhang Ruimin explained, "After the arrival of the Internet age, we realized that under this triangular hierarchical structure, people had a difficult time adapting to the requirements of the times. So we reorganized ourselves as an entrepreneurial platform."[18]

Risk

Nearly all of the internal innovators I interviewed cited a leader's willingness to accept risk-taking and failure as key to unlocking employee innovations. Plenty of research shows that an owner's tolerance for failure and risk-taking correlates with a firm's innovativeness.[19] Bezos says, "If failure is like a death knell for promotion, you won't have a lot of people being experimental. . . . It's not an experiment if you know in advance it's going to work. If you want to be inventive, you have to experiment a lot, which means you will fail a lot."[20]

We have yet to find compelling structural ideas among innovative outperformers for allowing risk-taking. Systematic solutions to this problem still evade us. But anecdotes abound of employees who took a risk, failed, and were patted on the back for their effort. Facebook is well known for celebrating the failures of employees, as is Google owner Alphabet. Astro Teller, who directs Google X, thinks of it as encouraging employees to search for big opportunities or "mountains," saying, "If you shame them when they come back, if you tell them that they've failed you because they didn't find a mountain, no matter how diligently they looked for it or how cleverly they looked for it, those scouts will quit your company."[21]

Internal innovators shared with me that in most companies, unfortunately, the cost of failure is acute. If you diagnose what happens to an employee's career when she or he fails, you should be able to identify the organizational norms suppressing risk-taking.

Organizational Freedom

To ensure greater organizational freedom—to create "freedom of movement," as one internal innovator I interviewed termed it—many innovative outperformers seek to break large hierarchical units into smaller teams. For example, Tencent forms small, fast-moving teams that launch "micro-innovations" that are tested and iterated on.

Another interesting practice that Amazon implements to encourage organizational freedom is to be technology agnostic. While many large companies, such as Apple and Google, create internal software tools and platforms employees are expected to use, Amazon follows the opposite approach, allowing employees to use the technology they think suits the project best. The company also eschews companywide policies and procedures, allowing for greater freedom in how employees operate.[22]

Many innovative outperformers rethink physical spaces as structures to encourage greater organizational freedom. Much of Facebook's space is reconfigurable, with moving walls and furniture, so people can create open innovation labs and private spaces at will. Fast Retailing, the owner of the fast-growing Japanese apparel retailer Uniqlo, created Uniqlo City Tokyo, which houses around 1,100 employees from across the company's business units. The office is designed to stimulate creativity and collaboration. Similarly, Naver built what it calls the Green Factory, featuring pods instead of office spaces surrounding a central open meeting area.

Shape the Right Culture

You have to catch people making mistakes and make it so that it's cool.
You have to make it undesirable to play it safe.
—PETER SIMS, AUTHOR OF *LITTLE BETS*

Even with leadership, talent, and structure in place, innovation is likely to peter out if not supported by the right culture. As described in chapter 9, corporate cultures that correlate with high levels of internal innovation encourage four values (note that these track closely with the attributes of successful innovation talent):

- Innovative thinking
- Autonomy and proactivity
- Market awareness
- Risk-taking

Innovative outperformers promote cultural norms that fit these four values remarkably closely. For example, Alibaba calls its company values the "Six Vein Spirit Sword," which CEO Jack Ma borrowed from a martial arts novel, *Demi-Gods and Semi-Devils* by Jin Yong. Each "vein" represents a company value—customer first, teamwork, embrace change, integrity, passion, and commitment. You will notice that these values touch on three of the four cultural attributes listed above. The company rates employee performance in part based on the extent to which employees fulfill these values.

Tencent's values—integrity, proactivity, collaboration, innovation—match two of the four. Illumina (the genomic company credited with helping bring down the cost of sequencing a human genome to $4,000 from $1 million ten years ago) adopts values—"innovative, collaborative, fast, open, dynamic-driven, and fun"[23]—that match two of the four. Similarly, Jeff Bezos has attributed Amazon's success to three ideas they have stuck with: "Put the customer first. Invent. And be patient." These match closely at least three of the four values listed above.

Contrast Mastercard's cultural values with those of American Express, and you will see that Mastercard's values (such as "agility" and "initiative") explicitly address all four while American Express's values (such as "a will to win" and "personal accountability") address only one ("customer commitment" links to market awareness). Mastercard's innovation strategy is multipronged and touches on all four sets of drivers (including leadership, talent, and structure), but culture has played a major role. Its success is evident in the numbers. Over the past five years, Mastercard has outpaced American Express across multiple performance dimensions: growth rate, profit

margins, return on invested capital (ROIC), and total return to shareholder (TRS).

Encouraging the right cultural norms takes many forms. To cultivate an innovative culture, for example, Activision Blizzard has, among other things, designated three employees with the title Loremaster. Their job is to "empower the other dungeon masters across the company so they can execute on their awesomeness."

Autonomy and proactivity are norms encouraged by nearly all innovative outperformers. Steve Jobs once described innovation as "people meeting up in the hallways or calling each other at 10:30 at night with a new idea, or because they realized something that shoots holes in how we've been thinking about a problem."[24] Alibaba has sought to drive such intense employee engagement in creative ways. In the early days at Alibaba, founder Jack Ma dictated that employees could not live more than fifteen minutes from the office so they could work late and come in at odd hours. The company has abandoned that practice, but it still has practices in place today to encourage intense work effort. For example, Alibaba does not discourage intracompany relationships, which become more common the more time employees spend at work. In fact, the company encourages it. Every year the company performs a "group wedding" for company employees, many of whom meet at work, with Jack Ma attending.

To encourage market awareness, Coloplast encourages employees to find a patient to visit once a year for a conversation in the patient's home over a cup of coffee. Market—or more precisely, patient—intimacy is particularly critical for Coloplast's success because its products assist patients with personal and private problems. Building trust between patients and employees is paramount.

Li & Fung, one of world's largest supply-chain managers for retailers around the globe, encourages market awareness through Fung Academy, through which they expose hundreds of senior managers to leading thinkers like Ray Kurtzweil and Peter Diamandis, the founders of Singularity University, and Tom Chi, a cofounder of Google X. They hired Deborah Weinswig, a global retail analyst, to lead a group of twenty-seven PhDs who examine the disruptive technologies that are altering the new retail ecosystem, such as the Internet of Things, digital payments, and omnichannel retail. This helps them keep employees ahead of the curve.[25]

Where We Are Headed

Opportunities of time vouchsafed by Heaven are not equal to
advantages of situation afforded by the Earth, and advantages
of situation afforded by the Earth are not equal to the
union arising from the accord of Men.
—MENCIUS

Ultimately, what we are experiencing today is the next step on a path
we have been walking for thousands of years. For the first five hundred
thousand years of human existence, we organized ourselves in small
tribes. We traveled in mobile units to hunt and gather food.

Around 7000 BC, we suddenly started planting seeds and cultivating gardens. We evolved from small bands of hunters into towns
and villages of farmers and created governments that maintained unity
through *hierarchies.*

We eventually discovered the power of specialization. People could
master more specific skills—a shoemaker, a stoneworker, an administrator—
and begin to think of themselves as belonging to *organizations*
which, like any organism, are composed of organs that each play their
own role.

Then, in the late 1700s, we discovered how to build machines and
harness energy and started coordinating work in *production lines.* Our
shoemakers could specialize even further, with one making the sole,
the next stitching on the outer shell, and another placing it on the shop
floor to sell. Today our concept of business is still dominated by the
production-line metaphor. We think of industries as chains (suppliers
hand goods to manufactures, who distribute them through channels).

But as the pace of change accelerates, and the costs of transacting
and coordinating decline, traditional forms of organizing are meeting
a breaking point. The centralized system is giving way to a new form
of organization. We see its outlines appearing, in different flavors and
under different names, all around us.

Team of Teams

In the military, General Stanley McChrystal found that reorganizing
the tight, hierarchical structure of the Joint Special Operations Task

Force into a "team of teams" made his forces more effective at fighting agile, asymmetrical enemies. Despite the U.S. military's advantages of size, equipment, and training, they were ineffective against Al Qaeda in Iraq. Al-Qaeda in Iraq was unlike anything traditional military principles had prepared him for. Composed of decentralized units, they would appear to attack and then melt into the population. Without a formal reporting hierarchy, they offered no clear power center to target.

McChrystal experimented with a new organizational philosophy he called a "team of teams." He broke his organization down into small independent teams, then overlaid an "umbrella" team, a team of teams, to help units coordinate with each other. His military force started winning.

Open Organization

Red Hat, the leading open-source software company, realized that its long history of organizing communities of independent developers to collaboratively develop software could also apply to how it organizes itself. They began adopting a model they call the "Open Organization," which has no top-down hierarchy but is composed of people with a common purpose. Decision-making is inclusive, and the CEO, rather than dictating, is tasked with convening conversations and encouraging debates.

Holocracy

Companies like Zappos are experimenting with a new organizing concept called "Holocracy," which CEO Tony Hsieh describes as "turning everyone into a mini-CEO." Instead of employees having permanent roles and titles, they sign up to perform the jobs that need to be done to help the organization succeed at that moment. Their roles may change week to week. These roles are broken into smaller pieces than full-time jobs, so at any given time you may have as many as twenty roles.

Platforms

The success of Uber and Airbnb has led numerous companies to explore the idea that instead of producing, owning, and selling things,

they might instead facilitate providers and users of things to find each other. Microsoft's recent resurgence is driven in part by its embrace of this philosophy. Its LinkedIn business helps professionals find each other and find employers, Skype helps users communicate, and its Xbox-only gaming platform helps game developers reach a massive community of gamers.

Blockchain

Blockchain started as alternative to traditional currencies, showing a currency can remain viable even without a central bank to control it. But the approach is now making its way into numerous new applications—education, digital-rights management, supply chains. Wherever a central authority exists today, a blockchain-like model might allow communities to regulate themselves instead.

These new concepts are popping up in pockets. But their commonalities are starting to align, pointing us toward a new emerging organizational form. While we have not yet named or defined what the next concept will be, its shape is coming into view. John Hagel calls the force driving us forward "institutional innovation," writing that in all our discussion of innovation initiatives we "can miss an underexploited and increasingly relevant opportunity for a more fundamental level of innovation, institutional innovation—redefining the rationale for institutions and developing new relationship architectures within and across institutions to break existing performance trade-offs and expand the realm of what is possible."[26] Economic theory, particularly the theory of the firm, shows that as costs of coordinating talent and capital continue to come down, the hierarchical model of corporations loses its role as the optimal way to allocate talent and resources. Centralized organizations will either shrink or evolve, pushing us into a new era. Gary Hamel has been pointing toward this future for years: "The outlines of the 21st-century management model are already clear. Decision-making will be more peer-based; the tools of creativity will be widely distributed in organizations. Ideas will compete on equal footing. Strategies will be built from the bottom up. Power will be a function of competence rather than of position."[27] If your organization does not adapt, history shows that it will fall behind.

The seven barriers outlined in this book point us to exciting future forms of organization:

Intent. Organizations that survive in the future are going to give employees their intent back and turn them into internal innovators.

Need. We're going to evolve from overly complex strategic plans into a simple statement of purpose that tells our employees what the company and the world need.

Options. We're going to see innovative ideas coming not from boardrooms but from our hallways.

Value blockers. Instead of just one established way of delivering value, we're going to see organizations adopt an ecosystem of business models that give employees greater freedom to change the world.

Act. We will move away from a model in which companies ask that employees prove their idea before they can act, because they will recognize that innovations require you to take action in order to prove the idea.

Teams. We're going to move from hierarchical siloed structures toward agile teams that can move quickly and reconfigure at will.

Environment. We will see a new environment evolve, as our organizations shift toward more open platforms where employees can find opportunities and rally resources to change things. We're going to see a seismic shift in organizations, from asking employees to operate within a confined job description to giving them an open structure that allows them to pursue and test ideas outside of their stated role.

Summary

There is no one right path to unlocking internal innovation. The challenge looks more perplexing than it needs to be because so much of what we think to do is merely "innovation theater." Removing the theater from what works reveals that by thinking through four sets of drivers—leadership, talent, structure, and culture—you can activate internal innovation and help your organization evolve toward the future. Doing so will unleash value and demand new forms of leadership and organization.

APPENDIX A

Are Entrepreneurs
the Innovators?

IN CHAPTER 1, I sought to test out the commonly held belief that entrepreneurs, rather than employees, are the drivers of innovation. Here I provide findings from that research.

Employees, not entrepreneurs, have been the primary source of the most transformative innovations over the past three decades, as shown in table 1.1 (chapter 1). But are things changing? The Kauffman Foundation, the leading research institution dedicated to the study of entrepreneurship, tracks a "Startup Activity Index," which integrates several timely measures of entrepreneurial activity into one composite indicator. It relies on three components to measure startup activity:[1]

- Rate of new entrepreneurs
- Opportunity share of new entrepreneurs
- Startup density (startups per 100,000 population)

As the graph in figure A.1 shows, with the exception of an uptick in 2015 and 2016 (the most recent years available as of this writing), startup activity has been in decline over the past two decades.

If it were true that entrepreneurs are increasingly becoming the innovators, we would expect to see the lists of highly innovative companies increasingly populated by younger companies. To test this, using the *Forbes* list of the most innovative companies from 2011 through 2017, we calculated how old each company was when it made the list. If younger companies are starting to replace older ones, the average age should come down. As the graph in figure A.2 shows, it does not.

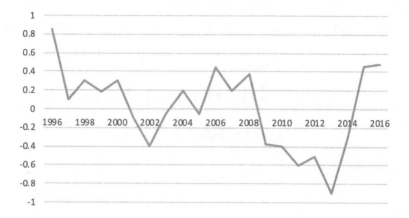

Figure A.1 Kauffman Foundation Startup Index. *Source:* "2017 Kauffman Index of Startup Activity," Ewing Marion Kauffman Foundation, 2017.

We may *think* old companies like GE and J&J are being replaced by younger innovators like Tesla or Spotify, but the data don't support that. If anything, the most innovative companies are getting older.

Perhaps "company" is the wrong unit of measure. After all, smaller, entrepreneurial companies don't yet have the scale to launch multiple innovations in any given year, so the "most innovative companies" list might skew toward larger organizations. We looked instead at the frequency of innovations. Using *R&D* magazine's annual list of one

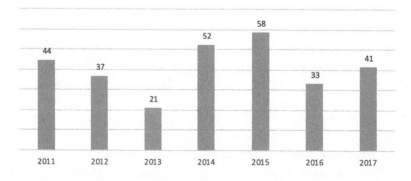

Figure A.2 Average age of companies on the *Forbes* most innovative list. *Source:* Forbes Most Innovative Company rankings 2011–2017, Author's analysis

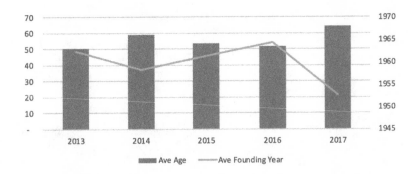

Figure A.3 Average age and founding year of organizations making the top 100 innovations list.

hundred top innovations from 2013 to 2017, we looked at how old the company behind each innovation was when its innovation made the list. If younger companies are starting to outinnovate incumbents, we should see an increasing prevalence of younger companies on the list. As the graph in figure A.3 shows, the data support no such trend.

Value Blockers Checklist

TO HELP YOU predict which value blockers your idea may confront, work through this checklist. For each item, answer "yes," "no," or "N/A" (not applicable).

Area of business model	Y	N	N/A
Position: your core customer and brand attributes			
Is the ideal core customer/user of your innovation idea the same as your organization's current core customer/user?			
Are the brand attributes that people associate with your organization's current offerings the same as the ideal brand attributes of your innovation idea?			
Product: what you offer (your core and ancillary products/services)			
Will your innovation idea avoid cannibalizing or otherwise threatening your organization's current products/services?			
Thinking about all of the ancillary services you will need to provide to deliver your innovation idea, including facilitating services like online ordering and augmenting services like order tracking, does your organization currently offer these?			

Area of business model (*continued*)	Y	N	N/A
Promotion: how you communicate to your core customer, including marketing, sales, public relations, and corporate communications			
Will your sales force be motivated to prioritize your innovation idea?			
Does your sales force have relationships with your innovation idea's target core customer?			
Will you be able to educate your sales force and arm them with the tools to promote your innovation idea?			
Do you have sufficiently strong relationships with, support from, and interest from your marketing, public relations, and corporate communications teams?			
Placement: how you deliver your product/service (e.g., channels, store locations, distribution methods)			
Does the ideal distribution structure for your innovation idea match your organization's current distribution capability? Do you already have the distribution points in place that you need?			
Pricing: how you price your product/service			
What is the ideal pricing structure for your innovation idea? Would pricing in this way fit with the way your organization prices its current offerings?			
Process: the internal processes that allow you to deliver on your value proposition			
Thinking through the processes you will need to deliver the value proposition of your innovation idea, are they in harmony with your organization's current processes? Consider:			
Inbound logistics			
Processes to add value to your inputs (e.g., manufacturing)			
Outbound logistics			
Customer service			
Procurement			
Technology			
Management			
Other: _____			

Area of business model (*continued*)	Y	N	N/A
Physical experience: the physical experience you create around your innovation idea, including what customers/users see, smell, hear, taste, and feel when interacting with your company and brand			
Is the physical experience your organization currently delivers to customers/users consistent with the ideal physical experience of your innovation idea?			
Is the physical experience your organization currently delivers to employees consistent with the ideal physical experience of your innovation idea?			
People: who you hire, how you organize them, and your culture			
Does your organization's current recruiting approach (who you recruit and how you attract them) fit with what you need for your innovation idea to succeed?			
Is your organization's incentive structure consistent with what your innovation idea needs?			
Is your organization's culture consistent with what your innovation idea demands?			
Is your organizational structure consistent with what you need for your innovation idea to succeed?			

APPENDIX C

Team Frameworks

IN CHAPTER 8, I referenced a number of frameworks and philosophies that are being successfully applied by organizations to form and activate innovation teams. You could dive deeply into any of these, attend classes, read blogs, and visit workshops. To save you time, I've done a good deal of that for you. Here is an executive summary of today's best approaches; I also synthesize them into one model that combines the best features of each. Five approaches have proven effective:

- **Objectives and key results (OKR).** A method introduced by Intel, propagated by Silicon Valley venture capitalists like John Doerr, and popularized by Google, this approach suggests that to scale quickly, you allow people to define their own objectives (qualitative mission statements), each supported by measurable key results. Have people focus on just a few OKRs at a time. Make OKRs available to everyone. Update them regularly. We have used a version of OKRs with our clients and found the approach and philosophy remarkably effective at accelerating the pace of strategy execution, increasing agility, and strengthening engagement, without interfering much with the core performance management process.[1]
- **John Kotter's** *Accelerate* **(XLR8).** Kotter has adapted his change-management framework for today. He argues that companies need to embrace a "dual operating system" in which the traditional hierarchy coexists with a more agile network structure. The two are loosely connected by the people who operate in both.

You not only have a formal hierarchical role (e.g., regional sales manager for XYZ) but also spend time as part of a multidisciplinary networked team scaling a particular innovation (e.g., the "Leopard" team with a mission to launch a new sales force and product). Kotter lays out eight key accelerators you need to drive your innovation team, including creating urgency, removing barriers, forming a change vision, and building a coalition.[2]

- **The Four Disciplines of Execution (4DX).** A good number of the internal innovators I interviewed have embraced and experienced this model, introduced by Chris McChesney, Sean Covey, and Jim Huling. The model suggests that you assemble a team around just one or two goals and then implement four disciplines: focus on "wildly important goals" (WIGs), act on lead measures (rather than lagging measures), keep a compelling scorecard that everyone can see, and create a cadence of accountability (frequent, short, efficient meetings to review progress).[3]

- **Growth teams.** Many fast-moving technology companies, including Uber, Pinterest, FanDuel, and HubSpot, have started adopting teams intensely fixated on accelerating growth. The common principles behind these growth teams include assembling an interdisciplinary team, focusing tightly on one or a few issues or objectives, generating quick wins, and implementing a rhythm of quick reviews. In a job posting, HubSpot describes its growth team this way: "The growth team is a small, versatile, focused, data-driven and aggressive group within HubSpot that works on new emerging products with massive audiences and a freemium business model (similar to Dropbox and Evernote). We are constantly pushing ourselves to learn new growth strategies, tactics, and techniques. As part of the growth team you'll have the opportunity to be involved in growing a product from thousands to millions of users while learning and working with some of the best along the way."[4]

- **Scrum teams.** "Scrum" is a teamwork philosophy first adopted in software development and now being adopted across a wide range of management activities. The key idea is that you divide a project into parts and create a prioritized backlog of work. You then focus on just one piece at a time, running a sprint to get that piece of work done quickly. To increase velocity, you ensure

that each piece of work is independent, actionable, and assigned, and has a clear definition of completion ("definition of done"). The team is organized under a "scrum master," with product owners and other experts rallying around each sprint. You also maintain a "scrum board" that visually displays the team's current progress.[5]

APPENDIX D

Innovative Outperformers

OUR RESEARCH INTO the 367 companies that have appeared on the *Forbes* or *Fast Company* "most innovative" lists over the past five years shows no correlation between appearing on such a list and firm performance. Adopting the practices from "most innovative" companies, therefore, may win recognition but not necessarily financial reward.

As described in chapter 10, to identify the companies whose innovation practices might lead to outperformance, we compared the five-year performance of companies that appeared multiple times on "most innovative" lists against their peers. We looked at five-year averages of:

- Annual revenue growth
- Earnings before interest and taxes (EBIT) margins
- Return on invested capital (ROIC)
- Total returns to shareholder (TRS)

Table D.1 summarizes our findings for companies that have appeared at least three times on "most innovative" lists. The number in each cell represents the percentage by which a company has over- or under-performed relative to its peers. For example, Tencent's average EBIT margins over the past five years is 49 percent of a standard deviation higher than its peers, and it has delivered an ROIC 53 percent of a standard deviation higher. If a company outperforms its peers by 30 percent of a standard deviation or more, its performance is highlighted in dark gray. Only thirteen "most innovative" companies outperform their peers across two or more metrics. We call these companies "innovative outperformers." These companies are highlighted in light gray.

TABLE D.1

Assessment of Innovative Outperformers

Name	Number of Appearances	Average Revenue Growth	Average EBIT Margins	Average ROIC	Average TRS
Tencent	5	−8%	49%	53%	17%
Apple	6	51%	130%	98%	14%
Regeneron Pharmaceuticals	4	41%	45%	53%	4%
Illumina	3	47%	43%	36%	50%
Coloplast	3	0%	141%	232%	13%
Mastercard	3	−18%	145%	279%	0%
Naver	3	−28%	30%	34%	17%
Netflix	9	88%	−88%	−52%	134%
Amazon	9	61%	−44%	7%	48%
Starbucks	4	73%	4%	104%	17%
Vertex Pharmaceuticals	4	46%	−20%	−107%	50%
Incyte	3	92%	−56%	−87%	89%
Visa	3	−21%	177%	47%	−3%
Facebook	3	−8%	42%	22%	7%
Hindustan Lever	4	−33%	5%	224%	N/A
Amorepacific	3	56%	−6%	2%	−1424%
Red Hat	4	79%	−29%	−3%	−6%
Adobe	3	15%	23%	15%	86%
Alexion Pharmaceuticals	4	83%	20%	−33%	−22%
Perrigo	3	39%	−72%	−78%	−9%
Activision	2	1%	45%	−12%	29%
Salesforce.com	4	14%	−25%	−4%	3%
Rakuten	3	3%	−7%	−127%	−78%
Expedia	2	−18%	15%	18%	−10%
Unilever	8	−15%	−4%	21%	−1%
Marriott	6	−49%	−60%	−29%	18%
Alphabet	5	−87%	−6%	−40%	−21%
Fast Retailing	4	17%	−8%	0%	−5%

Acknowledgments

THIS BOOK IS the culmination of an idea seeded years ago and cultivated through conversation, interviews, and insights from more people than I have the space to acknowledge here. I am grateful for the generosity of numerous thought leaders who, despite busy schedules, took time to share their thinking and guide mine. I especially would like to thank Bharat Anand, Ellen Auster, Gordon Bell, Steve Blank, Sarah Caldicott, John Camillus, Eric Clemons, Jack Daly, Joel Demski, Bob Dorf, Elizabeth Haas-Edersheim, Michael Gelb, John Hagel, Gary Hamel, Verne Harnish, Chuck House, Prescott Logan, Roger Martin, John Mullins, and Jeff Sutherland for their contributions. George Day and Rita McGrath played particularly influential roles in this book's development.

I was surprised by how much harder it was to uncover the stories of internal innovators than those of entrepreneurs, and I could not have done so without the willingness of people like Hector Aguilar, Wayne Barakat, David Bem, Alejandro Bernal, Debra Brackeen, Julie Copeland, Karen Dahut, Mariano Dall'Orso, Vince Danielson, Hoby Darling, Flint Davis, Heather Davis, Johanna Dwyer, Bran Ferren, Ellie Gates, Russ Gong, Doug Greenlaw, Greg Hale, Don Hastings, Dan Hess, Sunita Holzer, Sheila Hooda, Mir Imran, Michele Landon, Gary Lyons, Janice Maiden, Phil Marks, Fariba Marvasti, Vijay Mayadas, Carmen Medina, Sean Neff, Pat Pacious, Lee Pilsbury, George Pyne, Brendan Ripp, Joaquin Roca, Mark Saine, Keith Shah, Andrew Sherman, Robert Sinclair, and Marina Zhurakhinskaya to share their experiences. I owe special gratitude to Jean Feiwel for detailing, and allowing me to anchor this book to, her journey.

I've been blessed with the opportunity to interact with heads of strategy from across a wide range of industries. I particularly want to thank Jacques Antebi, Eric Chesin, Ken Eng, Kalina Nikolova, Russel Noles, Chris Nuttall, Caroline O'Connell, John Penney, and Milena Schafer, whose insights shed invaluable light on the organizational challenge of driving innovation from within.

My team at Outthinker—Charmian Hall, Katie Mullin, and Zach Ness—spent countless hours over the past several years helping to sharpen the core messages of this book. Additionally, the collaboration and efforts of an extended network of researchers, writers, editors, and friends such as Bill Ardolino, Mike Brassaw, Leslie DaCruz, Juan-Jose Gonzalez, David Greene, Erik Hane, Jill Hellman, Jody Johnson, Margaret McIntyre, Jonathan Muhlrad, Victor Saavedra, Karyn Strait, and Shannon Wallis were instrumental.

My wife, Pilar Ramos, despite a demanding career as a corporate executive and a commitment to being an amazing mother, made time to help untangle my ideas and gave me the space to spend weekends and late evenings writing. She has supported me unwaveringly through writing, now, five books. My remarkable children—Lucas, Kaira, and Makar—infuse this book, and my life, with passion and purpose.

In 1999, my agent, Laurie Harper, took a risk on a young, unknown business student who had written nothing longer than a term paper. She has been my guide and advocate ever since. I owe the opportunity to do what I love to her.

And finally, profound gratitude to my editor, Maggie Stuckey. To anyone who thinks that what editors do is fuss over the niceties of punctuation and grammar, let me introduce you to Maggie. This is our third book project together, and this time I did not make her job easy. Editing, when done by a true professional, is invisible. But I see Maggie's delicate touch on every page. She showed me where my logic had stumbled, and offered good fixes. She pushed me toward simplicity and clarity, with concrete suggestions. She pointed out where my writing had dipped in quality, and gave me improvements. She even saved me from making a silly mistake that would have been enormously embarrassing. And she did it all on a ridiculously tight schedule, with unfailing grace and good humor.

Notes

1. The Real Innovators Among Us

1. John Perlin, n.d. "Photovoltaics," California Solar Center, accessed July 31, 2018, http://californiasolarcenter.org/history-pv/.

2. Geoffrey Jones, *Profits and Sustainability: A History of Green Entrepreneurship* (Oxford: Oxford University Press, 2017).

3. Gifford Pinchot III, "Who Is the Intrapreneur?" in *Intrapreneuring: Why You Don't Have to Leave the Corporation to Become an Entrepreneur* (New York: Harper & Row, 1984), 28.

4. Peter F. Drucker, *Classic Drucker: Wisdom from Peter Drucker from the Pages of Harvard Business Review* (Boston: Harvard Business Review Books, 2006), 69.

5. "A World Transformed: What Are the Top 30 Innovations of the Last 30 Years?" Knowledge@Wharton, February 18, 2009, http://knowledge .wharton.upenn.edu/article/a-world-transformed-what-are-the-top-30 -innovations-of-the-last-30-years/.

6. Thomas S. Kuhn, *The Structure of Scientific Revolutions*, 3rd ed. (Chicago: University of Chicago Press, 1996).

7. Deborah Arthurs, "Now We Know Who to Blame! Flat-Pack Revolution Sparked When an IKEA Designer Sawed the Legs Off a Table to Fit in His Car," *Daily Mail*, July 19, 2013, http://www.dailymail.co.uk/femail /article-2370113/Ikea-designer-Gillis-Lundgren-sparked-flat-pack -revolution-sawing-table-legs-fit-car.html.

8. Emily Langer, "Gillis Lundgren, Designer of Ikea's Ubiquitous Billy Bookcase, Dies at 86," *Washington Post*, March 10, 2016, https://www .washingtonpost.com/world/europe/gillis-lundgren-designer-of-ikeas-ubiquitous -billy-bookcase-dies-at-86/2016/03/10/a1ec674a-e60b-11e5-a6f3 -21ccdbc5f74e_story.html?utm_term=.25184e5dd56b.

9. Marin Reeves, Simon Levin, and Daichi Ueda, "The Biology of Corporate Survival," *Harvard Business Review*, January–February 2016, https://hbr.org/2016/01/the-biology-of-corporate-survival.

10. "2017 Kauffman Index of Startup Activity," Ewing Marion Kauffman Foundation, 2017, https://www.kauffman.org/kauffman-index/reporting /startup-activity/~/media/c9831094536646528ab012dcbd1f83be.ashx.

11. Ray Kurzweil, *The Singularity Is Near: When Humans Transcend Biology* (New York: Viking, 2005).

12. Salim Ismail, *Exponential Organizations: Why New Organizations Are Ten Times Better, Faster, and Cheaper Than Yours (and What to Do About It)* (New York: Diversion Books, 2014).

13. "State of the Global Workplace," Gallup, 2017, https://www.gallup .com/workplace/238079/state-global-workplace-2017.aspx.

14. "State of the Global Workplace."

2. Six Attributes and Seven Barriers

1. Zoltán J. Ács, ed., *Global Entrepreneurship, Institutions and Incentives: The Mason Years* (Cheltenham, UK: Edward Elgar, 2015), 562.

2. Sjoerd Beugelsdijk and Niels Noorderhaven, "Personality Characteristics of Self-Employed: An Empirical Study," *Small Business Economics* 24, no. 2 (2005): 159–167.

3. George Pyne, interview by Kaihan Krippendorff, April 25, 2014.

4. Raymond L. Price et al., "Innovation Politics: How Serial Innovators Gain Organisational Acceptance for Breakthrough New Products," *International Journal of Technology Marketing* 4, no. 2/3 (2009): 181.

5. Hoby Darling, interview by Kaihan Krippendorff, May 2015.

6. Donald F. Kuratko and Michael G. Goldsby, "Corporate Entrepreneurs or Rogue Middle Managers? A Framework for Ethical Corporate Entrepreneurship," *Journal of Business Ethics* 55, no. 1 (2004): 13–30.

7. Israel Kirzner, *Competition and Entrepreneurship* (Chicago: University of Chicago Press, 1973); Robert A. Burgelman, "Intraorganizational Ecology of Strategy Making and Organizational Adaptation: Theory and Field Research," *Organization Science* 2, no. 3 (1991): 239–262.

8. Melissa Cardon, Richard Sudek, and Cheryl Mitteness, "The Impact of Perceived Entrepreneurial Passion on Angel Investing," in *Frontiers of Entrepreneurship Research* 2009, ed. Andrew L. Zacharakis (Wellesley, MA: Babson College, 2009); Melissa S. Cardon and Christopher E. Stevens, "The Discriminant Validity of Entrepreneurial Passion," *Academy of Management Proceedings* 2009, no. 1 (2009): 1–6.

9. Liam Kennedy, "Top 400 Asset Managers 2018: 10 Years of Asset Growth," *IPE*, June 2018, https://www.ipe.com/reports/special-reports/top-400-asset-managers/top-400-asset-managers-2018-10-years-of-asset-growth/10025004.article.

10. Donald Sull, Rebecca Homkes, and Charles Sull, "Why Strategy Execution Unravels—and What to Do About It," *Harvard Business Review*, March 2015, https://hbr.org/2015/03/why-strategy-execution-unravelsand-what-to-do-about-it.

3. Intent: Choosing to See and Seize Opportunities

1. Ashley Strickland, "Swoon Lets YA Readers Choose Which Books Get Published," *CNN*, October 16, 2014, https://edition.cnn.com/2014/10/15/living/crowdsourced-young-adult-swoon/index.html; Sally Lodge, "Macmillan Expands Scope of Swoon Reads," *Publishers Weekly*, November 22, 2016, https://www.publishersweekly.com/pw/by-topic/childrens/childrens-industry-news/article/72101-macmillan-expands-scope-of-swoon-reads.html; Alexandra Alter, "Publishers Turn to the Crowd to Find the Next Best Seller," *New York Times*, August 11, 2014, https://www.nytimes.com/2014/08/12/business/media/publishers-turn-to-the-crowd-to-find-the-next-best-seller.html.

2. Jay Yarow, "This Is an Awesome and Inspiring Quote from Jeff Bezos on What It Takes to Make Invention Happen," *Business Insider*, August 14, 2013, https://www.businessinsider.com/jeff-bezos-on-how-innovation-happens-2013-8.

3. "Cinnabon's Kat Cole: Savoring the Sweet Taste of Success," Knowledge@Wharton, February 6, 2015, http://knowledge.wharton.upenn.edu/article/141022_kw_radio_cole-mp3/.

4. Chuck House, interview by Kaihan Krippendorff, December 14, 2014.

5. Richard Wiseman, "The Luck Factor," *Skeptical Inquirer: The Magazine for Science and Reason* 27, no. 3 (2003): 26–30.

6. Wiseman, "The Luck Factor."

7. Lee Pilsbury, interview by Kaihan Krippendorff, July 23, 2015.

8. Shaun Neff, interview by Kaihan Krippendorff, January 6, 2014.

9. Kendra Scott, interview by Kaihan Krippendorff, May 30, 2018.

10. Norris F. Krueger and Alan L. Carsrud, "Entrepreneurial Intentions: Applying the Theory of Planned Behaviour," *Entrepreneurship & Regional Development* 5, no. 4 (1993): 315–330.

11. Albert Bandura, *Social Foundations of Thought and Action: A Social Cognitive Theory* (Englewood Cliffs, NJ: Prentice-Hall, 1986).

12. Adapted from Amanda Mortimer, *This Is It! It's Your Life, Live It* (Self-published, 2013), 185.

13. Steven Pressfield, *The War of Art: Break Through the Blocks and Win Your Inner Creative Battles* (New York: Black Irish Entertainment, 2002), 161.

4. Need: Knowing Where to Look

1. Janet Bumpas, "Innovation Track Record Study," Strategyn, 2010.

2. Google annual 10-Ks for 2001 and 2008.

3. Thomas Wedell-Wedellsborg and Paddy Miller, "Get More Actionable Ideas from Your Employees," *Harvard Business Review*, November 25, 2014, https://hbr.org/2014/11/get-more-actionable-ideas-from-your-employees.

4. "Our Company," Google, n.d., accessed July 31, 2018, https://www.google.com/about/our-company/; Timothy O'Keefe, "Because We LUV You!" *Southwest Airlines*, December 4, 2011, https://www.southwestaircommunity.com/t5/Southwest-Stories/quot-Because-we-LUV-you-quot/ba-p/36586; "We Pioneer," Amazon, n.d., accessed July 31, 2018, https://www.amazon.jobs/en/working/working-amazon; "Company Overview," Alibaba Group, n.d., accessed July 31, 2018, https://www.alibabagroup.com/en/about/overview; "A Purpose Beyond Profits," Johnson & Johnson, October 8, 2009, https://www.jnj.com/health-and-wellness/a-purpose-beyond-profits; Barbara Farfan, "Disney's Unique Company Mission Statement," *Balance Small Business*, November 12, 2017, https://www.thebalancesmb.com/disney-mission-statement-2891828.

5. Marina Zhurakhinskaya, interviewed by Kaihan Krippendorff, January 21, 2016.

6. Michael Treacy and Fred Wiersema, *The Discipline of Market Leaders: Choose Your Customers, Narrow Your Focus, Dominate Your Market* (Reading, MA: Addison-Wesley, 1995).

7. Mehrdad Baghai, Steve Coley, David White, and Stephen Coley, *The Alchemy of Growth: Practical Insights for Building the Enduring Enterprise* (Reading, MA: Perseus Books, 1999).

8. Vijay Govindarajan, *The Three Box Solution: A Strategy for Leading Innovation* (Boston, MA: Harvard Business Review Press, 2016).

9. Peter F. Drucker, *Innovation and Entrepreneurship* (New York: Harper Business, 2006).

10. Kevin Systrom, "Statement from Kevin Systrom, Instagram Co-Founder and CEO," *Instagram Press*, September 24, 2018, https://instagram-press.com/blog/2018/09/24/statement-from-kevin-systrom-instagram-co-founder-and-ceo/.

5. Options: How to Generate Disruptive Ideas

1. Jean Feiwel, interview by Kaihan Krippendorff, June 18, 2018.

2. Jeremy Schoolfield, "Keeping a Watchful Eye Over the Fun," IAAPA press release, November 2016, http://www.iaapa.org/news/newsroom/news -articles/keeping-a-watchful-eye-over-the-fun---november-2016.

3. "Greg Hale," AALARA Conference and Trade Show 2017, https:// aalara.com.au/wp-content/uploads/2017/04/Greg-Hale.pdf.

4. "Patents by Inventor Gregory Hale," JUSTIA Patents, April 5, 2018, https://patents.justia.com/inventor/gregory-hale.

5. Lois Kelly and Carmen Medina, *Rebels at Work: A Handbook for Leading Change from Within* (Sebastopol, CA: O'Reilly Media, 2014); Carmen Medina, interview by Kaihan Krippendorff, February 28, 2015.

6. John Szramiak, "This Story About Warren Buffett and His Long-Time Pilot Is an Important Lesson About What Separates Extraordinarily Successful People from Everyone Else," *Business Insider*, December 4, 2017, https:// www.businessinsider.com/warren-buffetts-not-to-do-list-2016-10.

7. "Vijay Govindarajan Quotes," Primo Quotes, n.d., accessed July 31, 2018, https://www.primoquotes.com/quotes/Vijay_Govindarajan.

6. Value Blockers: Neutralizing "Corporate Antibodies"

1. Michael Feiner, *The Feiner Points of Leadership: The 50 Basic Laws That Will Make People Want to Perform Better for You* (New York: Business Plus, 2005).

2. Gordon Bell, interview by Kaihan Krippendorff, January 2, 2015.

3. George Day, interview by Kaihan Krippendorff, May 31, 2018.

4. "The Xbox, the Duke, Jurassic Park: The Fascinating Career of Seamus Blackley," *IGN Unfiltered* 31, YouTube, May 15, 2018, https://www .youtube.com/watch?v=Xi7T80JJLsY; Dean Takahashi, "The Making of the Xbox: How Microsoft Unleashed a Video Game Revolution (Part 1)," *Venture Beat*, November 14, 2011, https://venturebeat.com/2011/11/14 /making-of-the-xbox-1/2/.

5. Brendan Ripp, interview by Kaihan Krippendorff, April 4, 2016.

6. Phil LeBeau, "Record Number of Americans Leasing Autos," *CNBC*, June 1, 2015, https://www.cnbc.com/2015/06/01/record-highs-of-americans -leasing-vehicles.html.

7. Kaihan Krippendorff, *Hide a Dagger Behind a Smile: Use the 36 Ancient Chinese Strategies to Seize the Competitive Edge* (Grand Prairie, TX: Platinum Press, 2008), 6.

8. Nidhi Srivastava and Anand Agrawal, "Factors Supporting Corporate Entrepreneurship: An Explorative Study," *Vision: The Journal of Business Perspective* 14, no. 3 (2010): 163–171.

9. Michael E. Porter and Victor E. Millar, "How Information Gives You Competitive Advantage," *Harvard Business Review* 63, no. 4 (1985): 149–160.

10. See, for example, George Day, *Innovation Prowess: Leadership Strategies for Accelerating Growth* (Philadelphia: Wharton Digital Press, 2013); Srivastava and Agrawal, "Factors Supporting Corporate Entrepreneurship."

11. Based on the Charles A. O'Reilly, David Nadler, and Michael Tushman, "Designing and Aligning Organizations: The Congruence Model," working paper, Harvard Business School, 2016.

7. Act: Getting Permission to Experiment

1. Thomas Wedell-Wedellsborg and Paddy Miller, "The Case for Stealth Innovation," *Harvard Business Review*, March 2013, https://hbr.org/2013/03/the-case-for-stealth-innovation.

2. Amar Toor, "Meet Harry Beck, the Genius Behind London's Iconic Subway Map," *Verge*, March 29, 2013, https://www.theverge.com/2013/3/29/4160028/harry-beck-designer-of-iconic-london-underground-map.

3. Peter Sims, *Little Bets: How Breakthrough Ideas Emerge from Small Discoveries* (New York: Free Press, 2011).

4. Andrew Leonard, "Reid Hoffman: To Successfully Grow a Business, You Must 'Expect Chaos,'" *Entrepreneur*, April 24, 2017, https://www.entrepreneur.com/article/292749; Steve Blank, *The Four Steps to the Epiphany: Successful Strategies for Products That Win* (California: S. G. Blank, 2007), 17; Jeff Sutherland: I found the quote here: https://www.linkedin.com/pulse/101-agile-leadership-quotes-every-business-leader-brian/.

5. Eric Ries, *The Startup Way: How Modern Companies Use Entrepreneurial Management to Transform Culture and Drive Long-Term Growth* (New York: Crown, 2017).

6. Michael Schrage, *The Innovator's Hypothesis: How Cheap Experiments Are Worth More Than Good Ideas* (Cambridge, MA: MIT Press, 2014).

7. Prescott Logan, interview by Kaihan Krippendorff, December 10, 2014; interview by Kaihan Krippendorff, June 12, 2015.

8. Steve Blank, "Why Founders Should Know How to Code," September 3, 2014, http://steveblank.com/2014/09/03/should-founders-know-how-to-code/.

9. Peter Cohan, "How P&G Brought Febreze Back to Life," *Telegram*, February 26, 2012, http://www.telegram.com/article/20120226/COLUMN70 /102269984.

10. Geoffrey A. Fowler, "The Man Who Got Us to 'Like' Everything," *Wall Street Journal*, August 13, 2011, https://www.wsj.com/articles/SB100 01424053111904007304576499220914732798.

11. "Wm. Wrigley Jr. Company 2007 Annual Report," https://www.sec .gov/Archives/edgar/data/108601/000119312508025818/dex13.htm.

12. Jeff Sutherland and J. J. Sutherland, *Scrum: The Art of Doing Twice the Work in Half the Time* (New York: Crown Business, 2014), 214.

8. Team: Building an Agile Team

1. John P. Kotter, "Accelerate!" *Harvard Business Review*, November 2012, https://hbr.org/2012/11/accelerate; see also John P. Cotter, *Accelerate: Building Strategic Agility for a Faster-Moving World* (Boston: Harvard Business Review Press, 2014).

2. "Redbox," *Wikipedia*, accessed July 31, 2018, https://en.wikipedia .org/wiki/Redbox; Davis Freeberg, "A Virtual Happy Meal: McDonald's Redbox a Smashing Success," *Seekng Alpha*, December 1, 2006, https:// seekingalpha.com/article/21558-a-virtual-happy-meal-mcdonalds-redbox-a -smashing-success.

3. Don Hastings and Leslie Hastings, interview by Kaihan Krippendorff, June 14, 2016; see also Donald F. Hastings and Leslie A. Hastings, *Behind the Mask: Embrace Risk and Dare to Be Better* (Bloomington: Xlibris, 2014).

4. George Day, "Research on Growth Leaders," unpublished paper, 2016.

5. Susan Douglas and Bernard Dubois, "Looking at the Cultural Environment for International Marketing Opportunities," *Columbia Journal of World Business* 12, no. 4 (1977): 102–118; Geert Hofstede, "The Cultural Relativity of Organizational Practices and Theories," *International Business Studies* 14, no. 3 (1983): 75–89; David K. Tse, John K. Wong, and Chin Tiong Tan, "Towards Some Standardized Cross-Cultural Consumption Values," *Advances in Consumer Research* 15, no. 1 (1988): 387–395.

6. Donald Sull, Rebecca Homkes, and Charles Sull, "Why Strategy Execution Unravels—and What to Do About It," *Harvard Business Review*, March 2015, https://hbr.org/2015/03/why-strategy-execution-unravelsand -what-to-do-about-it.

7. Chris McChesney, Sean Covey, and Jim Huling. *The 4 Disciplines of Execution: Achieving Your Wildly Important Goals* (New York: Free Press, 2012).

8. Hanneke J. M. Kooij-de Bode, Daan L. Van Knippenberg, and Wendy P. Van Ginkel, "Good Effects of Bad Feelings: Negative Affectivity and Group Decision-Making," *British Journal of Management* 21, no. 2 (2010): 375–392.

9. Brian Balfour, "Why Focus Wins," Brian Balfour, April 23, 2014, https://brianbalfour.com/essays/why-focus-wins.

10. Marc Benioff, "How to Create Alignment Within Your Company in Order to Succeed," *Salesforce* (blog), April 09, 2013, https://www.salesforce.com/blog/2013/04/how-to-create-alignment-within-your-company.html.

11. Tracy Stapp Herold, "Top Fastest-Growing Franchises for 2015," *Entrepreneur*, February 6, 2015, https://www.entrepreneur.com/article/241670; Ananya Barua, "Top 10 Largest Hotel Chains in the World," *List Surge*, September 14, 2015, https://listsurge.com/top-10-largest-hotel-chains-in-the-world/.

12. Pat Pacious, interview by Kaihan Krippendorff, March 8, 2016.

9. Environment: Creating Islands of Freedom

1. History.com Staff, "1926: New Sound Process for Films Announced," *History*, November 13, 2009, http://www.history.com/this-day-in-history/new-sound-process-for-films-announced.

2. Clifford A. Pickover, "Traveling Through Time: Part 2. The Future of Time Travel," *PBS*, November 2000, http://www.pbs.org/wgbh/nova/time/through2.html.

3. Josh Ong, "Apple Cofounder Offered First Computer Design to HP Five Times," *Apple Insider*, December 6, 2010, https://appleinsider.com/articles/10/12/06/apple_co_founder_offered_first_computer_design_to_hp_5_times.

4. Snopes Staff, "The Origins of Fedex," *Snopes*, May 28, 2009, https://www.snopes.com/fact-check/term-paper-goods/.

5. "Salon des Refusés," *Wikipedia*, May 3, 2018, https://en.wikipedia.org/wiki/Salon_des_Refus%C3%A9s.

6. Quoted in Mark Batterson, *ID: The True You* (Maitland, FL: Xulon, 2004), 56.

7. Canaan Mash, *Don't Give Up! You Are Stronger Than You Think* (Morrisville, NC: Lulu, 2015), 29.

8. Elaine M. Marconi, "Robert Goddard: A Man and His Rocket," NASA, September 3, 2004, https://www.nasa.gov/missions/research/f_goddard.html.

9. "E. E. Cummings Biography," *Encyclopedia of World Biography*, n.d., accessed July 31, 2018, http://www.notablebiographies.com/Co-Da/Cummings-E-E.html.

10. "The Greatest 'Bad Business Decision' Quotation That Never Was," *History of Phone Phreaking Blog*, January 8, 2011, http://blog.historyofphone phreaking.org/2011/01/the-greatest-bad-business-decision-quotation-that -never-was.html.

11. Jarrod Dicker, "Stupid Business Decisions: Decca Records Snubs the Beatles," Minyanville Media, April 23, 2010, http://www.minyanville.com /special-features/articles/worst-stupid-business-decisions-beatles-decca /4/23/2010/id/27014.

12. Sandra Larkin, "Ken Kutaragi 1950–," *Reference for Business*, n.d., accessed February 6, 2018, http://www.referenceforbusiness.com/biography /F-L/Kutaragi-Ken-1950.html.

13. ZDNet Staff, "Ken Kutaragi—Father of the Playstation," *ZDNet*, April 2, 2001, http://www.zdnet.com/article/ken-kutaragi-father-of-the -playstation/.

14. James Mielke, "The Original PlayStation Boss," *Polygon*, October 31, 2017, https://www.polygon.com/features/2017/10/31/16550652/the -original-playstation-boss-shigeo-maruyama.

15. IGN Staff, "History of the PlayStation," *IGN*, August 27, 1998, http://ca.ign.com/articles/1998/08/28/history-of-the-playstation.

16. Kenneth Li, "Meet the Man Behind Sony's PlayStation," *CNN*, September 1, 2000, http://www.cnn.com/2000/TECH/computing/09/01 /meet.ken.kutaragi.idg/.

17. Donato Piccinno, "Ken Kutaragi, the Ultimate Paradigm-Shifting Project Manager," *LinkedIn*, June 7, 2015, https://www.linkedin.com/pulse /ken-kutaragi-ultimate-paradigm-shifting-project-manager-piccinno/.

18. Jeffrey G. Covin and Dennis P. Slevin, "A Conceptual Model of Entrepreneurship as Firm Behavior," *Entrepreneurship Theory and Practice* 16, no. 1 (1991): 7–26; G. T. Lumpkin and Gregory G. Dess, "Clarifying the Entrepreneurial Orientation Construct and Linking It to Performance," *Academy of Management Review* 21, no. 1 (1996): 135–172.

19. One of the most popular cultural innovation assessments several of our clients have applied is the Situational Outlook Questionnaire (SOQ). "Situational Outlook Questionnaire (SOQ)," Creative Problem Solving Group, n.d., accessed July 31, 2018, http://www.cpsb.com/assessments /soq.

20. Interview with company executive by Kaihan Krippendorf, August 10, 2016.

21. Ellen R. Auster and Lisa Hillenbrand, *Stragility: Excelling at Strategic Changes* (Toronto: Univesity of Toronto Press, 2016).

22. Rita McGrath, "The End of Competitive Advantage," presentation, New York, March 22, 2017.

23. Jeff Bukhari, "Stock-Picking Fund Managers Are Even Worse Than We Thought at Beating the Market," *Fortune*, April 13, 2017, http://fortune.com/2017/04/13/stock-indexes-beat-mutual-funds/.

24. Robin Wigglesworth, "ETFs Are Eating the US Stock Market," *Financial Times*, n.d., accessed January 28, 2018, https://www.ft.com/content/6dabad28-e19c-11e6-9645-c9357a75844a.

25. Jim Wiandt, "Nate Most, Exchange-Traded Fund Inventor, Dies at Age 90," *ETF.com*, December 8, 2004, http://www.etf.com/sections/features/281.html?nopaging=1; Jack Willoughby, "Farewell, Mr. ETF," *Barron's*, January 3, 2005, https://www.barrons.com/articles/SB11044525 3365513525.

26. Wiandt, "Nate Most."

27. Jim Wiandt and Will McClatchy, eds., *Exchange Traded Funds: An Insider's Guide to Buying the Market* (Hoboken, NJ: Wiley, 2001).

28. Wiandt, "Nate Most"; Jennifer Bayot, "Nathan Most Is Dead at 90; Investment Fund Innovator," *New York Times*, December 10, 2004, http://www.nytimes.com/2004/12/10/obituaries/nathan-most-is-dead-at-90-investment-fund-innovator.html.

29. Wiandt and McClatchy, *Exchange Traded Funds*.

30. State Street Global Advisors, "SPY: The Idea That Spawned an Industry," *Securities and Exchange Commission Archive*, January 25, 2013, https://www.sec.gov/Archives/edgar/data/1222333/000119312513023294/d473476dfwp.htm.

31. Michael Doumpos, Panos M. Pardalos, and Constantin Zopounidis, eds., *Handbook of Financial Engineering* (New York: Springer Science & Business Media, 2008).

32. David Berman, "The Canadian Investment Idea That Busted a Mutual-Fund Monopoly," *Globe and Mail*, February 19, 2017, updated April 14, 2017, https://www.theglobeandmail.com/news/national/canada-150/how-a-canadian-etf-that-toppled-the-mutual-fund-monopoly/article34086222/; Doumpos, Pardalos, and Zopounidis, *Handbook of Financial Engineering*, 69.

33. Wiandt and McClatchy, *Exchange Traded Funds*.

34. Wiandt, "Nate Most."

35. State Street Global Advisors, "SPY."

36. State Street Global Advisors, "SPY."

37. Ben Eisen and Sarah Krouse, "The Dinner That Changed the Investing World," *Wall Street Journal*, January 22, 2018, https://www.wsj.com/articles/the-dinner-that-changed-the-investing-world-1516659948; State Street Global Advisors, "SPY."

38. State Street Global Advisors, "SPY."

39. Doumpos, Pardalos, and Zopounidis, *Handbook of Financial Engineering*, 70; Stephen D. Simpson, "A Brief History of Exchange-Traded Funds," *Investopedia*, January 22, 2018, updated October 11, 2018, https://www.investopedia.com/articles/exchangetradedfunds/12/brief-history-exchange-traded-funds.asp; Ari I. Weinberg, "Should You Fear the ETF?" *Wall Street Journal*, December 6, 2015, https://www.wsj.com/articles/should-you-fear-the-etf-1449457201.

40. Eisen and Krouse, "The Dinner That Changed the Investing World"; Simpson, "A Brief History of Exchange-Traded Funds."

41. Eisen and Krouse, "The Dinner That Changed the Investing World."

42. State Street Global Advisors, "SPY."

43. Wiandt, "Nate Most."

44. Gary Hamel, *What Matters Now: How to Win in a World of Relentless Change, Ferocious Competition, and Unstoppable Innovation* (San Francisco, CA: Jossey-Bass, 2012), 128.

10. For Leaders: How to Unleash Internal Innovation

1. Jake G. Messersmith and William J. Wales, "Entrepreneurial Orientation and Performance in Young Firms: The Role of Human Resource Management," *International Small Business Journal* 31, no. 2 (2011): 115–136; Jeffrey G. Covin, Kimberly M. Green, and Dennis P. Slevin, "Strategic Process Effects on the Entrepreneurial Orientation–Sales Growth Rate Relationship," *Entrepreneurship Theory and Practice* 30, no. 1 (2006): 57–81.

2. Nicholas F. Lawler, Robert S. McNish, and Jean-Hugues J. Monier, "Why the Biggest and Best Struggle to Grow," *McKinsey Insights*, January 2004, https://www.mckinsey.com/business-functions/strategy-and-corporate-finance/our-insights/why-the-biggest-and-best-struggle-to-grow.

3. Steve Blank, "Hacking Corporate Culture: How to Inject Innovation Into Your Company," *Venture Beat*, September 9, 2015, https://venturebeat.com/2015/09/09/hacking-corporate-culture-how-to-inject-innovation-into-your-company/.

4. CB Insights, "State of Innovation Report 2018: Survey of 677 Corporate Strategy Executives," April 24, 2018, https://www.slideshare.net/CBInsights/the-state-of-innovation-survey-of-677-corporate-strategy-executives.

5. Reena Jana, "Inside Facebook's Internal Innovation Culture," *Harvard Business Review*, March 7, 2013, https://hbr.org/2013/03/inside-facebooks-internal-inno.

6. Donald Sull, Rebecca Homkes, and Charles Sull, "Why Strategy Execution Unravels—and What to Do About It," *Harvard Business Review*, March 2015, https://hbr.org/2015/03/why-strategy-execution-unravelsand -what-to-do-about-it.

7. Taylor Soper, "Amazon's Secrets of Invention: Jeff Bezos Explains How to Build an Innovative Team," *Geek Wire*, May 17, 2016, https:// www.geekwire.com/2016/amazons-secrets-invention-jeff-bezos-explains -build-innovative-team/.

8. "Our Culture of Innovation," Vertex, n.d., accessed July 31, 2018, https://www.vrtx.com/we-are-vertex/innovation-programs.

9. David Bem, PPG's CTO and VP for Science and Technology, interview by Kaihan Krippendorff, May 22, 2017.

10. Stuart Lauchlan, "Digital Life at Starbucks After Schultz—New CEO Commits to Tech Innovation," *Diginomica*, March 23, 2017, https:// diginomica.com/2017/03/23/digital-life-starbucks-schultz-new-ceo-commits -tech-innovation.

11. Michael Mankins, "Reduce Organizational Drag," *Harvard Business Review*, March 2, 2017, https://hbr.org/ideacast/2017/03/globalization -myth-and-reality-2.html.

12. Anita Woolley and Thomas W. Malone, "Defend Your Research," *Harvard Business Review*, June 1, 2011. https://hbr.org/2011/06/defend -your-research-what-makes-a-team-smarter-more-women.

13. See "Discover Kickbox," Adobe, n.d., accessed July 31, 2018, https:// kickbox.adobe.com/what-is-kickbox.

14. "Apple's Product Development Process—Inside the World's Greatest Design Organization," Interaction Design Foundation, July 20, 2018, https://www.interaction-design.org/literature/article/apple-s-product -development-process-inside-the-world-s-greatest-design-organization.

15. Lulu Yilun Chen, "How Tencent, China's Most-Valuable Company, Pushes Employees for Growth," *Australian Financial Review*, September 19, 2016, https://www.afr.com/technology/social-media/how-tencent-chinas -mostvaluable-company-pushes-employees-for-growth-20160918-grj6r6.

16. "How Tencent Pushes Employees."

17. Jodi Kantor and David Streitfeld, "Inside Amazon: Wrestling Big Ideas in a Bruising Workplace," *New York Times*, August 15, 2015, https://www .nytimes.com/2015/08/16/technology/inside-amazon-wrestling-big-ideas -in-a-bruising-workplace.html.

18. Art Kleiner, "China's Philosopher-CEO Zhang Ruimin," *Strategy +Business*, November 10, 2014, https://www.strategy-business.com/article /00296?gko=8155b.

19. Xuan Tian and Tracy Yue Wang, "Tolerance for Failure and Corporate Innovation," *Review of Financial Studies* 27, no. 1 (2014): 211–255.

20. Soper, "Amazon's Secrets of Invention."

21. "Astro Teller," *Wikipedia*, June 20, 2018, https://en.wikipedia.org/wiki/Astro_Teller.

22. Timothy B. Lee, "How Amazon Innovates in Ways That Google and Apple Can't," *Vox*, December 28, 2016, https://www.vox.com/new-money/2016/12/28/13889840/amazon-innovation-google-apple.

23. Workday Staff Writers, "Illumina's Head of HR Information Systems on the Speed of Innovation," *Workday*, January 31, 2017, https://blogs.workday.com/workday-community-voices-illumina/.

24. "Steve Jobs: In His Own Words," *Telegraph*, October 6, 2011, https://www.telegraph.co.uk/technology/steve-jobs/8811892/Steve-Jobs-in-his-own-words.html.

25. Robert Sinclair, president of Li & Fung, interview by Kaihan Krippendorf, November 30, 2017.

26. John Hagel and John Seely Brown, "Institutional Innovation: Part of a Deloitte Series on Innovation," *Deloitte Insights*, March 12, 2013, https://www2.deloitte.com/insights/us/en/topics/innovation/institutional-innovation.html.

27. Joanna Barsh, "A Conversation with Gary Hamel and Lowell Bryan," *McKinsey Quarterly* 1, no. 1 (2008): 24–35.

Appendix A: Are Entrepreneurs the Innovators?

1. "2017 Kauffman Index of Startup Activity," Ewing Marion Kauffman Foundation, 2017, https://www.kauffman.org/kauffman-index/reporting/startup-activity/~/media/c9831094536646528ab012dcbd1f83be.ashx.

Appendix C: Team Frameworks

1. See John Doerr, *Measure What Matters: How Google, Bono, and the Gates Foundation Rock the World with OKRs* (New York: Portfolio, 2018).

2. John Kotter, *Accelerate: Building Strategic Agility for a Faster-Moving World* (Boston: Harvard Business Review Press, 2014).

3. Chris McChesney, Sean Covey, and Jim Huling, *The Four Disciplines of Execution: Achieving Your Wildly Important Goals* (New York: Free Press, 2016).

4. See Adam Berke, "What the Heck Is a Growth Team?" *Venture Beat*, November 19, 2016, https://venturebeat.com/2016/11/19/what-the-heck-is-a-growth-team/; Casey Winters, "What Are Growth Teams For, and

What Do They Work On?," *Greylock Perspectives*, November 27, 2017, https://news.greylock.com/what-are-growth-teams-for-and-what-do-they-work-on-a339d0c0dee3.

5. Jeff Sutherland and J. J. Sutherland, *Scrum: The Art of Doing Twice the Work in Half the Time* (New York: Crown Business, 2014).

Bibliography

"2017 Kauffman Index of Startup Activity," Ewing Marion Kauffman Foundation, 2017, https://www.kauffman.org/kauffman-index/reporting/startup -activity/~/media/c9831094536646528ab012dcbd1f83be.ashx.

Ács, Zoltán J., ed. *Global Entrepreneurship, Institutions and Incentives: The Mason Years*. Cheltenham, UK: Edward Elgar, 2015.

Alter, Alexandra. "Publishers Turn to the Crowd to Find the Next Best Seller." *New York Times*, August 11, 2014. https://www.nytimes.com /2014/08/12/business/media/publishers-turn-to-the-crowd-to-find -the-next-best-seller.html.

"Apple's Product Development Process—Inside the World's Greatest Design Organization." Interaction Design Foundation, July 20, 2018. https://www .interaction-design.org/literature/article/apple-s-product-development -process-inside-the-world-s-greatest-design-organization.

Arthurs, Deborah. "Now We Know Who to Blame! Flat-Pack Revolution Sparked When an IKEA Designer Sawed the Legs Off a Table to Fit in His Car." *Daily Mail*, July 19, 2013. http://www.dailymail.co.uk/femail/article -2370113/Ikea-designer-Gillis-Lundgren-sparked-flat-pack-revolution -sawing-table-legs-fit-car.html.

"Astro Teller." *Wikipedia*, June 20, 2018. https://en.wikipedia.org/wiki/Astro _Teller.

Auster, Ellen R., and Lisa Hillenbrand. *Stragility: Excelling at Strategic Changes*. Toronto: University of Toronto Press, 2016.

Baghai, Mehrdad, Steve Coley, David White, and Stephen Coley. *The Alchemy of Growth: Practical Insights for Building the Enduring Enterprise*. Reading, MA: Perseus, 1999.

Balfour, Brian. "Why Focus Wins." Brian Balfour, April 23, 2014. https:// brianbalfour.com/essays/why-focus-wins.

Bandura, Albert. *Social Foundations of Thought and Action: A Social Cognitive Theory.* Englewood Cliffs, NJ: Prentice-Hall, 1986.

Barsh, Joanna. "A Conversation with Gary Hamel and Lowell Bryan." *McKinsey Quarterly* 1, no. 1 (2008): 24–35.

Barua, Ananya. "Top 10 Largest Hotel Chains in the World." *List Surge,* September 14, 2015. https://listsurge.com/top-10-largest-hotel-chains-in-the-world/.

Batterson, Mark. *ID: The True You.* Maitland, FL: Xulon, 2004.

Bayot, Jennifer. "Nathan Most Is Dead at 90; Investment Fund Innovator." *New York Times,* December 10, 2004. http://www.nytimes.com/2004/12/10/obituaries/nathan-most-is-dead-at-90-investment-fund-innovator.html.

Bem, David. Interview by Kaihan Krippendorff, May 22, 2017.

Benioff, Marc. "How to Create Alignment Within Your Company in Order to Succeed." *Salesforce* (blog), April 09, 2013. https://www.salesforce.com/blog/2013/04/how-to-create-alignment-within-your-company.html.

Berke, Adam. "What the Heck Is a Growth Team?" *Venture Beat,* November 19, 2016. https://venturebeat.com/2016/11/19/what-the-heck-is-a-growth-team/.

Berman, David. "The Canadian Investment Idea That Busted a Mutual-Fund Monopoly." *Globe and Mail,* February 19, 2017, updated April 14, 2017. https://www.theglobeandmail.com/news/national/canada-150/how-a-canadian-etf-that-toppled-the-mutual-fund-monopoly/article34086222/.

Beugelsdijk, Sjoerd, and Niels Noorderhaven. "Personality Characteristics of Self-Employed: An Empirical Study." *Small Business Economics* 24, no. 2 (2005): 159–167.

Blank, Steve. *The Four Steps to the Epiphany: Successful Strategies for Products That Win.* California: S.G. Blank, 2007.

——. "Hacking Corporate Culture: How to Inject Innovation Into Your Company." *Venture Beat,* September 9, 2015. https://venturebeat.com/2015/09/09/hacking-corporate-culture-how-to-inject-innovation-into-your-company/.

——. "Why Founders Should Know How to Code." September 3, 2014. http://steveblank.com/2014/09/03/should-founders-know-how-to-code/.

Borch, Odd Jarl, Alain Fayolle, and Elisabet Ljunggren. *Entrepreneurship Research in Europe: Evolving Concepts and Processes.* Cheltenham, UK: Edward Elgar, 2011.

Bukhari, Jeff. "Stock-Picking Fund Managers Are Even Worse Than We Thought at Beating the Market." *Fortune,* April 13, 2017. http://fortune.com/2017/04/13/stock-indexes-beat-mutual-funds/.

Bumpas, Janet. "Innovation Track Record Study," Strategyn, 2010.

Burgelman, Robert A. "Intraorganizational Ecology of Strategy Making and Organizational Adaptation: Theory and Field Research." *Organization Science* 2, no. 3 (1991): 239–262. doi.org/10.1287/orsc.2.3.239.

Cardon, Melissa S., and Christopher E. Stevens. "The Discriminant Validity of Entrepreneurial Passion." *Academy of Management Proceedings* 2009, no. 1 (2009): 1–6.

Cardon, Melissa, Richard Sudek, and Cheryl Mitteness. "The Impact of Perceived Entrepreneurial Passion on Angel Investing." In *Frontiers of Entrepreneurship Research 2009*, ed. Andrew L. Zacharakis, 1–15. Wellesley, MA: Babson College, 2009.

CB Insights. "State of Innovation Report 2018: Survey of 677 Corporate Strategy Executives." April 24, 2018. https://www.slideshare.net/CBInsights /the-state-of-innovation-survey-of-677-corporate-strategy-executives.

Chen, Lulu Yilun. "How Tencent, China's Most-Valuable Company, Pushes Employees for Growth." *Australian Financial Review*, September 19, 2016. https://www.afr.com/technology/social-media/how-tencent-chinas -mostvaluable-company-pushes-employees-for-growth-20160918-grj6r6.

"Cinnabon's Kat Cole: Savoring the Sweet Taste of Success." Knowledge@ Wharton, February 6, 2015. http://knowledge.wharton.upenn.edu/article /141022_kw_radio_cole-mp3/.

Cohan, Peter. "How P&G Brought Febreze Back to Life." *Telegram*, February 26, 2012. http://www.telegram.com/article/20120226/ COLUMN70/102269984.

"Company Overview." Alibaba Group, n.d. Accessed July 31, 2018. https:// www.alibabagroup.com/en/about/overview.

Covin, Jeffrey G., Kimberly M. Green, and Dennis P. Slevin. "Strategic Process Effects on the Entrepreneurial Orientation–Sales Growth Rate Relationship." *Entrepreneurship Theory and Practice* 30, no. 1 (2006): 57–81.

Covin, Jeffrey G., and Dennis P. Slevin. "A Conceptual Model of Entrepreneurship as Firm Behavior." *Entrepreneurship Theory and Practice* 16, no. 1 (1991): 7–26.

Darling, Hoby. Interview by Kaihan Krippendorff, May 2015.

Day, George. *Innovation Prowess: Leadership Strategies for Accelerating Growth*. Philadelphia: Wharton Digital, 2013.

——. Interview by Kaihan Krippendorff, May 31, 2018.

——. "Research on Growth Leaders." Unpublished paper, 2016.

Dicker, Jarrod. "Stupid Business Decisions: Decca Records Snubs the Beatles." Minyanville Media, April 23, 2010. http://www.minyanville.com/special -features/articles/worst-stupid-business-decisions-beatles-decca/4/23 /2010/id/27014.

"Discover Kickbox." Adobe, n.d. Accessed July 31, 2018. https://kickbox .adobe.com/what-is-kickbox.

Doerr, John. *Measure What Matters: How Google, Bono, and the Gates Foundation Rock the World with OKRs.* New York: Portfolio, 2018.

Douglas, Susan, and Bernard Dubois. "Looking at the Cultural Environment for International Marketing Opportunities." *Columbia Journal of World Business* 12, no. 4 (1977): 102–118.

Doumpos, Michael, Panos M. Pardalos, and Constantin Zopounidis, eds. *Handbook of Financial Engineering.* New York: Springer Science & Business Media, 2008.

Drucker, Peter F. *Classic Drucker: Wisdom from Peter Drucker from the Pages of Harvard Business Review.* Boston: Harvard Business Review Book, 2006.

——. *Innovation and Entrepreneurship.* New York: Harper Business, 2006.

"E. E. Cummings Biography." *Encyclopedia of World Biography,* n.d. Accessed July 31, 2018. http://www.notablebiographies.com/Co-Da/Cummings-E-E.html.

Eisen, Ben, and Sarah Krouse. "The Dinner That Changed the Investing World." *Wall Street Journal,* January 22, 2018. https://www.wsj.com/articles/the-dinner-that-changed-the-investing-world-1516659948.

Farfan, Barbara. "Disney's Unique Company Mission Statement." *Balance Small Business,* November 12, 2017. https://www.thebalancesmb.com/disney-mission-statement-2891828.

Feiner, Michael. *The Feiner Points of Leadership: The 50 Basic Laws That Will Make People Want to Perform Better for You.* New York: Business Plus, 2005.

Feiwel, Jean. Interview by Kaihan Krippendorff, June 18, 2018.

Fowler, Geoffrey A. "The Man Who Got Us to 'Like' Everything." *Wall Street Journal,* August 13, 2011. https://www.wsj.com/articles/SB10001424053111904007304576499220914732798.

Freeberg, Davis. "A Virtual Happy Meal: McDonald's Redbox a Smashing Success." *Seeking Alpha,* December 1, 2006. https://seekingalpha.com/article/21558-a-virtual-happy-meal-mcdonalds-redbox-a-smashing-success.

Govindarajan, Vijay. *The Three Box Solution: A Strategy for Leading Innovation.* Boston, MA: Harvard Business Review Press, 2016.

"The Greatest 'Bad Business Decision' Quotation That Never Was." *History of Phone Phreaking Blog,* January 8, 2011. http://blog.historyofphonephreaking.org/2011/01/the-greatest-bad-business-decision-quotation-that-never-was.html.

"Greg Hale." AALARA Conference and Trade Show 2017. shttps://aalara.com.au/wp-content/uploads/2017/04/Greg-Hale.pdf.

Hagel, John, and John Seely Brown. "Institutional Innovation: Part of a Deloitte Series on Innovation." *Deloitte Insights,* March 12, 2013. https://www2.deloitte.com/insights/us/en/topics/innovation/institutional-innovation.html.

Hamel, Gary. *What Matters Now: How to Win in a World of Relentless Change, Ferocious Competition, and Unstoppable Innovation.* San Francisco, CA: Jossey-Bass, 2012.

Hastings, Donald F., and Leslie Anne Hastings. *Behind the Mask: Embrace Risk and Dare to Be Better.* Bloomington, IN: Xlibris, 2014.

——. Interview by Kaihan Krippendorff, June 14, 2016.

Herold, Tracy Stapp. "Top Fastest-Growing Franchises for 2015." *Entrepreneur*, February 6, 2015. https://www.entrepreneur.com/article/241670.

History.com Staff. "1926: New Sound Process for Films Announced." *History*, November 13, 2009. http://www.history.com/this-day-in-history/new-sound-process-for-films-announced.

Hofstede, Geert. "The Cultural Relativity of Organizational Practices and Theories." *International Business Studies* 14, no. 3 (1983): 75–89.

House, Chuck. Interview by Kaihan Krippendorff, December 14, 2014.

IGN Staff. "History of the PlayStation." *IGN*, August 27, 1998. http://ca.ign.com/articles/1998/08/28/history-of-the-playstation.

Ismail, Salim. *Exponential Organizations: Why New Organizations Are Ten Times Better, Faster, and Cheaper Than Yours (and What to Do About It).* New York: Diversion Books, 2014.

Jana, Reena. "Inside Facebook's Internal Innovation Culture." *Harvard Business Review*, March 7, 2013. https://hbr.org/2013/03/inside-facebooks-internal-inno.

Jones, Geoffrey. *Profits and Sustainability: A History of Green Entrepreneurship.* Oxford: Oxford University Press, 2017.

Kantor, Jodi, and David Streitfeld. "Inside Amazon: Wrestling Big Ideas in a Bruising Workplace." *New York Times*, August 15, 2015. https://www.nytimes.com/2015/08/16/technology/inside-amazon-wrestling-big-ideas-in-a-bruising-workplace.html.

Kelly, Lois, and Carmen Medina. *Rebels at Work: A Handbook for Leading Change from Within.* Sebastopol, CA: O'Reilly Media, 2014.

Kennedy, Liam. "Top 400 Asset Managers 2018: 10 Years of Asset Growth." *IPE*, June 2018. https://www.ipe.com/reports/special-reports/top-400-asset-managers/top-400-asset-managers-2018-10-years-of-asset-growth/10025004.article.

Kirzner, Israel. *Competition and Entrepreneurship.* Chicago: University of Chicago Press, 1973.

Kleiner, Art. "China's Philosopher-CEO Zhang Ruimin." *Strategy+Business*, November 10, 2014. https://www.strategy-business.com/article/00296?gko=8155b.

Kooij-de Bode, Hanneke J. M., Daan L. Van Knippenberg, and Wendy P. Van Ginkel. "Good Effects of Bad Feelings: Negative Affectivity and Group Decision-Making." *British Journal of Management* 21, no. 2 (2010): 375–392.

Kotter, John P. "Accelerate!" *Harvard Business Review*, November 1, 2012. https://hbr.org/2012/11/accelerate.

———. *Accelerate: Building Strategic Agility for a Faster-Moving World*. Boston: Harvard Business Review Press, 2014.

Krippendorff, Kaihan. *Hide a Dagger Behind a Smile: Use the 36 Ancient Chinese Strategies to Seize the Competitive Edge*. Grand Prairie, TX: Platinum, 2008.

Krueger, Norris F., and Alan L. Carsrud. "Entrepreneurial Intentions: Applying the Theory of Planned Behaviour." *Entrepreneurship & Regional Development* 5, no. 4 (1993): 315–330. doi: 10.1080/08985629300000020.

Kuhn, Thomas S. *The Structure of Scientific Revolutions*. 3rd ed. Chicago: University of Chicago Press, 1996.

Kuratko, Donald F., and Michael G. Goldsby. "Corporate Entrepreneurs or Rogue Middle Managers? A Framework for Ethical Corporate Entrepreneurship." *Journal of Business Ethics* 55, no. 1 (2004): 13–30. doi: 10.1007/s10551-004-1775-3.

Kurzweil, Ray. *The Singularity Is Near: When Humans Transcend Biology*. New York: Viking, 2005.

Langer, Emily. "Gillis Lundgren, Designer of Ikea's Ubiquitous Billy Bookcase, Dies at 86." *Washington Post*, March 10, 2016. https://www .washingtonpost.com/world/europe/gillis-lundgren-designer-of-ikeas -ubiquitous-billy-bookcase-dies-at-86/2016/03/10/a1ec674a-e60b -11e5-a6f3-21ccdbc5f74e_story.html?utm_term=.25184e5dd56b.

Larkin, Sandra. "Ken Kutaragi 1950–." *Reference for Business*, n.d. Accessed February 6, 2018. http://www.referenceforbusiness.com/biography /F-L/Kutaragi-Ken-1950.html.

Lauchlan, Stuart. "Digital Life at Starbucks After Schultz—New CEO Commits to Tech Innovation." *Diginomica*, March 23, 2017. https:// diginomica.com/2017/03/23/digital-life-starbucks-schultz-new-ceo -commits-tech-innovation.

Lawler, Nicholas F., Robert S. McNish, and Jean-Hugues J. Monier. "Why the Biggest and Best Struggle to Grow." *McKinsey Insights*, January 2004. https://www.mckinsey.com/business-functions/strategy-and-corporate -finance/our-insights/why-the-biggest-and-best-struggle-to-grow.

LeBeau, Phil. "Record Number of Americans Leasing Autos." *CNBC*, June 1, 2015. https://www.cnbc.com/2015/06/01/record-highs-of-americans -leasing-vehicles.html.

Lee, Timothy B. "How Amazon Innovates in Ways That Google and Apple Can't." *Vox*, December 28, 2016. https://www.vox.com/new-money/2016 /12/28/13889840/amazon-innovation-google-apple.

Leonard, Andrew. "Reid Hoffman: To Successfully Grow a Business, You Must 'Expect Chaos.'" *Entrepreneur*, April 24, 2017. https://www.entrepreneur .com/article/292749.

Li, Kenneth. "Meet the Man Behind Sony's PlayStation." *CNN*, September 1, 2000. http://www.cnn.com/2000/TECH/computing/09/01/meet.ken.kutaragi.idg/.

Lodge, Sally. "Macmillan Expands Scope of Swoon Reads." *Publishers Weekly*, November 22, 2016. https://www.publishersweekly.com/pw/by-topic/childrens/childrens-industry-news/article/72101-macmillan-expands-scope-of-swoon-reads.html.

Logan, Prescott. Interview by Kaihan Krippendorff, December 10, 2014.

——. Interview by Kaihan Krippendorff, June 12, 2015.

Lumpkin, G. T., and Gregory G. Dess. "Clarifying the Entrepreneurial Orientation Construct and Linking It to Performance." *Academy of Management Review* 21, no. 1 (1996): 135–172.

Mankins, Michael. "Reduce Organizational Drag." *Harvard Business Review*, March 2, 2017. https://hbr.org/ideacast/2017/03/globalization-myth-and-reality-2.html.

Marconi, Elaine M. "Robert Goddard: A Man and His Rocket." *NASA*, September 3, 2004. https://www.nasa.gov/missions/research/f_goddard.html.

Mash, Canaan. *Don't Give Up! You Are Stronger Than You Think*. Morrisville, NC: Lulu, 2015.

McChesney, Chris, Sean Covey, and Jim Huling. *The Four Disciplines of Execution: Achieving Your Wildly Important Goals*. New York: Free Press, 2016.

McGrath, Rita. "The End of Competitive Advantage." Presentation, New York, March 22, 2017.

Medina, Carmen. Interview by Kaihan Krippendorff, February 28, 2015.

Messersmith, Jake G., and William J. Wales. "Entrepreneurial Orientation and Performance in Young Firms: The Role of Human Resource Management." *International Small Business Journal* 31, no. 2 (2011): 115–136.

Mielke, James. "The Original PlayStation Boss." *Polygon*, October 31, 2017. https://www.polygon.com/features/2017/10/31/16550652/the-original-playstation-boss-shigeo-maruyama.

Mortimer, Amanda. *This Is It! It's Your Life, Live It*. Self-published, 2013.

Neff, Shaun. Interview by Kaihan Krippendorff, January 6, 2014.

O'Keefe, Timothy. "Because We LUV You!" Southwest Airlines, December, 4, 2011. https://www.southwestaircommunity.com/t5/Southwest-Stories/quot-Because-we-LUV-you-quot/ba-p/36586.

Ong, Josh. "Apple Cofounder Offered First Computer Design to HP Five Times." *Apple Insider*, December 6, 2010. https://appleinsider.com/articles/10/12/06/apple_co_founder_offered_first_computer_design_to_hp_5_times.

O'Reilly, Charles A., David Nadler, and Michael Tushman. "Designing and Aligning Organizations: The Congruence Model." Working paper, Harvard Business School, 2016.

"Our Company," Google, n.d. Accessed July 31, 2018. https://www.google.com/about/our-company/.

"Our Culture of Innovation." Vertex, n.d. Accessed July 31, 2018. https://www.vrtx.com/we-are-vertex/innovation-programs.

Pacious, Pat. Interview by Kaihan Krippendorff, March 8, 2016.

"Patents by Inventor Gregory Hale." JUSTIA Patents, April 5, 2018. https://patents.justia.com/inventor/gregory-hale.

Perlin, John. "Photovoltaics." California Solar Center. n.d. Accessed July 31, 2018. http://californiasolarcenter.org/history-pv/.

Piccinno, Donato. "Ken Kutaragi, the Ultimate Paradigm-Shifting Project Manager." *LinkedIn*, June 7, 2015. https://www.linkedin.com/pulse/ken-kutaragi-ultimate-paradigm-shifting-project-manager-piccinno/.

Pickover, Clifford A. "Traveling Through Time: Part 2. The Future of Time Travel." *PBS*, November 2000. http://www.pbs.org/wgbh/nova/time/through2.html.

Pilsbury, Lee. Interview by Kaihan Krippendorff, July 23, 2015.

Pinchot, Gifford, III. "Who Is the Intrapreneur?" In *Intrapreneuring: Why You Don't Have to Leave the Corporation to Become an Entrepreneur*, 28–48. New York: Harper & Row, 1984.

Porter, Michael E., and Victor E. Millar. "How Information Gives You Competitive Advantage." *Harvard Business Review* 63, no. 4 (1985): 149–160.

Pressfield, Steven. *The War of Art: Break Through the Blocks and Win Your Inner Creative Battles*. New York: Black Irish Entertainment, 2002.

Price, Raymond L., Abbie Griffin, Bruce A. Vojak, Nathan Hoffmann, and Holli Burgon. "Innovation Politics: How Serial Innovators Gain Organisational Acceptance for Breakthrough New Products." *International Journal of Technology Marketing* 4, no. 2/3 (2009): 165–184.

"A Purpose Beyond Profits." Johnson & Johnson, October 08, 2009. https://www.jnj.com/health-and-wellness/a-purpose-beyond-profits.

Pyne, George. Interview by Kaihan Krippendorff, April 25, 2014.

"Redbox." *Wikipedia*. Accessed July 31, 2018. https://en.wikipedia.org/wiki/Redbox.

Reeves, Marin, Simon Levin, and Daichi Ueda. "The Biology of Corporate Survival." *Harvard Business Review*, February 2016. https://hbr.org/2016/01/the-biology-of-corporate-survival.

Ries, Eric. *The Startup Way: How Modern Companies Use Entrepreneurial Management to Transform Culture and Drive Long-Term Growth*. New York: Crown, 2017.

Ripp, Brendan. Interview by Kaihan Krippendorff, April 4, 2016.

"Salon des Refusés." *Wikipedia*, May 3, 2018. https://en.wikipedia.org /wiki/Salon_des_Refus%C3%A9s.

Schoolfield, Jeremy. "Keeping a Watchful Eye Over the Fun." IAAPA press release, November 2016. http://www.iaapa.org/news/newsroom/news -articles/keeping-a-watchful-eye-over-the-fun---november-2016.

Schrage, Michael. *The Innovator's Hypothesis: How Cheap Experiments Are Worth More Than Good Ideas.* Cambridge, MA: MIT Press, 2014.

Scott, Kendra. Interview by Kaihan Krippendorff, May 30, 2018.

Simpson, Stephen D. "A Brief History of Exchange-Traded Funds." *Investopedia*, January 22, 2018, updated October 11, 2018. https:// www.investopedia.com/articles/exchangetradedfunds/12/brief-history -exchange-traded-funds.asp.

Sims, Peter. *Little Bets: How Breakthrough Ideas Emerge from Small Discoveries.* New York: Free Press, 2011.

Sinclair, Robert. Interview by Kaihan Krippendorff, November 30, 2017.

"Situational Outlook Questionnaire (SOQ)." Creative Problem Solving Group, n.d. Accessed July 31, 2018. http://www.cpsb.com/assessments/soq.

Snopes Staff. "The Origins of Fedex." *Snopes*, May 28, 2009. https://www .snopes.com/fact-check/term-paper-goods/.

Soper, Taylor. "Amazon's Secrets of Invention: Jeff Bezos Explains How to Build an Innovative Team." *Geek Wire*, May 17, 2016. https://www .geekwire.com/2016/amazons-secrets-invention-jeff-bezos-explains-build -innovative-team/.

Srivastava, Nidhi, and Anand Agrawal. "Factors Supporting Corporate Entrepreneurship: An Explorative Study." *Vision: The Journal of Business Perspective* 14, no. 3 (2010): 163–171.

"State of the Global Workplace," Gallup, 2017, https://www.gallup.com /workplace/238079/state-global-workplace-2017.aspx.

State Street Global Advisors. "SPY: The Idea That Spawned an Industry." *Securities and Exchange Commission Archive*, January 25, 2013. https:// www.sec.gov/Archives/edgar/data/1222333/000119312513023294 /d473476dfwp.htm.

"Steve Jobs: In His Own Words." *Telegraph*, October 6, 2011. https://www .telegraph.co.uk/technology/steve-jobs/8811892/Steve-Jobs-in-his -own-words.html.

Strickland, Ashley. "Swoon Lets YA Readers Choose Which Books Get Published." *CNN*, October 16, 2014. https://edition.cnn.com/2014 /10/15/living/crowdsourced-young-adult-swoon/index.html.

Sull, Donald, Rebecca Homkes, and Charles Sull. "Why Strategy Execution Unravels—and What to Do About It." *Harvard Business Review*, March 2015. https://hbr.org/2015/03/why-strategy-execution-unravelsand-what -to-do-about-it.

Sutherland, Jeff, and J. J. Sutherland. *Scrum: The Art of Doing Twice the Work in Half the Time*. New York: Crown Business, 2014.

Systrom, Kevin. "Statement from Kevin Systrom, Instagram Co-Founder and CEO." *Instagram Press*, September 24, 2018. https://instagram-press.com/blog/2018/09/24/statement-from-kevin-systrom-instagram-co-founder-and-ceo/.

Szramiak, John. "This Story About Warren Buffett and His Long-Time Pilot Is an Important Lesson About What Separates Extraordinarily Successful People from Everyone Else." *Business Insider*, December 4, 2017. https://www.businessinsider.com/warren-buffetts-not-to-do-list-2016-10.

Takahashi, Dean. "The Making of the Xbox: How Microsoft Unleashed a Video Game Revolution (Part 1)." *Venture Beat*, November 14, 2011. https://venturebeat.com/2011/11/14/making-of-the-xbox-1/2/.

Tian, Xuan, and Tracy Yue Wang. "Tolerance for Failure and Corporate Innovation." *Review of Financial Studies* 27, no. 1 (2014): 211–255.

Toor, Amar. "Meet Harry Beck, the Genius Behind's London's Iconic Subway Map." *Verge*, March 29, 2013. https://www.theverge.com/2013/3/29/4160028/harry-beck-designer-of-iconic-london-underground-map.

Treacy, Michael, and Fred Wiersema. *The Discipline of Market Leaders: Choose Your Customers, Narrow Your Focus, Dominate Your Market*. Reading, MA: Addison-Wesley, 1995.

Tse, David K., John K. Wong, and Chin Tiong Tan. "Towards Some Standardized Cross-Cultural Consumption Values." *Advances in Consumer Research* 15, no. 1 (1988): 387–395.

Vijay Govindarajan. *The Three Box Solution: A Strategy for Leading Innovation*. Boston, MA: Harvard Business Review Press, 2016.

"Vijay Govindarajan Quotes." Primo Quotes, n.d. Accessed July 31, 2018. https://www.primoquotes.com/author/Vijay+Govindarajan.

"We Pioneer." Amazon, n.d. Accessed July 31, 2018. https://www.amazon.jobs/en/working/working-amazon.

Wedell-Wedellsborg, Thomas, and Paddy Miller. "The Case for Stealth Innovation." *Harvard Business Review*, March 2013. https://hbr.org/2013/03/the-case-for-stealth-innovation.

———. "Get More Actionable Ideas from Your Employees." *Harvard Business Review*, November 25, 2014. https://hbr.org/2014/11/get-more-actionable-ideas-from-your-employees.

Weinberg, Ari I. "Should You Fear the ETF?" *Wall Street Journal*, December 6, 2015. https://www.wsj.com/articles/should-you-fear-the-etf-1449457201.

Wiandt, Jim. "Nate Most, Exchange-Traded Fund Inventor, Dies at Age 90." *ETF.com*, December 8, 2004. http://www.etf.com/sections/features/281.html?nopaging=1.

Wiandt, Jim, and Will McClatchy, eds. *Exchange Traded Funds: An Insider's Guide to Buying the Market.* Hoboken, NJ: Wiley, 2001.

Wigglesworth, Robin. "ETFs Are Eating the US Stock Market." *Financial Times,* n.d. Accessed January 28, 2018. https://www.ft.com/content/6dabad28-e19c-11e6-9645-c9357a75844a.

Willoughby, Jack. "Farewell, Mr. ETF." *Barron's,* January 3, 2005. https://www.barrons.com/articles/SB110445253365513525.

Winters, Casey. "What Are Growth Teams For, and What Do They Work On?" *Greylock Perspectives,* November 27, 2017. https://news.greylock.com/what-are-growth-teams-for-and-what-do-they-work-on-a339d0c0dee3.

Wiseman, Richard. "The Luck Factor." *Skeptical Inquirer: The Magazine for Science and Reason* 27, no. 3 (2003): 26–30.

"Wm. Wrigley Jr. Company 2007 Annual Report." https://www.sec.gov/Archives/edgar/data/108601/000119312508025818/dex13.htm.

Woolley, Anita, and Thomas W. Malone. "Defend Your Research." *Harvard Business Review,* June 1, 2011. https://hbr.org/2011/06/defend-your-research-what-makes-a-team-smarter-more-women.

Workday Staff Writers. "Illumina's Head of HR Information Systems on the Speed of Innovation." *Workday,* January 31, 2017. https://blogs.workday.com/workday-community-voices-illumina/.

"A World Transformed: What Are the Top 30 Innovations of the Last 30 Years?" Knowledge@Wharton. February 18, 2009. http://knowledge.wharton.upenn.edu/article/a-world-transformed-what-are-the-top-30-innovations-of-the-last-30-years/.

"The Xbox, the Duke, Jurassic Park: The Fascinating Career of Seamus Blackley." *IGN Unfiltered* 31. YouTube, May 15, 2018. https://www.youtube.com/watch?v=Xi7T80JJLsY.

Yarow, Jay. "This Is an Awesome and Inspiring Quote from Jeff Bezos on What It Takes to Make Invention Happen." *Business Insider,* August 14, 2013. https://www.businessinsider.com/jeff-bezos-on-how-innovation-happens-2013-8.

ZDNet Staff, "Ken Kutaragi—Father of the Playstation." *ZDNet,* April 2, 2001. http://www.zdnet.com/article/ken-kutaragi-father-of-the-playstation/.

Index